M000222967

Azusa, Rome, and Zion

Pentecostal Faith, Catholic Reform, and Jewish Roots

Peter Hocken

FOREWORD BY
Christoph Schönborn

PICKWICK *Publications* · Eugene, Oregon

AZUSA, ROME, AND ZION
Pentecostal Faith, Catholic Reform, and Jewish Roots

Copyright © 2016 Peter Hocken. All rights reserved. Except for brief quotations in critical publications or reviews, no part of this book may be reproduced in any manner without prior written permission from the publisher. Write: Permissions. Wipf and Stock Publishers, 199 W. 8th Ave., Suite 3, Eugene, OR 97401.

Pickwick Publications
An Imprint of Wipf and Stock Publishers
199 W. 8th Ave., Suite 3
Eugene, OR 97401

www.wipfandstock.com

PAPERBACK ISBN: 978-1-4982-2834-3
HARDCOVER ISBN: 978-1-4982-2836-7

Cataloguing-in-Publication Data

Hocken, Peter.

　Azusa, Rome, and Zion : Pentecostal faith, Catholic reform, and Jewish roots / Peter Hocken, with a foreword by Christoph Schönborn

　　xii + 232 p. ; 23 cm. Includes bibliographical references.

　　ISBN 978-1-4982-2834-3 (paperback) | ISBN 978-1-4982-2836-7 (hardcover)

　　1. Pentecostalism. 2. Messianic Judaism. 3. Jewish Christians. 4. Francis, Pope, 1936–. 5. Ecumenical movement. I. Schönborn, Christoph. II. Title.

BR1644 H63 2016

Manufactured in the U.S.A.　　　　　　　　　　　　　01/22/2016

The author and publisher gratefully acknowledge permission to include, as chapter 5, "Catholic Charismatic Renewal: Sources, History, Challenges," the English version of a paper whose French translation appeared in *Istina*

All Scripture quotations are taken from the Revised Standard Version of the Bible, copyright 1973 by the Division of Christian Education of the National Council of the Churches of Christ in the United States of America. Used by permission. All rights reserved.

Contents

Foreword

THIS BOOK IS BEING published at a most opportune moment. Pope Francis is challenging the Catholic Church to awaken to the creativity and the newness of the Holy Spirit. For most Catholics, this challenge is itself a surprise of the Spirit. Catholics are accustomed to seeing the primary task of the church as handing on intact the faith once delivered to the saints. Pope Francis insists on the constant presence and activity of the Holy Spirit. For him, the faith to be passed on is not an object like a family treasure, but faith in the Lord of history who creates each Christian, each community of faith, each generation, not as a replica of the past, but as a new creation issuing from the unchanging foundation in Christ.

In an address to members of the International Theological Commission, Francis emphasized two essential roles of the Catholic theologian:

> The theologian is first and foremost a believer who listens to the Word of the living God and receives it in his/her heart and mind. But the theologian must also humbly listen to "what the Spirit says to the churches" (Rev 2:7), through the various manifestations of the faith lived by the People of God.[1]

I see this collection of articles and lectures by Fr. Peter Hocken as a humble listening "to what the Spirit says to the churches" through some of the "manifestations of the faith lived by the People of God." This kind of reflection is badly needed. The movements he has singled out for examination and reflection are those in which he has had personal involvement or close personal relationships for many years, discerning them all to be in some way movements of the Holy Spirit. For various reasons, these major new currents of modern times have not received much attention from academic theologians. The new charismatic churches have only received

1. Address to members of the International Theological Commission, December 5, 2014. Online: http://w2.vatican.va/content/francesco/en/speeches/2014/december/documents/papa-francesco_20141205_commissione-teologica-internazionale.html.

the attention of specialists in sects, while the Messianic Jews remain generally unknown. These collected lectures do not offer a detailed study of these phenomena, but they provide a reliable and stimulating introduction, along with an initial theological reflection, that can alert the church to their significance.

A favorite word of Fr. Peter is "challenge." He understands well that every creative work of the Holy Spirit poses profound challenges, an awareness that rejoins the message of Pope Francis in his exhortation *Evangelii Gaudium*. The challenges are both pastoral and theological. To study these contemporary movements is to be faced with areas and subjects that have been out of fashion, but which remain vital for the church: deliverance and exorcism, signs and wonders, the role of prophets, the role of Jewish believers in Jesus, and above all eschatology.

While the actions and words of Pope Francis have been receiving wide circulation and much comment, his openness to Pentecostal and charismatic leaders has been given much less attention than his emphases on the poor, simplicity of lifestyle, the self-referential church, the throwaway culture, and the environment. But this opening to the Christian "peripheries" belongs to the pope's teaching on the surprises and the creativity of the Holy Spirit. This book can aid a deeper understanding of Pope Francis, opening hearts to the "pastoral and missionary conversion" of the church for which he calls.[2]

—Cardinal Christoph Schönborn, OP
Archbishop of Vienna
April 2015

2. *Evangelii Gaudium*, 25.

viii

Preface

INITIALLY THE PROPOSAL FOR this book was to put together a collection of papers and teachings that the author has presented, all concerning themes prominent in the distinctive ministry that he has been blessed to exercise for the last twenty years and more. The themes have arisen from his lengthy involvement as a Catholic priest in the charismatic movement (since 1971), his active participation in Pentecostal and charismatic studies (since 1980), and his developing relationships with Messianic Jews (since 1995).

The various contributions gathered in this book all address these relatively modern developments in the Christian world that bear evidence of being foundationally the work of the Holy Spirit. The new developments/ currents/movements considered in this collection are (1) the Pentecostal and charismatic movements; (2) the new charismatic churches and networks; (3) the Messianic Jewish movement; and (4) the conversionist and reforming impact of Pope Francis. All these developments have major significance for the whole Christian world, and have a particular significance for Christian unity. The first three all represent phenomena/developments to which Christian theologians, whether Catholic, Orthodox, or Protestant, have paid minimal attention. Much is being written about Pope Francis, but his openings toward Evangelical, Pentecostal, and charismatic leaders interest the theological commentators much less than other the pope's other initiatives and utterances.

Four years ago when I was invited to write a commendation for a collection of essays by Mark Kinzer, I wrote that its "coherence flows directly from the coherence of Mark Kinzer's life project."[1] Any coherence that this present collection possesses assuredly derives from the specific character of the author's ministry, and his stance of committed engagement. As this manuscript moves toward publication, an article on the author and his

1. Kinzer, *Israel's Messiah.*

ministry by Pentecostal scholar William K. Kay is due to appear.[2] Since Kay's article was written, a website has been created with many teachings and writings of the author.[3]

Since this ministry has focused on Pentecostal revival and charismatic renewal, on the renewal of the Catholic Church since the Second Vatican Council, and the significance of the Jewish people, the title *Azusa, Rome, and Zion* suggested itself. When it became necessary to omit one item from the collection, it seemed appropriate to write an additional chapter that would bring these themes together in a coherent ecumenical vision. So the final chapter is entitled "From Azusa via Rome to Zion."

Because the collected papers all treat in some way of new initiatives of the Holy Spirit they all present major challenges to our received ways of thinking and acting in the body of Christ. In these chapters I attempt in an initial way to spell out these challenges and to indicate the enormous potential there is for the future of the entire church, for the Jewish people, and for the contemporary world when these challenges are heard and received.

—Peter Hocken

Hainburg an der Donau, Austria

April 2015

2. See Kay, *Peter Hocken.*

3. www.peterhocken.org.

Abbreviations

CCC	*Catechism of the Catholic Church.* New York: Doubleday, 1994.
CCI	*Consultazione Carismatica Italiana*
CCR	Catholic Charismatic Renewal
CDF	Congregation for the Doctrine of the Faith
CEEC	Communion of Evangelical Episcopal Churches
CFCCCF	Catholic Fraternity of Charismatic Covenant Communities and Fellowships
CGM	Christian Growth Ministries
CRECES	*Comunión Renovada de Evangélicos y Católicos en el Espíritu Santo* (Renewed Communion of Catholics and Evangelicals in the Holy Spirit)
EG	*Evangelii Gaudium* English translation. London: Catholic Truth Society, 2013. (Apostolic Exhortation of Pope Francis)
EN	*Evangelii Nuntiandi* English translation. London: Catholic Truth Society, n.d. (Apostolic Exhortation of Paul VI)
EPCRA	European Pentecostal and Charismatic Research Association
EQ	*Evangelical Quarterly*
FIEC	Federation of Independent Evangelical Churches
GS	*Gaudium et Spes* (Constitution on the Church in the World of Today of the Second Vatican Council)
GCF	Global Christian Forum
HJ	*The Heythrop Journal.* Heythrop College, University of London, England

HTB	Holy Trinity, Brompton (London).
ICCRS	International Catholic Charismatic Renewal Services
IJSCC	*International Journal for the Study of the Christian Church*
JEPTA	*Journal of the European Pentecostal Theological Association*
JPT	*Journal of Pentecostal Theology*
LG	*Lumen Gentium* (Constitution on the Church of the Second Vatican Council)
MA	*Mortalium Animos*. London: Catholic Truth Society, 1928 (Encyclical Letter of Pius XI)
NA	*Nostra Aetate* (Declaration on Non-Christian Religions of the Second Vatican Council)
NARSC	North American Renewal Service Committee
NIDPCM	*The New International Dictionary of the Pentecostal and Charismatic Movements*. Edited by Stanley M. Burgess and Eduard M. van der Maas. Grand Rapids: Zondervan, 2002.
RH	*Redemptor Hominis* (Encyclical Letter of John Paul II). London: Catholic Truth Society, 1979
RT	*Redemption Tidings*
SC	*Sacrosanctum Concilium* (Constitution on the Liturgy of the Second Vatican Council)
SChr	*Sources Chrétiennes*
SPS	Society for Pentecostal Studies
TJCII	Toward Jerusalem Council II
TMA	*Tertio Millennio Adveniente* (Apostolic Letter of John Paul II). Vatican City: Libreria Editrice Vaticana, 1994
UR	*Unitatis Redintegratio* (Decree on Ecumenism of the Second Vatican Council)
UUS	*Ut Unum Sint* English translation. London: Catholic Truth Society, 1995. (Encyclical Letter of John Paul II)
WCC	The World Council of Churches
WEC	World Evangelization Crusade
WPC	World Pentecostal Conference

PART I

The Pentecostal and Charismatic Movements and Christian Unity

CHAPTER 1

A Catholic and Ecumenical Understanding of the Pentecostal Movement

SCHOLARS FROM PENTECOSTAL AND charismatic backgrounds are aware of the ways that significant experiences have shaped their thinking and understanding. One such decisive moment in my life occurred soon after I was baptized in the Spirit. I was taken to a "revival night" in a Pentecostal church, a totally new experience. Providentially, this church was a remarkably lively and impressive assembly, unusually so as I learned later. I knew instantly that they were living the same reality that I was discovering in the charismatic movement. From that point, I knew that Pentecostals were sisters and brothers in the Spirit (I say sisters advisedly as this assembly was pastored by two extraordinary women), and that it would be wrong to do what many charismatics were doing—to distance themselves from the Pentecostals and to see Pentecostals primarily as those whose excesses the charismatic renewal had to avoid.[1]

This positive encounter with Pentecostals motivated me after my move to the USA in 1976 to become involved in the Society for Pentecostal Studies. As one who had been heavily involved in ecumenical activities in Britain and who remained deeply committed to the search for Christian unity, I had to reflect on the central characteristics of the Pentecostal movement, and how it differed from other spiritual and theological traditions in the Christian world. I was immediately aware of the differences between the Pentecostal movement and Evangelical Christianity. I readily sympathized with those Pentecostal scholars who were critical of the tendency to classify

1. In effect, the chapter I wrote about Pentecostalism in *New Heaven and New Earth?* was almost entirely based on my experience at Hockley Pentecostal Church in Birmingham, England, between 1971 and 1976 (see Hocken, *Significance*).

Pentecostalism as a sub-section of Evangelicalism.[2] I knew in my guts that this tendency sells the Pentecostal movement short and fails to do justice to its originality as a work of the Holy Spirit. But as a Roman Catholic, I needed to integrate my appreciation of the Pentecostal movement into a Catholic and ecumenical theology of the church.

Four Ways in Which the Unity Issue Keeps Arising for Pentecostals

I see four main ways in which the unity issue keeps surfacing within the Pentecostal movement. Some raise very directly the question of Pentecostal attitudes to the ecumenical movement.

First, from Azusa Street onward there has been the sense that the Pentecostal revival was for all people and so for all Christians. Cecil M. Robeck Jr. has often reminded fellow Pentecostals that at Azusa Street William Seymour had expressed a vision for Christian unity: "We stand as assemblies and missions all in perfect harmony. Azusa stands for the unity of God's people everywhere. God is uniting his people, baptizing them by one Spirit into one body."[3] This conviction about unity presupposes that the Pentecostal revival is for all Christians. It was constantly expressed in Alexander Boddy's paper *Confidence* published from Sunderland, England. But it was with the spread of Pentecostal blessing outside the Pentecostal denominations in the charismatic movement that this question arises with a new insistence. Donald Gee was constantly referring to this challenge to Pentecostals in the editorials of *Pentecost* as he received reports from his friend David du Plessis about other Christians receiving the baptism in the Holy Spirit.[4] I give two examples, one from 1953 and one from 1954:

> Let us beware of making it our supreme aim to drag people into our own denomination. If they can maintain unsullied and intact their Pentecostal witness where they are, then let them do it. Our experience causes us to expect that they will have difficulty. . . . Our prayer will henceforth be that the floodgates of Pentecostal grace and power that should follow speaking with tongues may be manifested in any and all of the churches.[5]

2. I recall being impressed by the contributions of Gerald Sheppard from Canada.

3. *The Apostolic Faith,* Jan. 1907, cited by Robeck, *Azusa,* 96.

4. See chapter 3.

5. Gee, "Tongues."

> Perhaps the most urgent of all questions facing the Pentecostal people themselves is whether those elements of durability within the Movement shall lead them into becoming just one more distinctive denomination among all the others, or whether they shall still try and hold tenaciously to the original concept of the Pentecostal Movement as a *revival* to powerfully affect Christians everywhere without crystallising itself in the process.[6]

Second, the historical roots of the Pentecostal movement in earlier Evangelical revivals and in the Holiness movement necessarily raised for Pentecostals the question of their relationship as a movement to Evangelicalism. The understanding of the Pentecostal movement as revival implicitly inserted it into Evangelical Protestant history. But Pentecostal self-understanding was always that their movement represented something more, an intensification, a new thrust toward the climax of history, as the common labels Apostolic Faith, Latter Rain, and Pentecost indicate in their different ways. Pentecostalism was never just another revival, but a "revival plus." Similar to Evangelical revivals in bringing personal conversions of heart, with a deep repentance for sin, and a focus on the cross of the Lord, it had other features that marked it as different. Prominent among the differences was the restoration of the spiritual gifts as God's equipment for the body of Christ, among which speaking in tongues attracted the most attention. It brought a new teaching about baptism in the Holy Spirit, even before the Assemblies of God taught that speaking in tongues is the initial evidence of Spirit-baptism. Very importantly, through its African-American component, it brought a new degree of physical expression and bodily involvement. It was this plus factor, which made many of the existing Evangelical and Holiness denominations suspicious, sometimes leading to rejection and denunciation.

The revivalistic and missionary thrust of the Pentecostal movement meant that there was little incentive or time to reflect theologically on its distinctiveness. So Pentecostals typically took over Evangelical doctrinal positions and statements, adding clauses about speaking in tongues and divine healing. This embrace of Evangelical thinking would later favor the political alignment of Pentecostals with Evangelicals in the USA, and the entrance of Pentecostals into the National Association of Evangelicals in 1942. This relationship strengthened the view that Pentecostalism is a subsection of Evangelicalism. It also helped to ensure that the unity issue for

6. Gee, "Pentecost Re-Valued."

Pentecostals was largely limited to relationships with Evangelicals, and that they shared the increasing Evangelical negativity toward the ecumenical movement.

Third, the rise of the charismatic movement in the historic churches—especially in churches committed to the ecumenical movement—raised the ecumenical issue in a new way. A key issue for Pentecostals is whether the renewal of historic institutional bodies is possible, that is of churches and denominations. Donald Gee, the foremost Pentecostal teacher as the ecumenical movement was taking shape, had always seen the scope of the revival in merely personal terms. In effect, his "invisible church" ecclesiology precluded any vision for ecclesial renewal.[7]

But insofar as charismatic Christians in the historic churches understood this movement as for the renewal of their churches, they were uncomfortable with such an individualistic and non-ecclesial understanding. Yes, it was a form of spiritual revival for all participants, but it was also a renewal for the transformation of church life and its corporate expressions in liturgy, catechesis, and diaconal service. This ecclesial reference became even more marked with the spread of the renewal movement to the Roman Catholic Church. It raises the issue, ultimately theological, of the relationship between revival and renewal.[8] These are inherently ecumenical issues that affect inter-church relations. Moreover, as the Pentecostal movement enters its fourth or fifth generation, Pentecostals are inevitably faced with the need for renewal of their own denominations.

Fourth, as the Pentecostal movement has become a recognized force no longer on the margins, and as it has shed earlier hostility to theology and higher education, there has been a rise in the quality of Pentecostal scholarship and the emergence of a more articulate formulation of Pentecostal distinctives. Nowhere is this more evident than in the Society for Pentecostal Studies. So, for example, there has been much debate on a Pentecostal hermeneutic, distinctively different from Evangelical ways of handling the biblical texts. This same tendency is also leading to greater Pentecostal attention to the issue of ecclesiology. As I hope to demonstrate, the formulation of a Pentecostal ecclesiology cannot happen in isolation, but only in dialogue with Christian traditions that possess a more developed theology of the church. Ultimately, a genuine Pentecostal contribution to

---

7. Gee's attitude to ecumenism is treated in chapter 3. See in particular the citation in note 56.

8. See Hocken, "Pentecostal-Charismatic" and "Revival."

world Christianity cannot happen without the development of a Pentecostal ecclesiology.

A genuine Pentecostal ecclesiology will need to articulate a distinctively Pentecostal understanding of such questions as (1) the relationship between Jesus Christ and the Holy Spirit in the structuring and the constitution of the church, and (2) the relationship between the universal body of Christ and its visible expressions at national and local level. It will also need to ask what kind of entity the Pentecostal movement is theologically and what theological significance its organized expressions have within the ecumenical context. In many ways, the debates on a distinctively Pentecostal hermeneutic are preparing the ground for a distinctive Pentecostal ecclesiology.

The Contribution of Miroslav Volf

Possibly the most important book sketching the outline of a possible Pentecostal contribution to ecclesiology is Miroslav Volf's *After Our Likeness: the Church as the Image of the Trinity.* What Volf seeks to present is an authentic free church ecclesiology, that is not specifically Pentecostal, though his theology clearly draws upon his Pentecostal upbringing. It cannot be simply presented as a Pentecostal ecclesiology, as many Pentecostals do not share Volf's vision for the autonomy of the local church that is firmly "congregationalist," though not in a separatist sense, as Volf insists on the need for communion between local churches.[9] However, Volf's free church ecclesiology could be very helpful for Pentecostal theologians, in particular because of the emphasis placed on the Holy Spirit poured out on each believer, and because of the place he allocates to charisms in the structuring of the church.[10]

Equally applicable to Pentecostals is Volf's recognition that all free churches need to develop an ecclesiology that is not individualistic (that recognizes the social character of salvation) and that is not voluntaristic (not simply based on human choice and free association). His method implies that an adequate free church ecclesiology has to arise out of dialogue

---

9. For Volf, "every local church is indeed independent or 'self-complete'. It stands on its own spiritual feet because the whole Christ is present to it through the Spirit." (*After Our Likeness*, 154–55). But Volf takes "the *openness* of every church toward all other churches as an indispensable condition of ecclesiality" (ibid., 156).

10. See part II, chapter VI.

with the Christian traditions with a developed ecclesiology, from which the free churches need both to learn and to differentiate themselves. Thus, in *After Our Likeness*, he examines the ecclesiology of Joseph Ratzinger (Catholic)[11] and of John Zizioulas (Orthodox) to indicate what is acceptable and what is dangerous from a free church standpoint.

Four points from Volf's book are of major importance for an ecumenical ecclesiology and with which I am in fundamental agreement as a Catholic. First, Volf grounds the essentially communal and personal character of ecclesial communion in the triune communion of the one God, Father, Son, and Holy Spirit. He sees this rooting in trinitarian communion as the basic safeguard against the free church dangers of individualism and voluntarism. Volf presents Christian initiation as a "simultaneous incorporation into both trinitarian and ecclesial communion."[12] He roots this in an understanding of the social nature of the human person and the revealed pattern of trinitarian communion:

> Just as God constitutes human beings through their social and natural relations as independent persons, so also does the Holy Spirit indwelling them constitute them through ecclesial relations as an intimate communion of independent persons. As such, they correspond to the unity of the triune God, and as such they are instantiations of the one church.[13]

Second, Volf argues that an authentic ecclesiology has to respect both the divine element ("from above") and the human element ("from below"). He describes as a "false alternative" the juxtaposition of "the Free Church notion of 'from below' with the Catholic (or Orthodox) and allegedly genuinely Protestant notion of 'from above.'"[14] But Volf insists, "*no* church can arise and live without *also* being constituted 'from below.'"[15] In his view, the second element, the aspect of the church "from below," is the essential free church contribution to ecclesiology. This distinction is parallel to Volf's distinction between the "objective activities" of the church and the "subjective" acts of its members. This will protect the church from all forms of domination and imposition "from above": "if one defines the church *only* from the perspective of the objective activities (and thus 'from above'), the

11. Later Pope Benedict XVI.

12. Ibid., 197.

13. Ibid., 213.

14. Ibid., 176.

15. Ibid.

church hovers over the people of God and cannot be identified with that people."[16] So Volf concludes that "the question is not whether the church is constituted 'from below', but rather *how* one is to reflect theologically on this element 'from below' so that the church is not simply reduced to the result of these believing individuals' need for association."[17] The Catholic tradition, while heavily accenting the element of authority "from above," mediated through historic succession, has always recognized a comparison between the church and Christ in that the church is formed from the interaction of the divine and the human. This makes the simultaneous affirmation of "from above" and "from below" both orthodox and necessary.

Third, Volf asserts the necessary complementarity of offices and charisms. Their complementarity is in line with Volf's general refusal to opt for "either-or" positions.[18] However, at times, he departs from his own principles, as when he omits an "only" in the following judgment: "the presence of Christ does not enter the church through the 'narrow portals' of *ordained office*, but rather through the dynamic life of the entire church."[19] In my reading, Volf's statement that "'Offices' are a particular type of charismata"[20] does not pay enough attention to the fact that the charismata are poured out by the risen, ascended Christ, but the choice of the Twelve belongs to the earthly life of Jesus before his death and resurrection.[21] This may need a qualification in the statement that "the pneumatological structure of the church follows from the sovereignty of the Spirit in the bestowal of charismata."[22] Nonetheless it remains true that the charismata bestowed by the Holy Spirit on any and all believers belong to the nature and character of the church and should act as a check upon any one-sided emphasis on church office.

Fourth, Volf indicates that the most important ecclesiological debate of the future will be between the historic churches and the free churches.[23]

16. Ibid., 177.

17. Ibid., 177.

18. There is an interesting example of this in his affirmation that "the church is a mixture of the social type that Weber called 'church,' into which a person is born, and the social type he called 'sect,' which a person freely joins" (ibid., 180).

19. Ibid., 152.

20. Ibid., 246.

21. This observation is connected with Volf's neglect of the foundation of the church within Israel, on which see below.

22. Ibid., 232.

23. This insight is being confirmed in the initiatives of Pope Francis toward

As the ecumenical world opens up to recognize in a new way the significance of the revival currents, especially in the Pentecostal and charismatic movements, an important corrective is provided to the widespread "mainline" view that the free churches have nothing to contribute to ecclesiology.

For Volf, total exclusivity is "no longer credible."[24] His free church ecclesiology therefore makes ecumenism essential for both free churches and historic churches. He insists that "the dynamic life and the orthodox faith of the many, quickly proliferating Free Churches make it difficult to deny them full ecclesiality."[25] But he adds, "Equally untenable is the early, though still widespread Free Church position that denies ecclesiality to the episcopal churches."[26] It will become increasingly impossible for the ancient churches to ignore the challenge of the free churches. "Although the episcopal churches will probably not surrender their own hierarchical structures, they, too, will increasingly have to integrate these Free Church elements into the mainstream of their own lives both theologically and practically."[27]

Other Pentecostal Voices

I consider briefly the contributions of Simon Chan and Peter Althouse to a Pentecostal ecclesiology. Chan is highly critical of Volf's "social, egalitarian" understanding of trinitarian relations, which ignores "the constitutive role of the Father."[28] Chan sees this position as "less a reflection of biblical order" and to represent "a carryover of modern liberal democratic values."[29] In another book, Chan has written of the disastrous effects in Asia of individualism and the lack of a theology of the visible church.[30] Peter Althouse sides with Volf against Chan on the non-hierarchical structure of trinitarian relations and dismisses Chan's liturgical-sacramental understanding: "Ultimately, Chan's project is overburdened by hierarchical assumptions and a High Church episcopacy that many Pentecostals would

---

Evangelicals and Pentecostals. See chapters 11 and 12.

24. Ibid., 133.
25. Ibid.
26. Ibid., 134.
27. Ibid., 13.
28. Chan, *Pentecostal Theology*, 101, footnote 11.
29. Ibid., 101, note 11.
30. Chan, *Spiritual Theology*, 103.

find disconcerting."[31] But does Chan's insistence on the "constitutive role of the Father"[32] require the use of the historically-loaded term "hierarchical"? Maybe as an Asian, he sees how heavily European-North American history has weighed upon inherited theological terminology.

Chan and Althouse agree with Volf concerning the eschatological character of the church. For Volf, "The all-embracing framework for an appropriate understanding of the church is God's eschatological new creation. According to the message of Jesus, the gathering of the people of God is grounded in the coming of the Kingdom of God in his person."[33] Chan says: "The understanding of the church as the eschatological community constituted by the Spirit is extremely crucial for Pentecostal spirituality."[34] Althouse seeks to "construct a Pentecostal ecclesiology that is Trinitarian, missional, and eschatological in scope."[35]

A Key Question

In a Catholic understanding of the church, a key question has to be the identification of the church as a visible body in history. Volf affirms the visibility of the church, regularly and firmly, and less frequently the need for an historical continuity. "The Spirit unites the gathered congregation with the triune God and integrates it into a history extending from Christ, indeed, from the Old Testament saints, to the eschatological new creation."[36] My first question concerning Volf's ecclesiology is whether it bears much relation to free church life and interaction as it is actually lived and manifested. It is undoubtedly an impressive theological construction. As a Catholic with free church connections, I see the importance of Volf's book in his articulation of the challenges to the received ecclesiologies of the historic churches arising from free church life and thinking. But does this reflect how most free church leaders and members understand themselves and think of church?

Today many Pentecostal scholars acknowledge that ecclesiology has been a neglected theme in their theologies. But in the last fifty years there

31. Althouse, *Pentecostal Ecclesiology*, 238.

32. Chan, *Pentecostal Theology*, 101.

33. Volf, *After Our Likeness*, 128.

34. Chan, *Pentecostal Theology*, 109.

35. Althouse, *Pentecostal Ecclesiology*, 231.

36. Volf, *After Our Likeness*, 129.

has been an increasing interest. Several contributory factors can be identified. The more evident ravages of individualism and the growing breakdown of Western society have made those giving a primacy to evangelism aware of the issue of what converts are being "evangelized into." The church growth movement and the vogue for church planting have also focused attention on church. The ecumenical movement forces more thought about church. In fact, the new charismatic free churches may be devoting more attention to church than Pentecostals, with the widespread teaching on the restoration of apostles and prophets.

I interpret this growing interest and attention as a growing desire for church. I do not think that the desire itself can create church, but it can lead to the spread and deepening of elements that are important for church life. To become church in the Catholic sense it is necessary to connect to the church of history. The church as the gathering of God's people in Christ has had an historical existence since the time of Jesus. The new covenant in his blood has existed since that time. Today new local assemblies are not creations ex nihilo, but grow out of what has existed for two thousand years. "The church . . . is a spiritual reality that exists prior to the individual Christians. . . . For to be a Christian is to be identified as one who is baptized or grafted into a pre-existing reality, the Body of Christ."[37]

This weakness in Volf's ecclesiology is also connected with the lack of rooting of the church in the chosen people of Israel, for whom being part of a people in historic continuity with their father Abraham is intrinsic to their identity. The choice of twelve apostles is clearly based on the constitution of Israel in twelve tribes (see Matt 19:28 and Rev 21:12, 14). The distancing of the church from its Jewish roots produced the "spiritualizing" tendencies which still affect much Christian exegesis. Among these consequences is the ignoring of the visible embodied people of God in history and a separatist understanding of the remnant.

The historical and the liturgical-sacramental are closely linked to the eschatological. Key to the Jewish roots are the major feasts when all Israel gathered in memorial, thanksgiving, and anticipation. The structure of the symbolic acts later designated sacraments and the structure ongoing sending of the Spirit to form the church, and the longed-for eschatological fulfillment.

---

37. Chan, *Pentecostal Theology*, 97–98.

A second question concerns what the Catechism of the Catholic Church calls "the bonds of unity."[38] The Catechism first emphasizes the role of the Holy Spirit: "It is the Holy Spirit, dwelling in those who believe and pervading and ruling over the entire Church, who brings about that wonderful communion of the faithful and joins them together so intimately in Christ that he is the principle of the Church's unity."[39] Then the Catechism turns to the bonds of unity, the factors through which the Holy Spirit forms and preserves the church in unity: first, there is charity; and then three "visible bonds of communion":

1. profession of one faith received from the apostles;

2. common celebration of divine worship, especially of the sacraments;

3. apostolic succession through the sacrament of Holy Orders, maintaining the fraternal concord of God's family.[40]

In other words, the nature of the church requires both the invisible role of the Holy Spirit and the visible role of such instruments of communion as the creeds, the liturgy, especially the Eucharist, and the episcopate. It is a pity that the role of the Word of God and the complementary character of Word and sacrament, re-emphasized in post-conciliar Catholicism, are not mentioned here.[41] This phrase "instruments of communion" has been taken up in the Anglican context to describe bodies that facilitate communion without having constraining authority.[42] So I scrutinized Volf's book in search of any visible bonds of unity to bind the free churches together, and I have not found any. His key argument seems to be: "the Spirit present in many persons . . . exist with one another in the Spirit. . . . They do not . . . dissociate into a multiplicity of individuals standing in isolation from one another, since the same Spirit is present in every person, and the

---

38. CCC, 815.

39. CCC, 813.

40. CCC, 815.

41. It is surprising that the magisterium is not listed among these bonds, presumably because it is implied by apostolic succession, though of course the role of the papacy and the magisterium is emphasized elsewhere.

42. The Anglican instruments of communion are the Lambeth conference of bishops, the meeting of the primates, and the Anglican Consultative Council, together with the archbishop of Canterbury, as "the focus of unity." See http://www.anglicancommunion.org/resources/acis/docs/unity.cfm

same Spirit connects them all with one another."[43] I do not see how Volf can escape from the problem of free church voluntarism (unity resulting from chosen association) unless there are some visible "bonds of unity," or "instruments" of communion.

How to Understand the Pentecostal Contribution

In the year 2000 and again in 2007, the Vatican upset many other Christians by statements that the Protestant communions are not churches in the proper sense, i.e., in the sense that the Catholic Church means by church.[44] This declaration was not in fact anything new, and not a going back on Vatican II, but it was nonetheless a communications disaster. The statements did explain that this view of church flows from the tight connection between Christ and the church, and that between the church and the Eucharist, so that the fullness of the eucharistic mystery is needed for church to be truly church. The communications disaster came from the complete absence of any consideration of what the Protestant communions—and Pentecostal assemblies—positively contribute to the full understanding of church and to the fullness of the body of Christ.

At this point we can return to the basic Pentecostal perception of the Pentecostal movement as a revival, but a "revival plus." All the positive elements of Evangelical revivals can and should be affirmed, even if not all the theological presuppositions are. Similarly, the distinctiveness of the Pentecostal movement should be affirmed in its understanding of being "baptized in Spirit," and in the bestowal of charismata as tools for the church's task.

The historic church contribution is to insist that ultimately all new movements and outpourings of the Spirit are not ends in themselves, nor do they form the whole of Christian life. Authentic moves of the Spirit in Christian history are never only for the recipients, but they are a gift of the Lord for the whole body, to revive, renew, and refresh, to heal, and live again from the fullness of the biblical heritage.

---

43. Volf, *After Our Likeness*, 189.

44. The precise wording was " the ecclesial communities which have not preserved the valid Episcopate and the genuine and integral substance of the Eucharistic mystery, are not Churches in the proper sense" (*Dominus Jesus*, 2000, 17).

We can pick up from Volf's ecclesiology key elements that belong to the free church contribution to the one church and add some that are more specifically Pentecostal. Among the free church contributions are the following:

- the importance of the local church and its being equipped to fulfill its ministry (even though a strict congregationalism is not acceptable and there are differences about the contours of the local church);

- the necessity of the church being built "from below" as well as "from above";

- the preaching of the Word of God as necessary for personal conversion and for the church to be the servant not the master of the Word;

- the presence of a wholly active church membership not divided into active ministers and not so active laity.

The following elements can be added for Pentecostal and free charismatic bodies:

- the need for constant outpouring of the Holy Spirit upon the church (in addition to the historic church emphasis on receiving the full Christian heritage from the past);

- the need for an exegesis of Scripture that brings together the Spirit, the Word, and the faith community;[45]

- the role of the charisms in structuring and modelling the church;

- the role of trans-local ministries such as apostles and prophets.

It is probably necessary to outline what these proposals do not mean so as to avoid all misunderstanding, especially in view of past history. It does not mean that all Christian communions and fellowships not in communion with the sees of Rome or of Constantinople simply have to accept their authority and apply for rapid admission. The ancient churches have to go through their own form of conversion and renewal so as to be ready to receive what the free churches have to contribute. This will require a great humbling and much rethinking. The continuing habit among some Catholic and Orthodox leaders of dismissing all Pentecostal and free charismatic

---

45. This has been a major concern of Pentecostal theologian Amos Yong, e.g., in *Spirit*.

groups as "sects" shows how much humbling is needed, and the time that will be needed for new mentalities to develop.

The position I am advocating is not a reversion to the pre-Vatican II Catholic notion of *vestigiae ecclesiae*, literally vestiges of the church.[46] In this theory the surviving ecclesial elements in Protestant communions were simply survivals of what had not been rejected at the time or times of separation. These *vestigiae* then needed to be reintegrated into mother church. The *vestigiae ecclesiae* theory simply looked backwards and formed part of an ecumenism of "return," whereby all other church communities had simply to return to communion with Rome. It was a somewhat static view with the only possibilities for the separated *vestigiae* being longer survival or further disintegration and weakening of orthodox faith. By contrast, the position I am urging is looking at the present and the future, seeing the ecclesial elements in the Pentecostal and free charismatic churches as a new creative activity of the Holy Spirit, and thus not *vestigiae*. In this light, the Holy Spirit is at work also in the process whereby these churches are led to pay greater attention to the issue of church. Whereas in the *vestigiae* theory, the Catholic Church was held already to possess all these elements, in my understanding the Holy Spirit is drawing attention through the free churches to aspects of church forgotten or neglected in the Catholic tradition.[47] This work of the Spirit is then inherently directed towards a future fullness of the one church.

As the work of the Holy Spirit is always creative, and always has a reference to the formation of the church and the preparation of the coming kingdom, it requires constant attention to what is actually happening in the Pentecostal–charismatic world. Among the free charismatic groupings we find a major emphasis on the fivefold ministries of Eph 4:11, especially on apostles and prophets. The conviction that God is restoring apostles to the church represents a major departure from the congregational ecclesiology of Miroslav Volf, but it emphasizes in a different way the element of church "from above." This development also needs to be assessed in terms of its ecclesiological significance.[48]

46. The issue of *vestigiae ecclesiae* is also considered in chapter 8.

47. It is true that Catholic teaching still insists that in the Catholic Church in communion with Rome are found "the fullness of the means of salvation" (CCC, 816, citing Vatican II, UR, 3) and "the fullness of divine revelation." But in an ecumenical age these concepts are commonly understood to include a recognition that some of these elements may be more profoundly understood and more fully reflected in the actual life of other Christian bodies than in the Catholic Church.

48. See chapter 8.

This position does not mean that no separation is ever justified. But it does require that separations are never more than provisional.[49] The schism between the northern kingdom of Israel and the southern kingdom of Judah is highly relevant, since the separation is prophetically sanctioned, and represents neither a permanent split, nor the disinheriting of the Davidic kingship.[50] The sanctioning of a provisional and not lasting separation is presented as a consequence of the sin and corruption within the one kingdom, particularly in and through its leadership. While this may provide the justification for a division in its origins, the ongoing maintenance of separation can only be justified as long as the original failings have not been repented for and corrected. The historical inevitability of the Pentecostal movement developing into new ecclesial communities would seem to have a rather different rationale: viz., that the historic churches were not then ready to receive all that the Holy Spirit was giving. It can be plausibly argued that a time was needed for separate development and maturing, even though the separation and isolation produces its own distortions, before the historic expressions change enough for the Pentecostal gifting to be received.

So the Pentecostal and charismatic movements should be acknowledged as powerful currents of the Holy Spirit, though they obviously have their shadow sides and their weaknesses. As currents of the Spirit they are ultimately for the refreshing, healing, enrichment, and unity of the one church. It has not been my intention to discuss the much-debated question of the relationship of the Catholic Church in communion with Rome to the one church. I have rather focused on the necessity for the church to be visible and to manifest a historic continuity. This is the more important point to make to Pentecostals and it is one to which Volf refers. It is too premature to address the question as to how such currents can eventually flow into one church. But it is obvious that huge changes of mentality have to take place on every side for such an outcome to be possible. I argue this utopian vision because it seems to me to be required by the witness of the New Testament and by the reality of these revival-renewal currents.[51] But it is no more utopian than the original vision of the ecumenical movement based on John 17:21 that "all may be one."

49. See chapter 6.

50. See Lanne, "Notes," 67–86.

51. Since the presentation of this paper, the election and the initiatives of Pope Francis, especially toward Evangelicals and Pentecostals, are already making such changes appear less utopian. See chapter 12.

The reconstitution of visible unity is ultimately impossible without the Jewish component. Some Catholic scholars were recognizing at the time of the Second Vatican Council that Israel remains an intra-covenantal reality and that the first schism was between the church and the synagogue.[52] I have become much more aware of this dimension through my interest in and involvement with the Messianic Jews. In my study, *The Challenges of the Pentecostal Charismatic and Messianic Jewish Movements* I noted the charismatic impulses at the origin of the modern Messianic Jewish movement.[53] What is particularly interesting in the light of the debate concerning historic church and free church ecclesiology is that the Messianic Jews both represent something very old and something very new.[54] They are influenced as Jews by the Jewish rabbinic and synagogal heritage and as a new movement of the Spirit by free church patterns of organization. The Messianic Jewish insistence that their movement belongs at one and the same time to the historic people of Israel and to the church makes quite illogical any assertions about the necessary invisibility of the church.

Finally such an understanding requires that the Pentecostal and charismatic groupings play their full part in the movement of all Christians toward unity. What this means in terms of existing ecumenical instruments is for them to decide, but it is an encouraging sign that in most parts of the world the Pentecostal leadership has welcomed and taken part in the developments out of which the Global Christian Forum has been formed. The GCF arose from initiatives from deeply involved ecumenical leaders who understood that any initiatives for Christian unity that did not gain the support of leaders from the fast-growing Evangelical and Pentecostal movements would lack credibility and be missing a key ingredient of Christian witness. They realized that a new ecumenical methodology was needed, that did not privilege an European or North American theological agenda, and that would give greater attention to spirituality and the power of the Word of God. While GCF is at this stage a tender young plant, it is a highly encouraging development, for it brings the Evangelical and Pentecostal worlds into constructive inter-action with ecumenical church leadership.[55]

52. See Hocken, *Jewish*.

53. Ibid., 97–115.

54. Chapter 5 in Hocken, *Challenges*, is entitled "The Messianic Jewish Movement: New Current and Old Reality."

55. A full report on the GCF and its first global meeting in Limuru, Kenya in November 2007 is found in van Beek, *Revisioning*. See the GCF website www.globalchristianforum.org

CHAPTER 2

The Theological Task in Ecumenical Renewal as Purification from Ideology

THIS CHAPTER ARISES DIRECTLY from my personal history and experience. Such an approach should not require justification in a Pentecostal and charismatic context. However, I am a charismatic Catholic rather than a Pentecostal, and so my focus is on the renewal of theology through the Holy Spirit, rather than the formation of a distinctively Pentecostal theology. Because the charismatic movement has been a movement spanning virtually all Christian churches and traditions, I have seen my role as a charismatic theologian as inherently ecumenical. But in making this contribution, I am conscious of the necessary interaction between an emerging Pentecostal theology and the renewal of older theological traditions, as well as the need for an ongoing renewal of Pentecostal theology as it begins to acquire the status of a tradition.

Personal Background and Experience

Two elements in my life as a Christian have alerted me to the need for a purification from ideology. The first arose during my doctoral studies in the early 1980s. When I went to Birmingham to begin work on a PhD, I knew that the topic for my dissertation had to be connected with the charismatic movement, in which I had then been involved for eight years, and on which I had already done some theological writing.[1] During my first six months I

---

1. See Hocken *Significance* (1976); "Catholic Pentecostalism," (1974) "Charismatics and Mystics," (1975) and "Charismatic Movement" (1979).

read all that Catholic theological commentators on the charismatic movement had been writing.[2]

I found this reading increasingly unsatisfactory. I did not entirely agree with these scholars, and I wanted to avoid producing a work that was primarily critical of others. In practice, I could not even attempt such an overview, as at this stage I had not yet arrived at a distinctive overall understanding of the Renewal. It was at this point of frustration that I had an illumination: I sensed that the Lord was saying to me: "Study what I am doing, not what other people think about what I am doing." Later I was to discover that this word or light was not just for the completion of my dissertation, but was also a guide for my subsequent studies and writings.[3] Studying what the Lord is doing cannot but have an ecumenical scope. This word led me to pay much more attention to history, because the question "What is the work of the Holy Spirit today?" leads necessarily to the question "What was the work of the Holy Spirit in the past?" And in both cases, the question cannot be answered without a study of the empirical historical data.

It would seem to be easier for a Catholic than for an Evangelical or a Pentecostal to study and reflect theologically on the contemporary work of the Holy Spirit. Catholic theologians are not so preoccupied with being biblical, which is both a weakness and a strength. The Catholic theologians of the period between the Council of Trent and the Second Vatican Council typically started from traditional Catholic theological positions and from the teachings of the popes. The conservative majority sought to defend the traditional teaching and to repudiate "errors," often "Protestant errors," while more adventurous spirits explored the possibility of modifications in the received positions. The preparations for the Second Vatican Council, called by Pope John XXIII as a council of renewal, encouraged a reflection on the church as it actually is in the light of what it should be and could be. One of the great exponents of this approach was the German Jesuit, Karl Rahner.[4] This kind of theological writing did not normally start from Scripture, though Scripture played a role in the reflection. As a result, today there is much Catholic theological reflection on what is going on in the (Catholic) Church, and what should or could be going on. Although

2. In particular, the writings of Edward O'Connor CSC, Kilian McDonnell OSB, Simon Tugwell OP, and Donald Gelpi SJ.

3. This is most evident in my books *Glory* (1994) and *Strategy* (1996).

4. See, for example, many essays in Rahner, *Theological Investigations*, in particular Vol. 14, and in *Mission*, especially Vol. 2.

Catholic theologians are not accustomed to studying the contemporary movements of the Holy Spirit and have generally been slow to recognize the importance of the Pentecostal and charismatic movements, this study of the contemporary church makes it relatively easy for a Catholic theologian to reflect on the contemporary work of the Holy Spirit. Today I understand that just as the Holy Spirit sanctifies the Christian, so an authentic theology of the Holy Spirit purifies the church's theology.

The second major influence in the last two decades has been my involvement with the Messianic Jews. Before this, I had only a very general and hazy understanding of Judaism and things Jewish. My growing knowledge of the Jewish people made me aware of their absolute horror of idolatry. Through this awareness, I have understood that ideology is the idolatry of the mind. Ideology absolutizes what is merely created and contingent. Ideology enters theology when an importance is given to particular ideas and realities in the religious sphere beyond the importance they possess in God's overall plan, unveiled in the Scriptures. Karl Rahner describes ideology as "a fundamental closure in face of the 'wholeness' of reality, one which turns a partial aspect into an absolute."[5]

Through my association with the Messianic Jews, I have been led to participate in initiatives of reconciliation addressing the sins of the past, both concerning the Jewish people and concerning Christian divisions. These initiatives directly confront the participants with the need to purify ecclesial and denominational histories and theologies from all forms of ideology. It is above all the challenge of the Holocaust that has forced the Catholic Church to recognize the sin in the Catholic treatment of the Jewish people throughout the centuries, and for the "purification of memory" to be proposed as a necessary ingredient in all work for reconciliation.[6] Thus, through this experience with the Messianic Jews, where the past sins stare you in the face, I have been led back to the role of "purification" in the whole sphere of theology and ecumenical dialogue.[7]

---

5. Rahner, "Ideology," 44.

6. "The purification of memory" was described as the goal of repentance for the sins of the past by John Paul II in the document *Incarnationis Mysterium* (1998), para. 11. See also International Theological Commission, *Memory and Reconciliation* (1999).

7. See chapter 13.

Studying the Work of the Holy Spirit
in Revival/Renewal Currents

It is impossible to ignore the witness of the Scriptures when seeking to identify the work of the Holy Spirit in any currents of revival and renewal. It is also impossible to enter on such a reflection without accepted criteria from Christian tradition, though these will all have some biblical basis. There are patterns of behavior that the New Testament and the Christian tradition present as the work of the Holy Spirit: the confession of God as Father, and of Jesus as Lord come in human flesh; confession of sin leading to a transformed life; the love of those who appear to be the least lovable; the spontaneous praise of God; the love of the Scriptures; the desire to preach the gospel of Jesus; a concern for righteousness and justice; the practice of authority as service.

While theologians need to heed and respect the theological heritage of their own confessions, an objective theological reflection cannot be restricted by denominational or party boundaries. Here we encounter what may be the first stage of purification from ideology. The work of the Holy Spirit is never restricted to one church or one movement. An objective study will require us to challenge the ideological assertions in our ecclesial and theological camps. When I was writing my dissertation on the origins of the charismatic movement, I was faced with the uncomfortable fact of the new "non-denominational" streams within the charismatic movement: were they simply a deviation from "authentic renewal," as I was then thinking, or were they to be recognized in their distinctiveness as in a significant way a work of the Holy Spirit? I came to see that the historical evidence pointed to their being fully part of the charismatic movement, and to see that the first option was in effect ideological, preferring hallowed formulae of the past to the data of faith. So I was led to see that the renewal of the historic churches and the raising up of new streams outside are two complementary prongs of the work of the Holy Spirit.[8]

In this light, we can see the Catholic opening to ecumenism at the Second Vatican Council as a loosening of the ideological mindset among Catholics that nothing significant happens outside the Catholic Church. After centuries of exclusivist thinking it is recognized that the Holy Spirit is at work outside the Roman communion, not only in individuals but also in

---

8. This is the position advocated in Hocken, *Strategy,* and *Challenges.*

church communities.[9] This recognition soon made possible the acceptance by the Catholic Church of the charismatic movement which had begun outside its communion.

As the European Pentecostal and Charismatic Research Association (EPCRA) [10] and the Society for Pentecostal Studies (SPS) bear witness, the Pentecostal movement has been entering into a phase of greater theological maturity. However, the development of a movement and the inevitable processes of structuring and institutionalization bring new dangers of group (denominational) arrogance and ideology. I return to this danger in the next section. Here I note that the new independent charismatic streams, flourishing in most parts of the world, are mostly at a pre-reflective stage of their existence. Their colleges of formation and education are at an early stage of development and are mostly unrelated to the academic world. In most parts of the world, there are as yet no detailed studies of this phenomenon.[11] The natural tendency of those caught up in new currents of the Spirit is to think that their group is where the Holy Spirit is really working, that they are truly on the cutting edge of the Spirit's work today, and that those who do not act like them or speak their language do not know the deep work of the Holy Spirit. Here of course, it is the responsibility of mature leaders to fellowship more widely and to present a less sectarian view to their people.

It is no accident that the first studies of these new currents typically come from the social sciences, which are especially attentive to new patterns of human behavior and association. Many of these studies are of great value, but they rarely influence the participants because they are not written from a faith perspective. Until there are theological studies of the new currents of the Holy Spirit, that are seeking to understand them in the light of the Holy Spirit, the leaders are lacking an essential tool for their discernment and reflection. The theological reflection is essential for situating the phenomena studied in relation to other currents of the Spirit, in relation to the wider church, and in relation to the Christian past. It provides a protection against group ideology: the exaltation of one's own stream, the absolutization of teaching, and of the group's particular model and style. It

9. See UR, 3.

10. EPCRA is not formally constituted as a society, and does not have membership. Its continuity has been assured by a convener, Jean-Daniel Plüss (Switzerland).

11. There is more literature on the new charismatic churches in the United Kingdom than anywhere else to date. This was initiated by Walker (see especially *Restoring*) and has now reached more organized expression in Kay, *Apostolic*.

might even help to eliminate the terminology of "religious spirits," a phrase I dislike intensely! Though this negative use of the word "religion" attempts to describe a real spiritual condition, it is rooted in individualistic thinking, and makes difficult any real respect for a spiritual heritage.

The Purification of Received Theological Traditions

I now draw on the contribution of John Paul II. While strongly anchored in the Catholic tradition, John Paul II was a very creative thinker. Most of his encyclical letters contain some new insights, and this is especially true of his encyclical on Christian unity, *Ut Unum Sint* (1995). Although he nowhere spoke of purification from ideology in the church, John Paul II introduced a radically new element that is highly relevant to this theme: ecumenical dialogue necessarily includes an examination of conscience: "Such a radical exhortation to acknowledge our condition as sinners ought also to mark the spirit which we bring to ecumenical dialogue."[12]

Here the pope brings the church's relationship to God into his understanding of ecumenical encounter. "Dialogue cannot take place merely on a horizontal level, being restricted to meetings, exchanges of points of view or even the sharing of gifts proper to each Community. It also has a primarily vertical thrust, directed towards the One, who, as the Redeemer of the world and the Lord of history, is himself our Reconciliation."[13] From this God-centered vision comes a deep spiritual insight: it is the acknowledgment that "we are men and women who have sinned . . . which creates in brothers and sisters living in Communities not in full communion with each other that interior space where Christ, the source of the Church's unity, can effectively act, with all the power of his Spirit, the Paraclete."[14]

It is in our encounter with each other as separated Christian communions where we acknowledge our sinfulness in the presence of the Lord that the Holy Spirit can and will purify our minds and doctrinal formulations. It is the distinctive witness to the Holy Spirit in the other Christian traditions that confronts us with our own failings, our own lacunae, and our own biases. The point I am adding is that this purification—in the context of theology—is fundamentally a purification from ideology. Our theology

12. UUS, 34.

13. Ibid., 35.

14. Ibid.

and doctrine deteriorate into ideology when they lose sight of their never-ceasing foundation in the living Lord and in the Holy Spirit. The ideology is most evident in the ways that our denominations and institutions have come to be self-sufficient and to regard themselves as the norm by which all else is to be judged.

In other words, the area of our identities as churches is a fertile ground for ideology. Situations of major conflict produce a warfare psychology. Rejection produces judgmentalism. The opponents are demonized, and you define yourselves by what differentiates you from your enemies and detractors. In the Counter-Reformation, Catholic identity undergoes a major change. Protestants form their identity in opposition to everything Roman and papal. To be Catholic now becomes to be anti-Protestant. A true and loyal Catholic is now someone who believes in eucharistic transubstantiation, who singles out the role of Mary, and who exalts the authority of the pope. To uphold Protestant emphases, such as justification by faith or Bible-reading for all, has become suspect in the Catholic Church. Of course, the Catholic still believes in the incarnation, in the redemption, in the resurrection of Jesus, but the decisive distinguishing beliefs become those that Protestants deny. This warfare psychology produces a vicious spiral of distrust and self-concern. The more Catholics concentrate on the Mass, Mary, and the pope, the more these revealed realities become separated from their proper place in the full spectrum of biblical revelation and Christian doctrine. The more the forms of piety fed by Catholic institutional loyalty and anti-Protestantism flourish and develop, the more they are abhorrent to Protestants. The more the Protestants oppose and criticize, the more Catholic loyalty insists on "Catholic truth."

A parallel but different pattern occurs when revival movements are not accepted and are pushed "outside," becoming clusters of new Christian denominations. Here too there is a tendency to define yourself over and against those who reject you. Here the pressures are not as strong as in cases of outright conflict, so in the origins of the Pentecostal movement, we find an element of Pentecostals defining themselves in terms of who they are in relation to Jesus and the Holy Spirit, often in restorationist terms, along with an element of defining themselves over and against those who rejected them or who ignore them. The process of denominational formation strengthened the second tendency because each denomination had to define its own distinctive beliefs.

The only way out of this cul-de-sac is conversion to Jesus and the light of the Holy Spirit. The renewal of the church cannot happen without a breaking out of this cycle of mutual opposition, and without a re-centering on Christ and the Scriptures. The true identity of all is found in our relationship—personal and corporate—with the Triune God: our relationship to the Father in Jesus Christ through the Holy Spirit. This change from a church-centered to a Christ-centered church does not mean an abandonment of our distinctive convictions, but a re-centering of everything in Christ. This process of ecclesial conversion, which is never easy, is being freed from church-centered ideology by a return to a full Christ-centeredness. It would seem that distorted identities underlie all other ideological manifestations in our churches.

Two Applications

I want to take two examples: a Pentecostal example from Springfield, Missouri, and a Catholic example from Rome. I take the Springfield example first, because the history of the Assemblies of God is much shorter and less complex than that of the Roman Church. I receive the "Pentecostal ecumenism" of Mel Robeck as seeking to free the Pentecostal movement, and particularly the Assemblies of God, from ideological mentalities and self-understanding. As many Pentecostal scholars are aware, Mel wrote a courageous article suggesting some parallels between the "magisterium" in Springfield and the magisterium in Rome.[15] One major difference is that the Assemblies of God do not have a long-established theological tradition underpinning their practice in the same way as the Roman Catholic Church. But what Robeck is criticizing has all the trappings of ideology: the focus on institutional claims, a lack of interest in how one's methods are perceived by other Christians, a defensiveness in the face of criticism, the re-writing of past history to accord with current orthodoxy. He tells the story in some detail of the formulation of the Assemblies of God doctrine concerning speaking in tongues as "the initial evidence" of Spirit-baptism, how inconvenient data were excised from denominational publications, and critical voices were ignored or marginalized.

The Springfield example makes very clear the relationship between denominational ideology and hostility to ecumenism. This does not mean that the ecumenical movement cannot develop its own forms of ideology—one

15. Robeck, "Emerging."

of the criticisms legitimately made of some aspects of the WCC. Hostility to ecumenism protects our denominational ideology. It is the witness of other Christian communions—and all the more so when they are evidently manifesting the presence and the fruit of the Holy Spirit—that confronts each church community with its own lacunae, its own weaknesses, its own failure to honor and to be nourished by the full biblical revelation.

A Pentecostal theologian, Amos Yong, has addressed the danger of ideology, the idolatry of the mind, more philosophically, but his words seem applicable to the story told by Robeck: "the signs and symbols through which we encounter and engage the divine should never attain the kind of ultimacy that belongs to God alone."[16] Yong continues, "idolatry is the result of insisting on the reduction of the infinitude of the divine reality to solely finite terms."[17]

The Roman example can take as its starting point the Instruction from the Congregation for the Doctrine of the Faith (CDF), issued in July 2007, concerning the uniqueness of the Roman Catholic Church. How should this be interpreted? Is it a setback for ecumenism? Is it a reversion to pre-conciliar isolation? This document answers five questions that the CDF wants to clarify. The temptation to ideology seems to be most evident in the answer to the first question: "Did the Second Vatican Council change the Catholic doctrine on the Church?"

Here is their response: "The Second Vatican Council neither changed nor intended to change this doctrine, rather it developed, deepened and more fully explained it." The ideological tendency is fearful of admitting that there has been real change. The motto is "*Semper eadem*" [always the same]. A subsequent paragraph seeks to explain how this development and deepening did not involve change: "What the Church has taught down through the centuries, we also teach. In simple terms that which was assumed, is now explicit; that which was uncertain, is now clarified; that which was meditated upon, discussed and sometimes argued over, is now put together in one clear formulation." I find more honest the still rather cautious statement by John Paul II in his first encyclical letter: "Entrusting myself fully to the Spirit of truth, therefore, I am entering into the rich inheritance of the recent pontificates. This inheritance has struck deep roots

---

16. Yong , *Spirit*, 213.

17. Ibid., 213.

in the awareness of the church in an utterly new way, quite unknown previously, thanks to the Second Vatican Council."[18]

The ideological mindset has great difficulty in admitting mistakes and weaknesses. One of the most obvious new elements in the Vatican II Constitution *Lumen Gentium* on the church is the teaching on ecumenism. Can this really be regarded as development and explicitation rather than change? It is conveniently forgotten that in 1928 Pius XI issued an encyclical on unity totally rejecting the ecumenical movement and which presented a very different message from the Second Vatican Council and John Paul II.[19] Official Catholic documents typically cite previous magisterial teachings quite generously, but there is no reference in either *Lumen Gentium* or *Ut Unum Sint* to the 1928 encyclical *Mortalium Animos*.[20]

I see the opening to ecumenism at the Second Vatican Council as the beginning of a process whereby the Catholic Church was freeing itself from the ideological elements that had developed in its ecclesiology through the centuries. The Catholic Church in communion with Rome has always believed in its unique position, a uniqueness that is clearly bound up with the Roman primacy. The exclusiveness was once affirmed in the famous dictum *Extra Ecclesia nulla salus* (no salvation outside the church). At Vatican II, the uniqueness is reaffirmed, but the associated conclusions are modified: for the first time, it is acknowledged that other Christian communities can be means of salvation for their members. The other communities are no longer seen as simply "outside the church," but as "imperfectly within." The assumption that unity is only possible by the return of the others to an unchanged mother church is now abandoned. Thirty years later, in *Ut*

---

18. RH, 3.

19. "The energy with which this [ecumenical] scheme is being promoted has won for it many adherents, and even many Catholics are attracted by it, since it holds out the hope of a union apparently consonant with the wishes of Holy Mother Church, whose chief desire it is to recall her erring children and to bring them back to her bosom. In reality, however, these fair and alluring words cloak a most grave error, subversive of the foundations of the Catholic faith. Conscious, therefore, of Our Apostolic office, which warns Us not to allow the flock of Christ to be led astray by harmful fallacies, We invoke your zeal, Venerable Brethren, to avert this evil. We feel confident that each of you, by written and spoken word, will explain clearly to the people the principles and arguments that We are about to set forth, so that Catholics may know what view and what course of action they should adopt regarding schemes for the promiscuous union into one body of all who call themselves Christians." (MA, 11).

20. In LG chapter 2, there are two footnote references to other encyclicals of Pius XI issued in 1928!

Unum Sint John Paul II makes clearer the reciprocal element in ecumenical relations, when he writes, "Dialogue is not simply an exchange of ideas. In some way it is always an 'exchange of gifts.'"[21] At the end of *Ut Unum Sint* the pope recognized that the papacy had become an obstacle to Christian unity and so he invited the leaders and theologians of other churches and communions to join with him to see how the primatial ministry of the bishop of Rome could be exercised in a way that would serve the cause of unity rather than hinder it.[22] "I insistently pray the Holy Spirit to shine his light upon us, enlightening all the Pastors and theologians of our Churches, that we may seek—together, of course—the forms in which this ministry may accomplish a service of love recognized by all concerned."[23] While the insistence on a uniqueness of the Catholic Church remains, it is here re-interpreted in a less exclusivist way that recognizes the inherent reciprocity in ecumenical relations.

I see this process as a sifting of the Catholic tradition that is freeing the God-given foundation from ideological distortions. The ideological mentality is most evident in the total dismissal of the "others," on *a priori* grounds, without any study of the data. They are not part of us, therefore God is not at work among them. We do not need to know them, they are heretics, they are sects. The way out of ideology comes with relationship instead of apartness, with respect in place of disdain. With relationship and respect come an authentic knowledge of the "others" as they are gifted by the Lord, and the possibility of an authentic discernment in the Holy Spirit. In this process the Pentecostal and charismatic movements have an impor-tant role to play, because they remind the whole church of the essential role and gifts of the Holy Spirit, without which a full knowledge and authentic discernment of the "others" is not possible. This is why it is so tragic when Pentecostals and charismatics themselves adopt sectarian and ideological positions, for they are then refusing to look at everything with the eyes of Jesus, the prototype for all who are "Spirit-filled."

21. UUS, 28.

22. "This is an immense task, which we cannot refuse and which I cannot carry out by myself. Could not the real but imperfect communion existing between us persuade church leaders and their theologians to engage with me in a patient and fraternal dia-logue on this subject, a dialogue in which, leaving useless controversies behind, we could listen to one another, keeping before us only the will of Christ for his Church and allow-ing ourselves to be deeply moved by his plea "that they may all be one . . . so that the world may believe that you have sent me" (John 17:21)?" (UUS, 96).

23. UUS, 95.

In fact, however, the temptation to ideology affects the whole of the theological enterprise, as idolatry infects the whole of the human enterprise.[24] As I have already indicated, ideology develops when we forget that all our theology and doctrine have their authentic foundation in the living Lord and in the Holy Spirit, to whom the Scriptures bear a privileged and unique witness. I have an Evangelical contact in the United States, who is highly committed to the promotion of greater understanding and cooperation between Evangelicals and Catholics. He is always contacting leading Evangelical theologians, I would say trying to penetrate their ideology, and has recently been contesting the view of some Evangelical scholars that the Catholic Church has effectively replaced the gospel by the "sacramental system." There is ideology on both sides of this argument. On the Catholic side, the reaction to the Protestant Reformation did lead to an emphasis on the sacraments that led to what some Catholics have termed sacramentalization without evangelization. The phrase "sacramental system" does not strike me as unjust when applied to the period between the Council of Trent and the Second Vatican Council. The very word "system" points to an ideological element. But an ideological element also enters the Evangelical criticism when the belief that Catholics have replaced the gospel with a sacramental system becomes a kind of Evangelical dogma vigorously asserted without reference to renewal and reforms in Catholic teaching and practice.

I hope that the examples mentioned will help to demonstrate that an authentically ecumenical stance is essential for avoiding confessional, denominational, and sectarian ideology. The other Christian churches and traditions confront all our systems with the challenge of our lacks, our biases, and our distortions. There is no other way for the churches to be purified from ideology than a resolutely ecumenical way. This is not to deny that there can also be an ecumenical ideology! But in the ecumenical task between the traditions, the points of contention are important. They expose the most clearly where ideology has entered in.

---

24. The ideological danger also affects practical attitudes within our churches. Karl Rahner's article already cited (see note 5) notes the close link between ideology and praxis. A major part of the article is devoted to why Christianity is not an ideology, but Rahner acknowledges the presence of ideological currents within the church: "Christianity has often been used—sometimes in a revolutionary manner but mostly in a conservative and reactionary way—to justify social, economic, political, cultural and scientific conditions which cannot claim permanent validity" (*Art. cit.*, 46).

The Decisive Contribution
of the Jewish Dimension

My involvement with the Messianic Jews has convinced me that the Jewish issue confronts all the Gentile churches with the deepest ground of ideology. In particular, the existence and claims of the Messianic Jews confront Christians with all the consequences of "replacement theology," the view, now increasingly repudiated, that God had rejected the Jews as his chosen people, and that the church had taken the place of Israel. By asserting the rightness of Jewish believers in Jesus retaining their Jewish identity, and their right to live as Jewish disciples of Jesus, they face us with the abnormality of a totally Gentile church. They remind us that the original vision presented by Paul in Ephesians was of the church of the "one new man," made up of Jews and Gentiles reconciled through the blood of Jesus. In this vision, the Gentile disciples have now become "fellow citizens with the [Jewish] saints and members of the household of God, built upon the foundation of the [Jewish] apostles and prophets, Messiah Jesus himself being the cornerstone" (Eph 2:19–20). These verses contrast the condition of the Gentile believers with their pre-conversion state described in verse 12. This unity of Jew and Gentile in Messiah is "the mystery of Christ" (Eph 3:4), "that is, how the Gentiles are fellow heirs, members of the same body, and partakers of the promise in Christ Jesus through the gospel" (Eph 3:6). In other words, the church was formed by the Holy Spirit to have a dialogical character built into its constitution, the dialogue between Jews and Gentiles, whose identities, like those of man and woman, were irreducible. This polarity in the church represents a transformation of the traditional Old Testament relationship between Israel and the nations, re-shaped in the new covenant context.

In this perspective, the subsequent rejection and outlawing by the church of its Jewish component represented a capitulation to a Gentile ideology that exalts the nations over and against the Jewish people. It will later lead to a "Catholicism" of all the nations that was no longer grounded in the unique election of Israel. However, the original vision has not been entirely lost in the tradition of the church of Rome, which has always honored the apostles Peter and Paul as its founders.[25] These two apostles symbolize the bipolarity of the church, with Peter entrusted with "the mission

---

25. This is expressed in the celebration of the major feast of both apostles together on June 29 each year.

to the circumcised" (Gal 2:8) and Paul as the "apostle to the nations" (see Acts 9:15; 22:21; Gal 2:2, 9). In the biblical vision, not only found in the Old Testament, the orientation of the nations to Israel and especially to Jerusalem is their God-given protection against all self-exaltation and delusions of special grandeur as nations; that is, a protection against all forms of nationalistic ideology infecting the church. In the New Testament, this orientation to Jerusalem is expressed in the vision of the Jerusalem on high that will descend to earth, to which "the kings of the earth . . . shall bring . . . the glory and honor of the nations" (Rev 21:24, 26).

This is not the occasion to present a detailed study of the ways in which replacement theology opened the door to ideology in the church. I want simply to offer a few suggestions for further consideration. First, concerning the identity of Jesus himself. The very first verse of the New Testament presents us with the human identity of Jesus: "The book of the genealogy of Jesus Christ, the son of David, the son of Abraham" (Matt 1:1). From the start, it is clear that Jesus is an Israelite, of the tribe of Judah, and from the clan of David. In other words, Jesus is fully Jewish. It is only as a Jew—in fact as a son of David and a son of Abraham—that he can be the Messiah of Israel, and so fulfill the calling of Israel to be a blessing to all the peoples of the earth. What has this to do with ideology? The ideology enters when the Jewishness of Jesus is forgotten and the incarnation is presented simply as Jesus becoming a "man"—as though he became an all-purpose generic man without a particular people and heritage. The Italian biblical scholar, Francesco Rossi de Gasperis SJ, who lived and worked in Jerusalem for most of his academic life, repeatedly warned of the dangers of a Christianity, particularly of a Christology, cut off from its roots in Israel, becoming ideological. "The Christian churches have a great need to remain strongly connected to Israel so as to avoid being devastated by the dangers of "ideological Christianities" that are far from imaginary."[26] This danger arose from the disappearance of the Judeo-Christian church of the origins.[27]

26. "Le chiese cristiane hanno un grande bisogno di rimanere ben strette a Israele per non venire devastate dai pericoli non certo immaginari dei 'cristianesimi ideologici'" (Rossi de Gasperis, *Cominciando*, 161).

27. "Noi, cristiani provenienti dalle genti, non immaginiamo quanto la scomparsa visibile di una chiesa giudeocristiana, nel cuore della grande e unica chiesa del Messia Gésu, renda più ricorrente e più pesante per la nostra chiesa la tentazione gnostica e umanistica di ridurre la storia alla natura, l'evangelo a un messaggio anthropologico di giustizia et di welfare umanistico" (ibid., 85). English translation: "We, the Christians coming from the nations, do not imagine how much the disappearance of a Judeo-Christian church from the heart of the vast and one church of the Messiah Jesus renders more

Conclusion

As Karl Rahner indicated, all ideology absolutizes what is created and contingent. Ideology turns a part into the whole. The Holy Spirit reveals Jesus as Savior from all sin and ideology and as Lord of all. A theology guided and enlightened by the Holy Spirit will always demonstrate how each part fits into the whole. It will liberate us from the limitations and distortions of partial and one-sided presentations. The prophet Habakkuk mentions the workman who makes "dumb idols" as one who "trusts in his own creation" (Hab 2:18). The scholar led by the Holy Spirit is concerned not to produce his own theological creation in which to trust, but to throw the deeper light of the Holy Spirit upon the areas of study. As the place of each part—of creation, of the work of redemption, of the church, of the coming kingdom—is shown forth in relation to the whole, to what the Pauline writings calls "the mystery of Christ,"[28] we give glory to the one God, who alone is absolute, the Father, the Son, and the Holy Spirit.

---

frequent and heavier for our church the gnostic and humanistic temptation to reduce history to nature, the gospel to a human-centered message about justice and human well-being."

28. See Eph 1:9–10; 3:4–6; Col 1:26–27; 2:2–3.

CHAPTER 3

Donald Gee: Pentecostal Ecumenist?

IN MY STUDIES OF the Pentecostal movement, I quickly became aware of the key role played by British Pentecostal leader Donald Gee (1891–1966) in its development and maturing. Not surprisingly, the studies on Gee by fellow Pentecostals focus primarily on his role as a leader and teacher in the worldwide movement. John Carter calls Gee "Pentecostal statesman,"[1] while Colin Whittaker and Lois Gott describe him as "apostle of balance,"[2] an epithet apparently accorded from quite early years. Walter Hollenweger was one of the first scholars to emphasize Gee's more open attitude to other Christians, calling him a "Pentecostal gentleman"[3] noting Gee's openness at a time when Pentecostal relations with other Christians would not have been described as gentlemanly. It was Hollenweger who directed my attention to the importance of Gee's editorials in the magazine *Pentecost* that he edited from its foundation in 1947 until his death in 1966.[4]

In this chapter, I ask whether Donald Gee can be accurately described as a Pentecostal ecumenist. This is a significant question as Pentecostal scholars now open up to the ecumenical movement and the challenges of Christian division. It is important that they honor their pioneer figures as Catholic ecumenists honor men such as the Abbé Paul Couturier and Dom Lambert Beauduin, OSB. I begin by considering the unpublished dissertation on Donald Gee written by Brian Ross, whose sub-title includes

1. Carter, *Gee.*

2. Whittaker *Seven,* and Gott *Gee.*

3. Hollenweger, *Pentecostals,* 208.

4. In fact, *Pentecost* was so identified with Gee that the magazine ceased publication when he died.

the phrase "Sectarian in Transition."[5] Ross argues that Gee began his Pentecostal life and ministry as a sectarian, but that in his last twenty years Gee's attitudes changed significantly, with this period being described as "transition"[6] and "maturity."[7] Prior to 1947, Gee displayed the traits of a sectarian,[8] "but he was a thinking sectarian."[9] He was "a Pentecostal with a difference."[10] For Ross, "Donald Gee was a 'sectarian in transition,' not a transformed ecumenist."[11]

Ross's view of what Gee was leaving behind, namely sectarianism, is clearer than what he presents Gee as becoming, at least in terms of ecumenical relations. His title "Donald Gee: In Search of a Church: Sectarian in Transition" suggests that Gee was searching for something that he never really found. I am convinced that Ross was addressing an important element in Gee's life and thought, but that his conclusions are flawed. First, it is unhelpful and misleading to describe the pre-1947 Gee as sectarian. Secondly, I do not think that there is any evidence that Gee was "in search of a church." Thirdly, Ross is right in saying that Gee did not become a "transformed ecumenist," but that does not make him a "sectarian in transition." These observations raise further questions: first, was 1947 a turning point in Gee's ministry in terms of his openness to non-Pentecostal Christians? Secondly, if there was a transition in Gee's life, what was it from and what was it to? Was it to become a convinced Pentecostal ecumenist?

Was Gee Ever Sectarian?

The terminology of sects, like that of cults, is notoriously unsatisfactory and widely contested. However, I will take it that the essential characteristic of sectarianism is an exclusivism that usually manifests itself in (1) the refusal or severe limitation of fellowship with outsiders, (2) restricting salvation to insiders, and/or (3) claiming to be the sole provider of authentic doctrine.

---

5. Ross, *Donald Gee*. See also Ross' article in EQ (1978).

6. Ross distinguishes "transition" from "transformation" (Ross, *Donald Gee*, 158).

7. "Within a fellowship which has traditionally espoused a sectarian gospel, Gee demonstrated the uniqueness of maturity" (ibid., 259).

8. Ibid., 87.

9. Ibid., 158.

10. Ibid.

11. Ibid., 165.

On the basis of these criteria, it is very doubtful whether Gee could ever be fairly described as a sectarian. Ross weakens his own case by assuming that any attribution of uniqueness to one's creed is an inherently sectarian stance.[12] For Gee believed to the end of his life that there was something special and distinctive about the Pentecostal movement. If that made him a sectarian, then he was always a sectarian.

There are two main reasons for maintaining that Gee was never a real sectarian. The first is Gee's understanding of the Pentecostal movement as a "revival." The second is Gee's openness toward non-Pentecostal Christians.

"Pentecost" as Revival

Gee consistently understood the Pentecostal movement, that he often just termed "Pentecost," as a revival, not as a cluster of denominations. "It is possible to live as a denomination and die as a Revival."[13]

> Before we became so movement-conscious we thought more often of the Pentecostal Revival as a means of grace to quicken whomsoever the Lord our God should call. Denominational loyalties were a secondary consideration. Let them remain such. The vital necessity of the Movement is that it shall continue and grow as a Revival. Nothing less deserves to be called "Pentecostal."[14]

Gee presents, rightly I think, this understanding as the original vision of the movement.

> Perhaps the most urgent of all questions facing the Pentecostal people themselves is whether those elements of durability within the Movement shall lead them into becoming just one more distinctive denomination among all the others, or whether they shall still try and hold tenaciously to the original concept of the Pentecostal Movement as a *Revival* to powerfully affect Christians everywhere without crystallizing itself in the process.[15]

12. "The revival was to be maintained: Pentecostalism was to remain extraordinary. These were the marching orders of Donald Gee, sectarian" (Ross, *Donald Gee*, 132).

13. Gee, "Movement or Message?"

14. Gee, "Are We Too 'Movement' Conscious?"

15. Gee, "Pentecost Re-Valued." "The Pentecostal Revival is something bigger and grander than the Pentecostal denomination" (Gee, "Orientation.")

Gee's conviction that the Pentecostal movement was essentially a re-vival led him to see the Pentecostals as having a witness and a contribution for the rest of the Christian world.[16] This is not the stance of a sectarian.[17]

Early Attitudes to Other Christians

Gee was never bigoted in his evaluation of other Christians. Nor was this simply a characteristic of his later years.[18] It was reflected in his reading be-fore it was expressed in his personal contacts and friendships. It would seem that Gee's habit of reading widely, at least in historic Protestant sources, began during his pastorate at Bonnington Toll, Edinburgh, in the 1920s.[19] He was evidently an attentive reader of the *British Weekly* for many years.

In 1927, WEC (the World-wide Evangelization Crusade) issued a statement in opposition to the Pentecostal movement, attributing to it po-sitions and doctrines which were repudiated by the Assemblies of God, as Gee pointed out.[20] Gee wrote at the end of his refutation:

> We pray for God's richest blessing, and nothing worse than such
> an attitude of truly Christian charity, to rest upon the magnificent
> work of the World-wide Evangelization Crusade.[21]

In 1936, when Gee visited France for a conference held by the French Assemblies of God in Lyon, he took the opportunity to visit Charmes-sur-Rhône, the center of the charismatic revival in the Ardèche under the lead-ership of Louis Dallière.[22] Gee's description of this visit and his impression

---

16. Ross notes this conviction in Gee as early as 1928 in his book *Concerning Spiritual Gifts* (Ross, *Donald Gee*, 131, note 66).

17. It is interesting to recall here that when Louis Dallière, always a man of the church in its Reformed expression, first studied "le mouvement de Pentecôte" in his book *D'Aplomb*, his major question was whether it was an authentic revival or something sec-tarian, he concluded that the evidence pointed to the former.

18. It is interesting to recall that a Pentecostal prayer meeting was held regularly on Anglican premises at Sion College in London from 1908 until the 1930s, originally through the influence of Cecil Polhill. Gee wrote in 1934: "Its beautiful hall is available for religious gatherings, and Pentecostal people have appreciated this gracious hospital-ity of a Church of England establishment for many years" (Gee, "Sion College," 9).

19. I owe this information to the late Desmond Cartwright.

20. Gee, "The World-Wide Evangelization Crusade," 14–15.

21. Ibid., 15.

22. It appears that Gee had already met with the Pentecostal outbreak in Reformed circles in Belgium, associated with Pastor Henri de Worm of Paturages, who collaborated

of this French Reformed group can be found in *Redemption Tidings*.[23] The attitude that Gee would adopt toward the charismatic movement from the late 1950s was already present in 1936:

> For the present the Revival is beautiful in its infancy and inno-
> cence; and the pastors are humble servants of God with a very
> loving spirit. They long to see the Holy Spirit working once again
> in *old-time power* in their beloved Churches.[24]

A letter to Stanley Frodsham of March 6, 1939 mentions that the "Swiss Union for Revival among their National Church ministers have asked me *again* for a Convention in September. D.V."[25] Presumably the Lord was not willing as the outbreak of World War II would have prevented Gee traveling to Switzerland at that time. In view of the "again" we may assume that he had previously spoken at a meeting organized by a group within the Swiss Reformed Church.[26]

These two factors come together in Gee's explicit repudiation of the exclusivism and the anti-denominationalism of the Brethren. Gee pointed out in a 1943 article that the correct designation of his denomination was "Assemblies of God in Great Britain and Ireland," not "*The* Assemblies of God."[27] Later in the article he insists,

> It needs to be affirmed constantly and boldly that the unity of the
> Spirit often exists far more truly between believers who are con-
> nected with different denominations than it does between those

---

closely with Louis Dallière: this contact with Paturages is mentioned in Douglas Scott's tribute many years later after Gee's death: "Son premier contact, à Dampremy, fut par-ticulièrement béni—car un vrai réveil avait éclaté dans le Borinage sous l'égide du Pasteur Worms [sic] dans la région de Charleroi." (*Viens et Vois* 34/10 Oct. 1966, 3). Eng. Trans. "His first contact at Dampremy was particularly blessed—for a real revival had broken out in the Borinage under the pastorate of Pastor Worms [de Worm] in the region of Charleroi."

23. Gee, "A Day," 1–2.

24. Ibid., 2.

25. Most of this letter is reporting on visits Gee paid to Finland and Estonia. On the way back he passed through Germany and reports in his own hand-writing how overjoyed a Jewish couple were at reaching safety in Holland.

26. This group was probably associated with Pastor F. de Rougemont, whose death Gee records in *Pentecost* 53 (Sept.–Nov. 1960) 16.

27. "[W]e notice that among the local assemblies in our Fellowship the definite article quite frequently is incorrectly inserted. No 'The,' please." (Gee, "Not 'The' Assemblies," 5).

who mistakenly think that they can only achieve unity by with-drawing from all, and urging others to do the same.[28]

The two aspects of revival and non-exclusive attitudes come together in Gee's view of Pentecostal denominations. In March 1947, Gee answered the criticism that Pentecostals represent "a superfluous sect:"

> The answer to this is easy. Those who have formed Pentecostal Assemblies all over the world, and have united in Pentecostal Fellowships, have not wanted to leave their former church associations, but have been forced to do so by the very ones who now find fault. To have remained within denominations that rejected the Pentecostal testimony necessitated nothing less than quenching the Spirit (1 Thess 5:19) and this we dare not do.[29]

While Gee's pre-1947 attitudes cannot accurately be termed "sectarian," it is true that his experience of fellowship with non-Pentecostals was much more limited than it would later become. His response to the criticisms of WEC and his attitude to Louis Dallière show that he had a degree of openness to recognize the Spirit at work elsewhere when he did have such encounters.

In What Sense Was 1947 a Turning Point in Gee's Life and Thinking?

Ross is correct in seeing a particular significance for Donald Gee in the year 1947. It was the year of the first World Pentecostal Conference (WPC) in Zürich, at which Gee was commissioned to edit a new periodical *Pentecost* to serve the world-wide Pentecostal community. This appointment represented a recognition by the world Pentecostal leadership present at Zürich of Gee's qualities as teacher, diplomat, and church leader. It made more public (one should avoid saying "more official" in view of the sensitivity of Pentecostals to the informal and non-permanent character of the WPC), and thus strengthened the international role Gee had already been playing since he began his world-wide travels in 1928. *Pentecost* gave Gee a regular platform for international influence of which he took full advantage, especially in his editorials. It had the advantage of not being a denominational

---

28. Ibid., 5.

29. Gee, "Superfluous," 2.

journal—it was in his terms a "Movement" journal[30]—and so it is in the editorials of *Pentecost* that we find Gee's boldest thinking. No doubt the readership of *Pentecost* was more selective and discerning than that of the Pentecostal denominational journals.[31] The reopening of civilian travel following the end of World War II and the increasing ease of air travel also facilitated this international role.

Zürich and the following WPCs manifested sharp disagreements within Pentecostal ranks, particularly between the strongly congregationalist Scandinavian groupings and the greater pragmatism of the English-speaking world. Gee's emergence as a world-level Pentecostal statesman placed him in a unique position to oppose all divisive narrowness and to work for greater reconciliation and fellowship. The WPCs were also the occasion for a much closer relationship between Donald Gee and David du Plessis, who emerged into an international role as secretary of the WPCs.[32] This growing relationship and friendship, which was of decisive importance for Gee's ecumenical involvement, is not mentioned by Ross. However, du Plessis's distinctive contribution to the development of Gee's thinking only began several years later (see below).

Thus, 1947 was a significant year for Gee and for his role in world Pentecostalism, but it did not represent any emergence from sectarianism in the way portrayed by Ross. Gee was remarkably consistent in his understanding and his attitudes, and there was nothing in the period from 1947 in Gee's understanding of the Pentecostal movement or his basic attitude to other Christians that was not present between the early 1920s and 1947. The differences are to be located in terms of opportunity and influence.

An example of his extraordinary consistency is Gee's attitude to non-Pentecostals being baptized in the Spirit. He never disputed the authenticity of the Spirit's work; he never told such people they must join Pentecostal churches. He was not dogmatic about the impossibility of non-Pentecostal churches being renewed, but pragmatically he expected the task to be

30. Gee wrote that "This journal has been commissioned to give news of all truly Pentecostal Revival wherever it occurs throughout the world, without fear or favour." ("Are we too 'Movement' Conscious?" *Pentecost* 2 (Dec. 1947).

31. It is in *Pentecost* editorials that we find the bulk of Gee's probing critiques of Pentecostal weaknesses and follies.

32. It is important to bear in mind that there were no permanent officials of the WPC, and that du Plessis's service as secretary was only for the duration of each conference. He was accused by other Pentecostals, and politely but firmly challenged by Gee in several letters, for acting as though his role as secretary was less temporary.

difficult. The attitudes he expressed in 1936, 1953, and 1965 are remarkably consistent:

1936: "How this 'new wine' can ultimately be contained in such 'old bottles' remains to be seen."[33]

1953: "If they can maintain unsullied and intact their Pentecostal witness where they are, then let them do it. Our experience causes us to expect that they will have difficulty. Our hope is that such difficulty will grow less as truth wins its certain victories. Our prayer will henceforth be that the flood-tide of Pentecostal grace and power that should follow speaking with tongues may be manifested in any and all of the churches. For Pentecost is more than a denomination; it is a *Revival*."[34]

1965: "The trouble with some Pentys is that they have become so denominationally minded. They came out, and so everyone else must also! They want to rope everybody into their sect. But those who try to remain in the older denominations to revivify them will have a job on. But I hope history will not repeat itself."[35]

It would seem then that 1947 was not a turning point in any transition out of Pentecostal narrowness, but that it did mark Gee's entry into the role of an international Pentecostal statesman to a new degree and with an increasing level of recognition.[36]

The Development of Gee's Wider
Christian Contacts and Fellowship

If there is any point at which Gee's wider Christian sympathies were translated into an active commitment that shaped his "ecumenical" behavior, the Billy Graham crusade at Harringay, London, in 1954 is the prime candidate. He wrote an editorial in *Pentecost* defending the crusade, in which he said: "The unity of the Spirit, as it exists among all who are truly in Christ

33. Gee, "A Day," 2. This comment concerns Louis Dallière's French Reformed congregation in Charmes.

34. Gee, "'Tongues' and Truth" *Pentecost* 25 (Sept. 1953). It is interesting to speculate on what gave rise to this editorial. It was probably the news of the beginnings of Pentecostal blessing in Reformed circles in the Netherlands.

35. Letter to Michael Harper dated June 24, 1965.

36. Gott disputes Ross's contention that Gee was a "sectarian in transition," arguing that through him there was a "movement in transition." (Gott, *Gee*, 179).

Jesus, carries with it solemn obligations."[37] Gee's stance over the Graham crusade may have been helped by his regular contact with David du Plessis, whose ecumenical ministry had begun around 1952.[38]

Richard Massey cites a tribute paid by Gilbert Kirby of the Evangelical Alliance at Donald Gee's funeral, in which Gee is said to have been "one of the most faithful attenders" in an informal study group of Evangelical leaders, chaired by John Stott, the undoubted leader among Evangelical Anglicans.[39] This seems to have been an exaggeration, as John Stott later had no recollection of such a group.[40] Gilbert Kirby's comment was: "I can well understand that John Stott does not recall the small group that used to meet occasionally to discuss different theological issues. It was way back in the late 1950s but I feel sure Donald Gee attended it. The group had no particular title and I do not think it lasted very long."[41]

The following year (1955) Gee received an invitation to address a major gathering of non-Pentecostals. The International Conference on Divine Healing, held at High Leigh in July, gathered Christians involved in healing ministry, including figures from the Church of England (both Evangelical and Anglo-Catholic).[42] Gee, who was accompanied by Leslie Woodford of Elim, gave a talk that was unremarkable, being mostly facts about Pentecostal belief and practice in regard to healing.[43] After distancing himself from aspects of big healing campaigns,[44] he concluded with the most interesting paragraph in the talk:

> We realize that we are only one section among other sections of the Church that are seeking to come to a fuller understanding and richer actual experience of the truth in this matter. We would confess in all humility that we have much to learn and we want to learn it as the Spirit of Truth shall be our One Teacher and Guide.

37. Gee, "Billy Graham."

38. Du Plessis's first mention to Gee of ecumenical contacts appears to be in a letter dated January 22, 1952: "Last month I attended a conference of the Foreign Missions Department of the National Council of Churches of Christ in the United States."

39. Massey, *Another Springtime*, 193.

40. Letter from John Stott's secretary to Peter Hocken dated April 6, 1995.

41. Letter from Gilbert Kirby to Peter Hocken dated May 19, 1995.

42. The proceedings of the conference were published in a booklet *Report of International Conference on Divine Healing*, published by the London Healing Mission (Anglican).

43. Gee, "The Work," 112–16. This talk is not mentioned in Ross's text or bibliography.

44. Gee did that in much greater detail in several editorials in *Pentecost*.

> We offer our own contribution to our brethren in Christ for what
> they think it is worth. For that reason I greatly esteem the privilege
> you have extended to me of participation with you in this impor-
> tant Conference.[45]

Gee's capacity to recognize the work of God among non-Pentecostal
Christians, beyond the ranks of Evangelicalism was even extended to a Roman Catholic, as was demonstrated in his friendly correspondence with a
Benedictine monk, Dom Benedict Heron OSB, whom he first mistook for
an Anglican.[46] It was to Heron that he described the Catholic ecumenical
pioneer, the Abbé Paul Couturier, as "surely a saint of God."[47]

Donald Gee was cognizant of the first stirrings of what came later to
be termed the charismatic movement and that Gee often called "Pentecost
outside Pentecost." His information was chiefly supplied by David du Plessis, though he heard about early signs in the Netherlands when he visited
that country. Gee never manifested any hesitation in accepting such reports
as genuine, though, as with the Ardèche revival in France in 1935, he won-
dered whether the older churches would be able to retain the new wine. He
naturally interpreted the charismatic movement as another element within
Pentecostal-type revival. It reinforced his regular theme that "Pentecost"
was a movement arising from revival, rather than a denomination or cluster of denominations.

David du Plessis was in constant contact with Donald Gee as du Plessis's ecumenical contacts developed. It was through the influence of John A.
Mackay in particular that du Plessis had been invited to the International
Missionary Council meeting at Willingen, Germany, in 1952 and to the
second WCC Assembly at Evanston, USA, in 1954.[48]

While many Pentecostal leaders, especially in the United States, were
suspicious of du Plessis's contacts with the WCC, Gee stood behind his
friend, publishing his reports and publicizing his activities, and writing editorials addressing this issue.[49] Gee wrote a *Pentecost* editorial on Evanston,

45. Ibid., 116. The "We," which is rather like a kind of royal plural, says something
about Gee's confidence of being an authoritative figure, though what he then affirms
would probably have been endorsed by very few Pentecostals.

46. Heron was baptized in the Spirit around August 1973, is author of several books
on charismatic themes, and is known for a healing ministry.

47. Letter to Dom Benedict Heron, Aug. 24, 1964 (see Hocken, *Streams*, 197).

48. See Curlee and Isaac-Curlee, "Bridging," 141–56, esp. 146–47.

49. The *Pentecost* editorials dealing with the ecumenical movement and the WCC
are: "Amsterdam" (6, Dec. 1948), "Pentecost and Evanston" (30, Dec. 1954), "Contact"

whose final positive affirmations about the authenticity of faith among WCC participants come from the impressions of du Plessis, as Gee had no first hand experience of them at that time.[50]

In 1960, through the introduction of du Plessis, Gee attended part of the Faith and Order conference of the WCC at St. Andrews in Scotland. There he met leaders, such as Dr. Michael Ramsey, then the Archbishop of York,[51] and Fr. Bernard Leeming, a leading Jesuit ecumenist. As a result, he received an invitation to be an observer at the third WCC Assembly at New Delhi in 1961. The news that Gee had received this invitation caused consternation in some Pentecostal quarters, headquarters in fact, and he was forced into a position in which his only responsible decision was to decline the invitation.[52]

Gee's disappointment over the New Delhi furore was shown in his responses to his Pentecostal critics.

> When we have said our last word against the World Council of Churches and the Ecumenical Movement there still remains the great prayer of our Lord that His disciples may all be one (John 17:21–23). What are we doing about it? What is our constructive alternative? Those who testify to the fullness of the spirit of Christ cannot tamely accept the divided state of Christendom, and particularly of Protestantism. Our many divisions call for hearty

---

(53, Sept.–Nov. 1960), "Pentecostals at New Delhi" (59, Mar.–May 1962), and "The Pentecostal Churches and the WCC" (67, Mar.–May 1964). The final article is the text of a talk given by Gee in a BBC series, also published in *Redemption Tidings* (Feb. 21, 1964) 12–15.

50. This editorial contains the anti-extremist sentiments, characteristic of Gee: "the radical attitude of some extreme fundamentalists who see nothing in the WCC but a movement towards anti-Christ is deplorable and does little service to the truth. The violent and abusive language that has been used in some obscurantist quarters has been a disgrace. Deep, and sometimes bitter, as our theological differences may be, we lie and do not the truth if we do not confess to a consciousness that among these brethren in the WCC there is a real love for Jesus Christ and a sincere faith in Him as Saviour and Lord." ("Pentecost and Evanston" *Pentecost* 30 Dec. 1954). The final phrases about the authenticity of faith among WCC participants must have owed much to du Plessis's letters to Gee.

51. Subsequently Archbishop of Canterbury.

52. There is a short statement of Gee under the heading "Donald Gee and the WCC" in *Pentecost* 57 (Sept–Nov 1961) 16. This episode is fully discussed and documented by Robeck in "A Pentecostal."

repentance before God. They are a constant scandal, and not least when we project them on to our mission fields."[53]

Not long before his death, Gee wrote: "We are working in a time of strong ecumenical currents. It is unworthy of what the Pentecostal experience stands for if blind prejudice prevents us from being open to proper areas of unity."[54]

In What Sense Did Donald Gee Become a Pentecostal Ecumenist?

It is clear from the developments described that Gee truly did develop an ecumenical heart in the sense of having (1) a respect and love for Christians belonging to many other traditions, and (2) a sense of the importance of the Lord's prayer and command that "all may be one."

However, Gee's ecclesiology did not readily allow him to develop a consistent ecumenical methodology. For Gee did not really have a theology of ecclesial traditions. So he did not see Christian unity in terms of separated churches or communions coming into organic relationship. "It is impossible to achieve the unity for which Christ prayed by making unions out of denominations."[55] As a Catholic commentator on the Pentecostal movement I would want to distinguish between denominations, more a sociological than a theological term, and church communities bonded by more than doctrinal agreements. But what counted for Gee was the interior spiritual unity of individual believers.[56] His Pentecostal interpretation of the invisible unity of the church was expressed in these words:

> We are fundamentally one in Christ Jesus, but that one-ness in Christ is something more than a unity of faith and hope and love in our Blessed Redeemer. It is sealed home to our hearts by

---

53. Gee, "Pentecostals at New Delhi" *Pentecost* 59 (Mar–May 1962).

54. Gee, "Deserving."

55. Gee, "Possible." See comments of Kay in *Inside*, 220.

56. "The Pentecostal churches are committed to the concept of the true church being a spiritual entity composed of all who are truly in Christ by virtue of the new birth, apart from membership of an outward organization. Even among themselves, they regard ecclesiastical organization with profound suspicion" (Gee, "The Pentecostal Churches," 16).

participation in the One Spirit. This is the unique blessing of Pentecost in the realm of fellowship.[57]

However, some of Gee's writings about the local church have a less individualistic flavor. Certainly he was constantly working for more positive relations between most of the Pentecostal denominations, though he never found it easy to apply his generosity of spirit to the Apostolic Church.[58] Perhaps Gee's ecclesiology is most accurately described as one of visible local churches (congregations not denominations) and the invisible universal body of Jesus Christ. I see here no grounds for Ross's assertion that Gee was "in search of a church." I do not find any indication that Gee was dissatisfied with the stance described.

Gee often acknowledged Pentecostal weaknesses and he affirmed the need for Pentecostals to learn from other Christian traditions.[59] But without a theology with any room for ecclesial transformation and renewal beyond the local level, Gee lacked the tools for an ecumenical strategy. However, he did not have a closed mind. In a 1963 article for a new journal of the Student Pentecostal Fellowship, he wrote: "The time has come for the phenomena connected with the Pentecostal Movement to be integrated with older systems of theology."[60]

A further reason why Gee did not develop such an ecumenical methodology was that, for all his writing, he was a practical man, not a scholar or a theologian; thus, his ecumenical outlook translated into positive relationships across church boundaries rather than into theologies of church renewal through ecumenical sharing. This can be seen in an editorial of characteristic openness on Lesslie Newbigin's ground-breaking book *The Household of God*. Here Gee did manifest a modest degree of recognition

57. Gee, "I Believe."

58. "It is on my heart to do what I can to strengthen the unity between our Scottish work and the other Pentecostal Assemblies. We are very isolated in Scotland and have practically got our backs to the wall in contending against the advance of the erroneous practices of the Apostolic Church" (Letter of D. Gee to E. J. Phillips, Feb. 23 1923). Although Gee did not hold out for their exclusion, Phillips reminds Gee that he had led the opposition to the Apostolic Church being invited to the first WPC in Zürich in 1947: "Let me first deal with the matter of the Apostolic Church being invited to send delegates to Zürich. We all seem to remember that the proposal to exclude these people came from yourself" (Extract from letter of E. Phillips to D. Gee dated March 24, 1947).

59. See citation in note 45 from Gee's address to the International Conference on Divine Healing.

60. Gee, "Pentecostal Theology," 23.

that Pentecostals need to learn from other traditions: "If there is any truth in the analysis before us, and I believe there is, it indicates the need for a Pentecostal type of church to give more attention to order and to faith."[61] However, this editorial was based on reading a review of Newbigin in *The British Weekly*: he was not sufficiently impacted to go and buy a copy of the original and read that! He was a Pentecostal with a generous heart and an inquiring mind. Was he in the end a Pentecostal ecumenist? I would answer, Yes and No. Yes, in heart and attitudes; No in policy and practical strategy.

61. *Pentecost* 32 (June 1955).

CHAPTER 4

Liturgy and Eschatology in a Pentecostal-Charismatic Ecumenism

THIS CHAPTER ADDRESSES ESCHATOLOGY as a key issue in the relationship between the historic churches and the newer Evangelical–Pentecostal revivalist currents. It is a crucial theme for Catholic–Pentecostal dialogue. Eschatology as the science of ultimate destiny shapes all Christian life and provides the contours for our understanding of the present and the past. Eschatology is closely related to liturgy and worship, for it is in a church's worship that its fundamental faith in God, in Jesus, in the Holy Spirit, and corporate destiny in Christ, are expressed and nourished. Where there is no operative eschatology, there is no ultimate hope, and where there is no ultimate hope, there is diminished life in the present and no forward dynamic toward the future.

Eschatology is especially important for dialogue between the historic churches and the Pentecostals for other reasons too, of which it is important to mention two at the outset. The first is that Pentecostalism is at heart a revival movement, and revival movements have typically served to reawaken eschatological expectation. This is all the more so with the Pentecostal movement as a current emphasizing the power of the Holy Spirit and the centrality of the event of Pentecost. In consequence, Pentecostalism has from the beginning given a major place to the imminence of the coming of the Lord Jesus in glory. The two poles of Pentecostal faith, clearly manifest at Azusa Street, were expressed in the banners: "Pentecost Has Come," and "The Lord is Coming Soon." Here the Pentecostal revival takes up and intensifies the eschatological thrust present in all movements of Evangelical revival. The strong missiological dynamic unleashed at Azusa Street combined these two elements: the power of the Holy Spirit poured out, with the spiritual gifts as Holy Ghost equipment, to bring the gospel to the ends of the earth before the soon-coming of the Lord Jesus.

The second factor arises from the fact that Pentecostal eschatology has almost all been taken over from Evangelical eschatology, and that Evangelical–Catholic differences and oppositions are at their most glaring in the area of eschatology. The issues connected with millennialism fuel a constant Evangelical debate, with some Pentecostal denominations officially embracing pre-millennial dispensationalist positions and believing in a rapture of the saints. The pre-millennialist position has generally been linked with the restoration of Israel, with many Evangelicals and Pentecostals seeing the return of the Jewish people to the land and the establishment of the state of Israel as the fulfillment of biblical prophecy, and as heralding the soon-coming of the Lord. The timing of the "great tribulation" has been a recurring theme. There has been much interest in apocalyptic imagery concerning the identity of the antichrist, the beast, and the scarlet woman of Revelation 17, still occasionally identified with the church of Rome and its bishop. The major themes of Evangelical–Pentecostal eschatology are not simply absent from Catholic theological discourse, they are experienced as totally alien elements coming from a world with quite different theological presuppositions and Christian experience. Even as the Catholic Church has rethought its relationship to the Jewish people and has repudiated the historic "replacement" view of Israel in relation to the church, there has been no sympathetic interest in Evangelical eschatology and no detectable influences crossing the Evangelical–Catholic divide as a result of ecumenical dialogue. Some charismatic Catholics have been influenced by Evangelical teaching concerning the end-times, but this has not penetrated the Catholic charismatic renewal as an organized movement.

Eschatology as Consummation

I suggest that the great differences over eschatology are bound up with and in some way sum up the profound differences between the historic church traditions and the streams of revival that have produced Evangelical and Pentecostal denominations. I want to outline these major differences in approach, in presuppositions, and in framework, so as better to perceive the radical necessity of tackling the issue of eschatology in historic church dialogue with Evangelicals and Pentecostals. In the following chart, some Evangelical–Catholic contrasts are generally valid for the last three hundred years, but a few represent the ideal proposed more than the reality on the ground.

Points of Contrast	Evangelical–Pentecostal	Catholic–Orthodox
Starting Point	PERSONAL	CORPORATE
Basic Conviction	IMMEDIATE ACCESS	MEDIATION OF GRACE/DIVINE PRESENCE
Major Focus	SPIRITUAL	SACRAMENTAL
Worship Patterns	WORD & FREE	LITURGICAL
Action of Holy Spirit	REVIVAL & EVANGELISM	RENEWAL & SANCTIFICATION
Success in Goal	PERSONAL ON MASS SCALE	ECCLESIAL
God's Action in History	DISCONTINUITY	CONTINUITY
How?	NEW WAVES	DEVELOPMENT & PROCESS
Recommended Stance	ACTIVIST ZEAL	REFLECTIVE-CON-TEMPLATIVE
Primary Outreach	EVANGELISM	CHARITY/JUSTICE & PEACE
Vision of Church	GATHERED CHURCH OF THE SAVED	MIXED CHURCH OF WHEAT & TARES
Eschatology	PERSONAL HOPE	CORPORATE HOPE

Whatever the limitations of such a list, it can demonstrate the interconnectedness of our distinctive convictions and our stances as Christians. It highlights the centrality of liturgy and forms of communal worship that express how each Christian community understands and expresses their relationship to the one God, Father, Son, and Holy Spirit, God's dealings with humankind, and the nature of the Christian community before the all-holy God. Key Evangelical-Catholic differences in understanding and emphasis are expressed in our patterns of worship: for example the relationship between the individual believer, the church, and society; issues of the personal and the corporate; the relationship of the physical/bodily order to the spiritual; as well as the different ways in which we approach and make use of the Sacred Scriptures. In other words, the discussion of eschatology cannot prescind from the issue of liturgy.

However, it may be helpful to note a largely unnoticed paradox that exists between the historic churches and the newer Evangelical–Pentecostal revivalist currents. On the one hand, in the historic churches there is little preaching and teaching on the end-times, but their liturgies are full of the eschatological hope. On the other hand, the Evangelical, Pentecostal, and charismatic currents give an important place to eschatology in their preaching and teaching, especially in their initial phases and inspiration, but they are suspicious of liturgical forms.

I shall focus on Catholic–Pentecostal relations, as clearly embodying these issues, while recognizing that most points apply also to the other historic church traditions on the one side and to the newer charismatic churches on the other side, though the latter have been less influenced by dispensationalist thinking than the Pentecostals.

Historic Church–Revival Stream
Dialogues to Date

If we examine the themes treated in the many bilateral dialogues that have been taking place in the last forty-five years across the historic church–revival stream divide, we will find that eschatology has rarely featured. What is perhaps more surprising is that this neglect of eschatology in ecumenical dialogue has also extended to the Catholic–Pentecostal dialogue, which is now in its sixth quinquennium. Although the first five years (1972–77) were in effect between Catholics officially nominated and some of the friends of David du Plessis, mostly charismatics, this dialogue subsequently involved only Catholics and Pentecostals,[1] with a slow increase in the number of Pentecostals mandated in some way by their denominations. The most sig-

---

1. The exception was Howard Ervin, listed among the Pentecostal participants at some meetings, but described as an American Baptist.

nificant document to come from this dialogue has been the statement on Evangelization, Proselytism, and Common Witness (1997). At the end of the first two quinquennia, reports were prepared containing a list of themes for further discussion. But eschatology does not feature among them.[2] An Orthodox–Pentecostal dialogue has only recently got under way, and it may be that eschatology will reach its agenda more quickly in view of the stronger eschatological awareness of the Orthodox churches.

A first series of occasional meetings between the Pontifical Council for Promoting Christian Unity (Catholic) and the World Evangelical Fellowship took place between 1977 and 1984,[3] and a second series between 1993 and 2002,[4] with a more regular five-year dialogue beginning in 2009. A second series of conversations between representatives of the Baptist World Alliance and a Catholic team appointed by the Pontifical Council has just been completed.[5] Likewise, despite the chasm between most Evangelical eschatology and historic church eschatology, the subject has not yet made it to these dialogues either.

The more these new "frontier" dialogues start to address the biggest differences and the neuralgic issues, the more important becomes the level of trust and rapport among the dialogue participants. It is significant that the Catholic–Pentecostal dialogue was only possible because of the life and ministry of David du Plessis, who was neither a scholar nor a theologian, but who traveled the world making contacts and developing friendships so as to build bridges of reconciliation, having the courage to visit the Vatican. In fact, the ecumenical movement from its beginning has been aided by some remarkable friendships, a fascinating potential theme for a doctoral dissertation.[6]

2. Baumert and Bially, *Pfingstler*, 15, 33.

3. Documented in Meeking and Stott, *Evangelical–Roman Catholic Dialogue*.

4. Documented in the report "Church, Evangelization, and the Bonds of Koinonia." See *Information Service* of the Pontifical Council for Promoting Christian Unity, 113 (2003) 85–101.

5. A first phase lasted from 1984–88, while the second phase (2006–10) has treated "The Word of God in the Life of the Church: Scripture, Tradition, and Koinonia."

6. One of the highly significant ecumenical friendships was formed between Fr. Fernand Portal, a French Catholic priest, and Lord Halifax, a prominent Anglo-Catholic in British society and political affairs. From their friendship eventually issued the Malines Conversations (1921–26). Also significant was the friendship between Dom Lambert Beauduin, OSB, and Archbishop Angelo Giuseppe Roncalli, the future John XXIII. More recently, the friendship between Matteo Calisi and Giovanni Traettino paved the way for the friendships of Pope Francis with Bishop Tony Palmer and with Traettino (see

In commenting on the absence of eschatology from these dialogues, I am first simply making an observation, not a criticism. It can be argued that avoiding eschatology is not getting to the root of the differences. But it can also be argued that the delay in taking up eschatology reflects a practical wisdom and the timing of the Lord. It may be that the time will only be ripe to take up the eschatological issues when both Catholic and Evangelical or Pentecostal teams are composed of men and women who have all had a prolonged exposure to the real life of the other "side" and through their mutual relationships have developed a love for the Holy Spirit's work in the other.

Areas of Mutual Complementarity?

I ask now how a full Christian eschatology faithful to the biblical revelation requires the complementary witnesses of the Evangelical–Pentecostal revival streams and of the ancient churches of East and West, Orthodox and Catholics. The complementarity of the fundamental convictions on both or all sides is a necessary component in the preparation for the eschatological completion. Briefly, it is to argue first that we need each other, and then that the Lord needs this coming together to make the eschatological consummation possible.[7]

The Personal and the Corporate

The necessary polarity of the personal and the corporate is not difficult to accept. Both dimensions are clearly present in the Scriptures. The eschatological hope is both corporate and personal, the hope of God's covenant people, now become the body of Christ, and the hope of every believer. The cry "*Marana tha*, come Lord Jesus" is the cry of the Spirit and the bride (Rev 22:17). It is the cry of the one bride in process of purification (see Eph 5:27; 1 John 3:2–3), and it is the cry arising from the heart of each believer who has received the "first fruits" of the Holy Spirit (Rom 8:23). The cry of the church is first a liturgical cry, evidenced in the Didache around the year 100 CE,[8] and also expressed in many *anaphorae* (eucharistic prayers) in the

chapter 11).

7. See also chapter 6.

8. "May your grace come and may the world pass away. Hosannah to the God of David! If anyone is holy, let him come; if he is not holy, may he do penance, *Marana tha*" (end of Eucharistic prayer in the Didache).

Trisagion, Holy, Holy, Holy, through the messianic salutation: "Blessed is he who comes in the name of the Lord."[9]

While it is not hard to affirm that the kingdom hope is both personal and corporate, there is a chasm between the Evangelical–Pentecostal world and the heritage of the ancient churches. The Pentecostals with a strong eschatological thrust from their beginnings affirm that the hope is for all the saved, but can this really be said to be a corporate hope? Is it not rather a hope for all the saved en masse, but not for a living body in history "joined and knit together by every joint" (Eph 4:16)? The ancient churches express their eschatological hope in their liturgies, but is not the real hope of most Catholics an individual hope that they will eventually get to heaven after they die?[10] The Catechism of the Catholic Church teaches, "Since the apostolic age the liturgy has been drawn toward its goal by the Spirit's groaning in the Church: *Marana tha!*"[11] But how much is this goal the experienced and lived hope of participants in Catholic liturgy? Most Catholics would probably be very surprised to hear that at Mass they are longing for the Lord to come in glory. Pentecostals do not need to be judgmental to suggest that the weakness or lack of the hope is due to inadequate preaching of the gospel and to a lack of a conversion among many Catholics that would transform the theory into a living hope. There is a tension here between the eschatological gathering of the individually saved in the Evangelical–Pentecostal world and the corporate body of the ancient churches including wheat and tares, alive and dead members, who will be separated on the last day.

The Spiritual and the Physical–Sacramental

The revival streams (Evangelical, Holiness, Pentecostal, and charismatic) all privilege the spiritual. What matters above all is the inward, not the outward, the inner transformation of the heart, brought about by the Word of God and the direct action of the Holy Spirit upon each believer. By contrast, the ancient churches see God's grace mediated through liturgy and sacraments, the spiritual being conferred in and through the physical, bodily order. Even though the Pentecostal and charismatic movements

---

9. See Luke 19:38.

10. It is for Orthodox readers to comment on the real hope in the hearts of the Orthodox people.

11. CCC, 1130.

have promoted bodily expression in physical gestures and movements as vehicles of the Spirit, the overall paradigm remains largely in place.

In the Pentecostal–charismatic world, this focus on the spiritual has been accentuated in recent years by the expectation of rapid and visible spiritual results. The twentieth century has seen a certain subversion of Evangelical–Pentecostal faith by an ideology of success, particularly in the Western world. This world does not understand the role of hiddenness that is intrinsic to the age of the church when spiritual realities are only partially visible through their embodiment within the physical order. By contrast, the historic churches which profess faith in the spiritual efficacy of liturgy and sacraments often hardly seem to expect any tangible results. In its worst expressions, it can assume that spiritual reality is totally invisible, a position that is hard to reconcile with the incarnation. There can result a blindness to evident signs of spiritual deadness and hopelessness, and a blindness to the ravages of evil spiritual powers. In some places, the historic churches are being reduced to planning future decline. It is not that no long-term fruit is expected, but there is a suspicion of dramatic sudden effects, until there has been a long-term testing of their authenticity and depth.

A renewed liturgy and a renewed eschatology are both necessary to move the Christian world beyond these polarizations and extremes. A renewed liturgy, within which the transforming power of the Spirit through the Word of God is affirmed and manifested, manifests the right relationship between the invisible and the visible, between the spiritual reality and its visible signs, during this age of the church. A renewed liturgy makes clear its inner ordering toward the eschatological completion when all that is hidden will be manifest, and the age of signs comes to an end. A healthy eschatology presupposes a holistic anthropology affirming God's salvific purpose for the whole created order, for the whole of human society, and for the whole human person. A renewed liturgy and a renewed eschatology can together provide the necessary corrective to all naïve forms of optimism and to all forms of pessimistic fatalism.

Revival and Renewal: Radical Newness in Radical Continuity

In many ways the Evangelical movement has been born of revivals, and is always longing for new waves of revival. By contrast, the historic church world has not sought such dramatic unexpected inbreakings of the Spirit of God, but in recent and more difficult times has more readily recognized the need for renewal.[12] These two terms, revival and renewal, encapsulate many major differences in emphases between the two worlds.[13] Revival envisages a new outpouring of the Spirit of God upon a city, region, or nation that brings large numbers of people—unbelievers, backslidden, and lukewarm—to conversion and living faith in Jesus. Revival presupposes a discontinuity and a radical newness in God's workings. Renewal envisages a process within the churches in continuity with the past that involves a return to biblical roots and first principles producing new life for individuals, communities, and churches.

Revival typically revivifies the eschatological hope. Renewal often has no particular eschatological awareness, tending to see the church continuing to labor through the ages without any concrete expectation of a sudden and dramatic consummation.[14] I see revival and renewal as complementary concepts describing different emphases that ultimately belong together. This means in particular that we need a theology of the church in history that recognizes the necessary element of discontinuity and the essential element of continuity. The ecumenical question is how to relate the two. The foundation for a satisfactory answer has to lie in the elements of discontinuity and of continuity in the incarnation of the Son of God and in his death and resurrection. It seems highly plausible that the relationship of the discontinuous and the continuous in the second coming of the Lord in glory follows the pattern of the incarnation and of the death and resurrection of Jesus. A theology of the church that wishes everything to be continuous without any inbreaking from the sovereign Lord is unlikely to take seriously the ultimate unpredictable inbreaking of the parousia.[15]

12. I am conscious here that the term "renewal" has been adopted by currents influenced by the "Toronto blessing" of the mid-1990s to describe their understanding of the work of God that they have experienced. This seems to me an unfortunate choice of terminology. Perhaps the term "refreshing" might have been more appropriate.

13. See Hocken, "Revival," for a fuller treatment of these differences. See also an earlier article, Hocken, "Pentecostal–Charismatic."

14. However, it is the renewal of biblical studies in the Catholic Church that has led over a half-century to a clearer recognition of the eschatological hope of the New Testament church and that has made possible the much greater eschatological awareness expressed in the Catechism of the Catholic Church.

15. Close observers of the Roman Catholic world will be aware of a major discussion in the Vatican under Benedict XVI emphasizing a "hermeneutic of continuity" as against a "hermeneutic of rupture" in the interpretation of the Second Vatican Council. Benedict himself spoke of a "hermeneutic of renewal."

Return to the Jewish Roots

The currents of ecumenical bridge-building and reconciliation can hardly ignore the role of Israel and the Jewish people. For all Christians have to recognize that the roots of Christian faith lie in the covenant between Israel and the God of Abraham, Isaac, and Jacob. Moreover, the unity of the new covenant in Jesus has its roots in the unity of the first covenant, and the eschatological hope of the church has its roots in the messianic hope of Israel.

The historic churches today are much more aware of the theological importance of the Jewish people through the self-examination provoked by the unprecedented horror of the Holocaust. The Evangelical and Pentecostal world has been paying attention to Israel largely because many see the return of the Jews to the land of Israel as a fulfillment of biblical prophecy. The new openness to the Jews in the historic churches has led in several countries to the establishment of Jewish–Christian councils and to patterns of regular dialogue between Christian leaders and Jewish rabbis.[16] The openness to the Jews in the Evangelical–Pentecostal world has led to the creation of groups supporting the state of Israel,[17] and among some a strong support for the Messianic Jewish movement of Jewish believers in Jesus, seeking to live out a corporate commitment as Jewish disciples in congregations promoting a Jewish life-style.

The return to the Jewish roots is fundamental for the renewal of Christian eschatology because the existence of the Jewish people is grounded in the messianic hope. It is central to the Jewish tradition to be the bearers of the messianic hope. The synagogue liturgy and the Jewish feasts are strongly impregnated with the hope for the coming of the Messiah to save his people.[18] This messianic hope for a fulfillment in this world is strongly present among those Jews least affected by modern rationalism. I remember once meeting the mayor of an Israeli city who saw the growth of his city and the cultivation of the land as preparation for the coming of the Messiah.

The liturgical and eschatological character of the Jewish tradition is the obvious starting point for a dialogue with the Catholics and the Orthodox

---

16. This openness at official levels does not mean that there is little remaining anti-Semitism at the local level.

17. For example, Christian Friends of Israel and the International Christian Embassy Jerusalem.

18. An example from the Ashkenazi liturgy for Sabbaths and festivals: "Gladden us, Hashem, our God, with Elijah the prophet, Your servant, and with the kingdom of the House of David, Your anointed, may he come speedily and cause our heart to exult."

about eschatology. There is a basic earthiness about the Jewish heritage with the promise of descendants to Abraham, the promise of the land, the rite of circumcision as entry into the covenant, and the role of blood sacrifice in the covenant. Just as sin has polluted the human conscience, the corporate life of Israel, her leaders (priests, prophets, and wise men) and the land, so the promise and hope of redemption is for the cleansing and deliverance of the people, the leaders, and the land. The prophecies of messianic restoration and deliverance speak both of salvation coming from above, and also of salvation springing up or sprouting from below, from the earth, and Israel as being in gestation. This double movement of preparation is a recurring theme in the Roman liturgy for Advent when this verse is repeated: "Shower, O heavens, from above, and let the skies rain down righteousness; let the earth open, that salvation may sprout forth, and let it cause righteousness to spring up also; I the Lord have created it" (Isa 45:8).

Pre-Millennial Dispensationalism

In a paper focusing on the centrality of eschatology for Catholic–Pentecostal dialogue, it is necessary to say something about the system of pre-millennial dispensationalism, as fashioned by John Nelson Darby, a key figure in the origins of the Brethren movement in Great Britain.[19] While many today seek to pursue an ecumenical method of repudiating all the false "either–or" oppositions that have fractured the body of Christ, Darby was a specialist in such separations.[20] His system of dispensations is founded on the idea of the failure of each successive dispensation through human disobedience and divine judgment, and its replacement by a new dispensation operating according to different principles. In his system, the total separateness of Israel and the church is central. Israel and the church have separate destinies, Israel an earthly destiny and the church a heavenly destiny. It was this separation of destinies that necessitated the theory of the "rapture of the church," as Israel's destiny can only unfold on earth after the removal of the church. The age or era of the church is even described as "parenthetical," being a parenthesis between God's two periods of dealing with Israel.

I mention Darby's teaching because of the paradoxical fact that some aspects of his millennialism have been widely received by Pentecostals,

19. On Darby, see also chapter 10.
20. See Bass, *Backgrounds*, 48–63.

despite Darby's cessationism in relation to the spiritual gifts. To a Catholic, Darby's system appears irredeemably individualistic; in his system of sequential dispensations, all doomed to failure, any corporate renewal becomes impossible, and salvation becomes entirely individualistic. His teaching on "the ruin of the church" following the failure of the church dispensation meant that God's work of salvation is continued only through a remnant of faithful believers, so he wrote:

> The doctrine of succession, and all its accompaniments, becomes the stamp and mark of recognized and sanctioned, because perpetuated, apostasy; for if the church has failed, as these texts declare, the provision of its perpetuation becomes the provision for the perpetuation of the failure, and the maintenance of the object of the Lord's sure judgment.[21]

This separation of Israel from the church and the doctrine of the rapture deny the apostle Paul's vision of the church in Ephesians as "the one new man," made up of Jew and Gentile, reconciled through the cross. The most fundamental criticism of the eschatology of "Darbysme"[22] that I have read comes from Pastor Louis Dallière (1897–1976), the founder of the Union de Prière in France, who argued that the doctrine of the rapture removes the central task of the church to prepare for the coming of the Lord on the last day:

> If the Jews, according to this plan [of Darby], are converted by sight, without faith, after the rapture of the church, there is a profound reason for this: it is that the message of faith only ever converted individuals, but never built up a church. What is raptured is an invisible church, that is to say not a church at all; but an ensemble of individuals completely isolated one from another.[23]

However, there is an insight of John Nelson Darby that appears both valid and important, and that can serve as a potential bridge between revivalist eschatology and the historic churches. It is the marked difference between the this-worldly character of Israel's messianic expectation already noted and the heavenly character of the eschatological hope in the New Testament. It is clear that the heavenly dimension is decisively opened by

21. Darby, *Collected Writings: Ecclesiastical No. 1*, 123.

22. The French term coined by Dallière to describe Darby's dispensationalist system.

23. Notes from Dallière's teaching at the 1947 retreat of the Union de Prière, on the theme of "Le Retour de Jésus," 4 (author's translation).

the resurrection and ascension of Jesus. A key question then becomes: what is the relationship between the establishment of the kingdom of God on earth and the heavenly character of the promised kingdom?[24]

The Messianic Jews

Over the past forty years there has been a growing Christian awareness that return to the biblical sources means return to the sources in Israel, for the New Testament is really just as Jewish as the Old. But it is also during these years that the movement has sprung up of Messianic Jews who believe in Jesus as Messiah of Israel, Son of God, and Savior of the world. The Messianic Jews belong at one and the same time to modern currents of revival and to the Jewish heritage that is the root within which Christian faith took shape. It is both modern and ancient. The question raised by the theme of this paper is the difference made by the Messianic Jews to the ecumenical task in the area of eschatology. I will address this question by considering the challenges posed by the Messianic Jews to the Evangelical–Pentecostal world and to the historic churches.

Challenges to Evangelicals and Pentecostals

The challenges that an authentic encounter with the Jewish heritage poses to Evangelical and Pentecostal Christians are lessened by the strong influence of Evangelical thought and theology on the Messianic Jewish movement.[25] Thus, the majority of Messianic Jews have, at least initially, imbibed the anti-liturgical and anti-tradition animus of Evangelicalism. But this suspicion of liturgy and tradition does not make sense for a Jew, because Judaism is essentially a liturgical faith with divinely-appointed feasts and observances. It belongs to the heart of the Jewish heritage to be descendants of Abraham, and to transmit the Torah of Moses to each subsequent generation. Only as the Messianic Jews integrate these elements of Judaism

24. This question is addressed more directly in chapter 10.

25. The first Christians to take seriously the ongoing relevance of Old Testament prophecy and to found missions to the Jews were Evangelicals. In consequence, the Messianic Jews of today relate more readily to Evangelicals than to other parts of the Christian world. Because the Messianic Jews are majority charismatic in their faith, they have an affinity with the Pentecostals, and their emerging structures are similar to those of the new networks of charismatic free churches.

into their corporate life will they present a challenge to Evangelicals and Pentecostals in these areas.[26] Similarly, the Messianic Jews by virtue of being Jewish carry a definite sense of corporate identity. By virtue of being Jewish and their profound connection to the land of Israel, they are earthed and rooted. Most profoundly, their existence as a people is grounded in the messianic hope. The Messianic Jews fully share this messianic hope, only for them it is the second coming of the Messiah, this time in glory. It is above all in Israel that this messianic hope is most central to their faith in Jesus as Messiah and Savior. Not only do the Messianic Jews carry the Jewish hope for the coming Messiah and the realization of the messianic age, but the Jewish hope is a corporate hope, the hope of a people. It is the hope for the coming of the Lord Jesus to his own city and his own people for the establishment of his reign on earth. It is notable that the apostle Paul continues to speak of "the hope of Israel" when preaching Jesus to his people: "it is because of the hope of Israel that I am bound with this chain." (Acts 28:20).[27] This provides an important challenge to Evangelical–Pentecostal eschatology which is affected by the individualistic emphases of these revival streams.

The challenge to Evangelicals and Pentecostals from the Jewish heritage and from the historic churches focuses on the corporate and on the relationship of the corporate to the bodily/physical order. The corporate and physically-based character of historic faith communities is rooted in their liturgies. When Evangelicals look at the ancient churches of East and West, they typically see the apparatus of institutional religion, which can obscure their most essential features. For the ancient churches will all affirm that the most foundational structural element in their life is their liturgy, which is the continuous heritage of community worship of the Christian people. The bureaucratic elements can come and go, being clothed in very different forms in different epochs. In the Catholic tradition, this absolute centrality of the liturgy is expressed in the teaching of the Second Vatican Council

---

26. By virtue of their conviction that they are to be Jewish disciples of Jesus, Messianic Jews have a connection to the original tradition, and cannot long ignore the liturgical character of Jewish life and worship. This process can be seen at work in Messianic Jewish congregations as they seek to discover how to live as Jewish followers of their Messiah.

27. See also the discourse of Paul to King Agrippa: "And now I stand here on trial for hope in the promise made by God to our fathers, to which our twelve tribes hope to attain, as they earnestly worship night and day. And for this hope I am accused by Jews, O king!" (Acts 26: 6–7). Paul suggests that there is a deep irony in this accusation.

and of the Catechism of the Catholic Church. It is encapsulated in the dictum *Lex credenda lex orandi*: that is to say, the law or canon of faith is the law or canon of prayer-worship. Or, in the words of the Catechism of the Catholic Church: the liturgy "makes the Church present and manifests her as the visible sign of the communion in Christ between God and men."[28] The point is made in relation to the particular (local) church in the Constitution on the Liturgy of the Second Vatican Council:

> the principal manifestation of the church consists in the full, active participation of all God's holy people in the same liturgical celebrations, especially in the same Eucharist, in one prayer, at one altar, at which the bishop presides, surrounded by his college of priests and by his ministers.[29]

It is this foundational liturgical–sacramental structure of the historic churches that renders impossible any concept of a "rapture of the saints" before the coming of the Lord in glory. For in the sacramental framework, the sacramental signs belong to the entire "age of the church" which lasts from Pentecost to Parousia. This is the pattern for the Eucharist mentioned by the apostle Paul: "For as often as you eat this bread and drink the cup, you proclaim the Lord's death until he comes" (1 Cor 11:26). This would also seem to be the implication of the words of Jesus to Jerusalem just before his passion concerning his return as Messiah: "For I tell you, you will not see me again, until you say, 'Blessed be he who comes in the name of the Lord'" (Matt 23:39).

The Challenge to the Historic Churches

By contrast, the Messianic Jews present two major challenges to the historic churches. The first is different to those facing the Evangelicals and the Pentecostals, that is the challenge to their amillennialist eschatology that they have espoused through the centuries in the West since the time of St. Augustine. The second is also posed to the Evangelical world, namely the common assumption that the Christian destiny is translation to a highly spiritualized heaven, that leaves the earth behind.

The key question is what happens when the Christ comes in glory. The Jewish expectation is that the returning Messiah will be enthroned in

28. CCC, 1071.

29. SC, 41.

Jerusalem and will establish righteousness in Israel and from there among the nations throughout the earth. Ironically, this promise is at the heart of the angel's message to Mary in a passage otherwise dear to the Catholics and the Orthodox: "the Lord God will give to him the throne of his father David, and he will reign over the house of Jacob for ever; and of his kingdom there will be no end" (Luke 1:32–33). In this Jewish understanding the Messiah–Savior is coming back to establish his reign of righteousness on the earth, starting from Jerusalem. In his book *Surprised by Hope*, Anglican bishop Tom Wright strongly criticizes the widespread belief that the destiny of Christians is to go to heaven when they die. He writes of the expectation of the first Christians: "They believed that God was going to do for the whole cosmos what he had done for Jesus at Easter."[30] This conviction of Wright in fact fits with the teaching of the Catholic Catechism that "The Church will enter the glory of the kingdom only through this final Passover, when she will follow her Lord in his death and resurrection."[31]

It is the organic coherence of all Catholic and Orthodox doctrine that understands the whole age of the church as the time for the preparation and purification of the bride. The bride is not just an agglomeration of holy Christians, but the body of the church. This preparation and purification will continue from Pentecost to Parousia. So in Ephesians:

> Christ loved the church and gave himself up for her [that is from the beginning], that he might sanctify her, having cleansed her by the washing of water with the word, that the church might be presented before him in splendor, without spot or wrinkle or any such thing, that she might be holy and without blemish.[32]

This presentation of the totally cleansed bride will not happen before the parousia, a conviction that requires the healing of divisions and separation before the last day.

In the ancient tradition, this preparation of the body of Christ takes place primarily in the liturgy. So in the renewed eschatology taught in the Catechism of the Catholic Church it is said, "The Holy Spirit's transforming power in the liturgy hastens the coming of the kingdom and the consummation of the mystery of salvation."[33]

30. Wright, *Surprised*, 104.

31. CCC, 677.

32. Eph 5:25–27.

33. CCC, 1107. See also CCC, 1130.

But, in Catholic imagination, the destiny of the church has been seen as our transference to the heavenly realms. In popular Catholic piety, our destiny is immediate after death, whether heaven immediately or after a "period" of purgatorial cleansing. The resurrection of the body, which is prominent in all funeral liturgies, has little place at this level. In popular piety, the salvation of the cosmos has little or no place, though it survives in the liturgical traditions.

The Catechism of the Catholic Church has two rather different sections under the heading "I Believe in Life Everlasting:" one simply on heaven, and the other on "The Hope of the New Heaven and the New Earth." The section on heaven repeats the received focus of many centuries with most of the footnotes referring to passages from popes and church fathers.[34] The section on "The Hope of the New Heaven and the New Earth" is quite new, without parallel in previous catechisms, a fruit of the renewal in Catholic biblical studies, that also draws on the Vatican II Constitution *Gaudium et Spes*.[35] It must be confessed that in the teaching on heaven[36] it is difficult to see what significant difference is made by the resurrection of the body on the last day, also clearly taught in the Catechism.[37]

But here again we enter the realm of paradox. There is a line of continuity from this Jewish vision of the redemption of the whole earthly order to the concept of the millennium. The liturgical churches that have a tradition of the physical mediating the spiritual have not accepted the idea of a literal messianic reign on the earth. The Evangelicals have widely received this concept, while having a suspicion both of the role of the physical in salvation and of liturgy. A key question concerns the role of death-resurrection in the coming transformation not only of the earthly church, but also of the whole created order.

34. CCC, 1023–29.

35. CCC, 1042–50.

36. "Heaven is the ultimate end and fulfillment of the deepest human longings, the state of supreme, definitive happiness" (CCC, 1024)

37. CCC, 1101. The Catholic practice of the beatification and canonization of holy people who lived lives of heroic faith also contributes, though unintentionally, to this impression of the non-consequentiality of the resurrection of the body on the last day. Canonization is also practiced by the Orthodox Churches.

Conclusion

One conclusion is that the coming together of liturgy and eschatology that has always existed in the Jewish tradition is necessary for the reconciliation of the ancient liturgical churches and the newer revival traditions.

I have argued that liturgy and eschatology are basic components for integrating the dimensions of the corporate, intrinsic to the ancient liturgical traditions, and the personal, that has been the focus of the revivalistic traditions of the West. The bodily character of liturgy is intrinsic to its church-forming capacity, and the constitutional role of the liturgy in Christian worship makes the liturgy the key resource for maintaining the continuity and the orthodoxy of the Christian faith. The liturgy holds the key for a right relating of the corporate and in the personal in relation to the church's use, transmission, and exegesis of the Scriptures. The absence of liturgy in the revivalistic currents has caused eschatology to become individualistic: so the doctrine of the rapture is spoken of as "the rapture of the church," but in effect it is the rapture of millions of individual believers, as Louis Dallière pointed out.

However, the reawakening of eschatological hope is a hallmark of movements of the Holy Spirit throughout the centuries. It appears unlikely that the historic churches can recover a vibrant eschatological hope without a profound interaction with the revivalistic currents: Evangelical, Holiness, Pentecostal, and charismatic. A major obstacle in the past has been the entanglement of the church with empires and states that encouraged a settledness in this world that made any eschatological message a threat to the political order. The loosening of the ties between nation-states and established churches frees the churches from such political entanglement at the same time as we are seeing an intensification in the outpouring of the Holy Spirit. We thus live at a particularly propitious moment for a serious interaction of the historic church world and the revivalistic world that could bring unimaginable blessings and help to resolve some of the unsatisfactory dichotomies that have long plagued both sides.

CHAPTER 5

Catholic Charismatic Renewal: Sources, History, Challenges

A SYMPOSIUM ON THE theme of baptism in the Holy Spirit, organized by the community of Chemin Neuf at St. Niklausen in Switzerland in March 2013, gathered scholars and leaders from many churches and confessions to discuss what is an inter-denominational and potentially ecumenical phenomenon on a global scale.[1] The paper that constitutes this chapter specifically addresses the Catholic Charismatic Renewal (CCR) in the awareness that the symposium as a whole was contributing a wider Christian reflection on a phenomenon that has impacted and affected much of the Christian world on all continents.

The theme of CCR is broader than the issue of baptism in the Holy Spirit. However, all participants in the Renewal are agreed that baptism in the Spirit is its foundational spiritual reality from which all its other characteristics derive. This paper is then a reflection on baptism in the Spirit in the context of the whole Renewal. But it has wider relevance as the theme of baptism in the Spirit is wider than the CCR, for it is the foundational grace of the Pentecostal and charismatic movements as a whole.

I deliberately describe baptism in the Spirit as the "foundational spiritual reality" rather than as the fundamental experience, so as to avoid the subjectivist associations of experiential terminology. There is an objective character to baptism in the Spirit. It is not merely a subjective interior state. The charisms provide a clear witness to this objectivity. So does the fact that

1. This impact has been charted statistically by David Barrett and since his retirement and death by Todd M. Johnson in the *World Christian Encyclopaedia* and in annual statistical reports published in the January issues of the *International Bulletin of Missionary Research*.

these endowments of the Spirit can be exercised together with others. This objective character of baptism in the Spirit makes clear that it is intended as a gift for the church, a point recognized by Paul VI during the first major CCR gathering in Rome in 1975, when he said: "How then could this 'spiritual renewal' be other than a blessing for the Church and for the world?"[2]

The Origins

To address the challenges raised by CCR, it is necessary to look at its history and particularly its beginnings. In its first years, it was recognized that this movement had begun outside the Catholic Church. Baptism in the Spirit in the sense in which it has been lived within the Renewal can be traced back to the beginnings of the Pentecostal movement in the first decade of the twentieth century.[3] This work of the Holy Spirit first spread into the Protestant churches in the 1950s and 1960s, leading to its appearance in the Catholic Church from 1967.[4] From 1967, many Catholics were baptized in the Spirit through the imposition of hands by Pentecostals or charismatic Protestants.[5] The inter-church character of the origins was recognized as early as 1974 in the first Malines document written by a group of participant-scholars at the invitation of Cardinal Suenens: "It is evident that the charismatic renewal is a major ecumenical force and is *de facto* ecumenical in nature."[6]

Several things are clear from the beginnings. First, those involved recognized that they were experiencing the same grace of the Lord. These features include the prominence of praise in worship, including spontaneous praise, a heightened sensitivity to evil spirits, and the manifestation of

2. Pesare, *Then Peter*, 19.

3. There was a pre-Pentecostal history to the concept of baptism in the Spirit within Protestant milieux focused on sanctification; see Dayton, *Theological Roots*. There was a significant mutation from the Holiness usage to the Pentecostal usage that witnesses to the distinctive Gestalt of the Pentecostal movement.

4. There were Catholics baptized in the Spirit in the Pentecostal sense before February, 1967: for example, Fr. Jan Biesbrouck from Belgium at Utrecht, Netherlands in 1965, and several lay Catholics in the Episcopal parish of charismatic pioneer, Fr. Dennis Bennett, in Seattle, USA, also in 1965. But these instances did not give rise to a movement.

5. There are notable examples of Protestants baptized in the Spirit through the ministry of Catholics.

6. *Theological and Pastoral Orientations*, 49. This statement was cited by Pope Francis in an address to CCR on June 1, 2014.

the *charismata pneumatika*, listed by Paul in 1 Cor 12:8–10. Common to all these features is a clear sense of the present Lordship of Jesus Christ, who speaks and acts now in recognizable ways, symbolized most evidently in the exercise of charisms such as prophecy, healing, words of wisdom, and knowledge. This conviction of a shared grace of the Holy Spirit led to several of the first charismatic communities formed in the USA having an ecumenical dimension and vision.

Second, at the beginning, everyone used the same terminology. So this event-experience was called baptism in the Holy Spirit. The Catholic recipients, at least the theologically aware among them, recognized that confusion with the sacrament of baptism must be avoided, and that an adequate theological account of this reality must be formulated. Despite the early reservations of several theologians,[7] the terminology of baptism in the Spirit has become the standard usage in the English-speaking sector of CCR.[8] In some other linguistic groupings alternative terms were developed, such as *l'effusion de l'Esprit* in French, sometimes accompanied by the argument that baptism in the Spirit was an inherently Protestant concept. Why did baptism in the Spirit remain the English-language usage? Some might answer that the English-speaking Catholic world is more pragmatic and less theologically sensitive. There is some truth in this observation, but I am convinced that the deeper reasons were (1) the stronger sense in the English-speaking world of the ecumenical significance of the one term describing the same basic gift of the Lord, and (2) sensing how this phrase connects the contemporary experience to the event of Pentecost.

Baptism in the Spirit had been an identifying marker in the Pentecostal movement. When the Pentecostal movement became a number of new

---

7. "To avoid from now on all ambiguity it would be better not to speak of 'baptism in the Spirit' but to look for another expression" (Suenens, *A New Pentecost?* 83). "Such a moment may also be legitimately designated 'a baptism in the Holy Spirit,' that is, a deeper plunging into the Spirit received in baptism. It may be called 'an experience of Spirit-baptism.' But it may not be called 'the baptism in the Holy Spirit,' for the simple reason that there is much more to 'Spirit-baptism' than the experience of a Pentecostal breakthrough" (Gelpi, *Charism*, 151).

8. From the beginning Kilian McDonnell sought to retain this terminology by distinguishing between two senses of the phrase: "'Baptism in the Holy Spirit' is used in the renewal in two senses. First, there is the theological sense. Anyone who has been initiated has received the baptism in the Holy Spirit in this theological sense. Secondly, there is the experiential sense. When at the popular level persons ask, 'Have you received the baptism in the Holy Spirit?' it is to this experiential sense that they refer" ("The Holy Spirit and Christian Initiation" in McDonnell. *Holy Spirit*, 81–82).

denominations needing to formulate their own declarations of faith, baptism in the Spirit acquired the status of a doctrine, in fact a central defining doctrine. So, for example, the Assemblies of God taught that speaking in tongues is the necessary "initial evidence" of baptism in the Spirit. This position became a majority Pentecostal teaching, but it was not universal. Nonetheless all Pentecostals expected visible evidence of baptism in the Spirit, whether or not it was speaking in tongues. For them it was unthinkable that someone could be baptized in the Spirit and remain unaware of it.

When the pentecostal grace spread to the Protestant churches, it was entering spheres that already had doctrinal traditions shaped in most cases by historic confessions of faith. For the traditions believing in baptismal regeneration, the immediate issue was, as it would become for Catholics, the relationship between baptism in the Spirit and the sacrament of baptism. It was presupposed that charismatics were not creating a new doctrine, but clarifying how this grace enjoyed by some was to be understood in relation to the sacramental foundation for all. For the free church traditions, particularly those refusing infant baptism and practicing "believer's baptism," there was a parallel issue of the relationship between the rite, often described as "water-baptism" and the experience of Spirit-baptism, but in this context the debate typically focused on experience and the relationship between conversion-regeneration and a subsequent second experience or "blessing" of Spirit-empowerment-endowment.[9] The focus on experience more easily led to making Spirit-baptism mandatory and elevating it to a quasi-doctrinal status, a tendency that could lead to schisms. However, in their unenthusiastic response to the charismatic movement the Protestant churches typically saw the irrationality of speaking in tongues as more problematic than claims to a baptism in the Spirit.[10]

With the Catholic response to the charismatic movement, we should note some features that distinguished it from the origins in the Protestant communions. First, the Catholic movement had a much greater coherence

9. There was a debate among Pentecostals between three-stage (conversion, sanctification, Spirit-baptism) and two-stage (conversion, Spirit-baptism) that is still reflected in the differences between the Pentecostal denominations stemming from the radical Holiness movement (Church of God, Church of God of Prophecy, Pentecostal Holiness Church) and those stemming from Keswick Holiness or Baptist backgrounds (Assemblies of God).

10. There were some Lutherans, e.g., in the Lutheran Church–Missouri Synod in the USA, for whom the most problematic area in the charismatic movement was the attribution of any authority to prophetic utterances, that was seen as endangering the unique authority of the Word of God.

which contributed to a more rapid growth and diffusion; this coherence was linked to the close communications between key university campuses in the USA,[11] and the rise of well-organized charismatic communities in these places. Second, in the first decade far more theologians and scholars became involved in CCR than was ever the case in the Protestant world.[12] Third, in the Catholic renewal there was a strong sense that this movement was for the whole church, so that there was a deep motivation to interpret baptism in the Spirit in ways coherent with the Catholic tradition. Fourth, the close collaboration of Pope Paul VI and Cardinal Suenens led to the production of the Malines documents, of which the first included some comments on baptism in the Spirit, and to the remarkably quick papal endorsement of the movement in 1975, only eight years after its beginnings.

The major issue for the Catholic theologians closely involved with the Renewal was the relationship between baptism in the Spirit and the sacraments of initiation (many here linked together baptism and confirmation). Since the first exploration of this topic in the years 1972 to 1974 one interpretation has been dominant, that tied baptism in the Spirit strongly to the sacraments of initiation and in particular to the sacrament of baptism. This understanding explained baptism in the Spirit as the entry into conscious experience of graces objectively received in the sacraments of initiation, as the "actualization" of those graces and as a "release" of what was already within but not yet clearly manifest.[13] A second account attracted some attention, but never dislodged the first as the preferred Catholic account, explaining baptism in the Spirit as a new mission of the Spirit, and invoking St. Thomas Aquinas in support of new post-baptismal missions of the Spirit.[14] In the later 1970s the language of *l'effusion de l'Esprit* was preferred by some in France (particularly in the Emmanuel community), while the term *l'effusione dello Spirito* was taken up in Italy (particularly in that part of the

11. Notre Dame, Indiana; Michigan State, Lansing, MI; and the University of Michigan, Ann Arbor, MI in particular, plus in the earliest stages Duquesne University in Pittsburgh, PA.

12. Edward O'Connor, CSC, Francis Sullivan, SJ, Donald Gelpi, SJ, John Haughey, SJ, Francis Martin, George Montague, SM, Kilian McDonnell, OSB (more a close friend and supporter than participant). These were soon followed in Europe by Cardinal Suenens, Paul Lebeau, SJ, René Laurentin, and Heribert Mühlen (who always had reservations about CCR as an international movement). Some of the lay leaders such as Kevin Ranaghan, later ordained deacon, had also received a solid theological formation.

13. This theory received its major expression in McDonnell and Montague, *Christian Initiation*. This book was subsequently translated into many languages.

14. This account was particularly developed by Sullivan in *Charisms*.

Renewal known as Rinnovamento nello Spirito Santo).[15] In France, Père Congar raised some questions concerning the terminology arising within the charismatic renewal.[16]

Before examining these positions more closely, I want to draw attention to the ecumenical dilemma. The charismatic movement was marked by this unexpected grace of a work of the Holy Spirit that spanned virtually all Christian traditions and manifested the same characteristics in these very varied contexts. Recognition of this commonality led to affirmations of its ecumenical significance.[17] But all charismatics committed to their churches and denominations recognized the need to relate this grace to their distinctive theological and spiritual heritage. One largely unnoticed consequence was that the unity in the spiritual reality was threatened by the elaboration of differing accounts of baptism in the Spirit, as for example between Catholic and baptistic positions, that were in marked contrast to each other. So I raise the question as to whether such a process was inevitable. The pioneers in ecumenical charismatic community had been convinced that the God who had brought them together could keep them together. Was there a way in which baptism in the Spirit could be understood across the Christian spectrum that would affirm and not threaten the inchoate spiritual unity in the foundational event-experience?

Reflection on the Two Principal Catholic Presentations

My first comment is that both these explanations are Catholic positions for CCR. Both accounts clearly have as their principal aim the legitimation of the pentecostal experience within the Catholic tradition. Neither pays attention to the ecumenical or inter-confessional character of the charismatic movement. But within the whole charismatic movement, there is a variety of understandings of the sacrament or ordinance of baptism, ranging from the Catholic (regeneration through the liturgical-sacramental action) to the baptistic (testimonial, but no causal role of the water-action)

15. The Spanish-speaking world did not adopt a uniform terminology.

16. "Charismatiques, ou quoi?" *La Croix*, 19 Janvier 1974. McDonnell comments extensively on this article in *Holy Spirit*, 63–73.

17. "We believe that the Charismatic Renewal is called to fulfill an ecumenical vocation" (Suenens, *Ecumenism*, 4).

and beyond these to those Christian groups that reject all sacraments.[18] Whatever their merits, can accounts that ignore the inter-confessional dimension of the movement really do justice to this reality shared across so many traditions?

Next, the "actualization" theory seems to reflect a pre-ecumenical understanding of the sacraments. It pays little attention to the character of symbols and to baptism as a sign. In particular, the language of "graces actually received" at the moment of baptism seems to suggest that what later becomes manifest is somehow already inside the one baptized, presumed to be an infant.[19] There is an unsatisfactory objectivization of "graces" here, and inadequate attention to how the sacramental action of baptism symbolizes the whole Christian life through to the eschatological completion. This view often speaks of the release of what is already within, without mentioning any new element or influence coming from outside that occasions the release.[20] In my view, it is preferable to use the language of the foundations laid in sacramental baptism and the status of sonship then conferred.

This all-coming-from-inside position draws our attention to the absence from these theories of any role for the Word of God. In advocating a new mission of the Spirit, Sullivan strongly criticizes the all-from-within position, but does not advert to the Word of God.[21] These positions fail to ask the question: what proximate instrumental cause is producing this combination of blessings? It ignores the correlation between what is experienced/received and what is preached/taught. While a study of charismatic testimonies will indicate that a few people have been overwhelmed by this grace without prior knowledge of the charismatic movement or any evident predisposition to such an experience, the more typical pattern is for reception to follow teaching about a fullness of the Holy Spirit, as in Life in the Spirit seminars, or the hearing/reading the witnesses of others. A balanced position will surely acknowledge that there is a confluence between the

---

18. For example, the Quakers and the Salvation Army.

19. The paragraph in CCC about the seal or character imparted in the sacraments of baptism, confirmation, and holy orders may be helpful: "it remains for ever in the Christian as a positive disposition for grace, a promise and guarantee of divine protection, and as a vocation to divine worship and to the service of the Church" (1121).

20. "[W]e are concerned here with a new coming of the Spirit already present, of an 'outpouring' which does not come from outside, but springs up from within" (Suenens, *New Pentecost?* 83).

21. See Sullivan, *Charisms*, 59–75, especially 69–70.

grace of the Lord coming from outside (the Word of God, testimonies, new encounters) and the work of grace within the baptized Christian.

Personally I do not think that the Catholic theological accounts of baptism in the Spirit pay sufficient attention to the biblical data, in particular to the prophetic context of its usage by John the Baptist—only in verbal form—and the limitation of its prophetic fulfillment to two occasions, the day of Pentecost and the "Gentile Pentecost" in Caesarea (Acts 1:5; 11:15–16). The deep conviction that this outpouring of the Holy Spirit in our day is in some way a new Pentecost marked both the Pentecostal and the charismatic origins.[22] Almost twenty years ago I made a suggestion concerning the usage of the term "baptism in the Spirit" by the first Pentecostals. Even when we disagree with the Pentecostal doctrine concerning baptism in the Spirit "it is possible . . . to recognize that the Pentecostals were led by the Spirit in this identification with Pentecost and their naming of this central experience, without accepting all their exegesis. This can be done by insisting that the original Pentecostal use of the term 'baptism in the Spirit' was primarily prophetic. It is an interpretation of contemporary experience in the light of the Scriptures rather than exegesis of the Scriptures illuminated by present circumstances."[23] The Pentecostals in the first decade of the twentieth century were doing what the apostle Peter did at Pentecost in citing the prophecy of Joel and saying "this is what was spoken by the prophet Joel" (Acts 2:16).

Neither theory does much to investigate the significance of this phenomenon, why it has appeared at this point in Christian history, and what challenges it presents to received theology and pastoral practice. Probably the time was not ripe in the first decade of the Renewal, when there was a real need to justify its existence within the Catholic Church.

The Institutional and the Charismatic

In the drafting of the ICCRS document on baptism in the Holy Spirit, Mary Healy and I sensed the importance of the address of John Paul II at Pentecost 1998 to the new ecclesial movements and communities, particularly concerning the complementarity of the institutional and charismatic dimensions of the church. John Paul II had said:

22. This dimension is often mentioned in the teaching of Fr. Raniero Cantalamessa.
23. Hocken, *Glory*, 46.

Whenever the Spirit intervenes, he leaves people astonished. He brings about events of amazing newness; he radically changes persons and history. This was the unforgettable experience of the Second Vatican Ecumenical Council during which, under the guidance of the same Spirit, the Church rediscovered the charismatic dimension as one of her constitutive elements.[24]

The pope added that the institutional and the charismatic dimensions are as it were co-constitutive of the church.[25]

In the ICCRS document this distinction is described in the following way:

The institutional is passed down from generation to generation and belongs to the permanent visible structure of the Church. The charismatic is given by the Lord in an unpredictable way and cannot be codified. Baptism in the Spirit, as a manifestation of the spontaneous working of the Spirit, belongs to the charismatic dimension, but at the same time it brings new life and dynamism to the institutional dimension of Christian life grounded in the sacraments.[26]

The sacrament of baptism belongs to the institutional element (the Word of God, all the sacraments and the ministerial structures), while baptism in the Spirit belongs to the charismatic element. This distinction enables us to uphold the distinctive grace of baptism in the Spirit as it has been experienced in the Pentecostal and charismatic movements, while at the same time giving proper weight to the church's tradition concerning the foundational character of the sacraments of initiation.

This distinction raises the question of the relationship between doctrine binding on all and other forms of Christian utterance (biblical and theological interpretation, preaching, exhortation). It would seem that doctrine subsequent to the apostolic age that is binding on all cannot be based on charismatic elements, for the charismatic elements come and go. Theological reflection is needed on the charismatic irruptions, but they cannot form the basis of new doctrine that is binding on all. In this light, I suggest that any attempt to formulate a doctrine of baptism in the Spirit is misguided, being based on a confusion of categories. It seems to me that this temptation to subsume baptism in the Spirit as known in these modern

24. Pesare, *Then Peter*, 149.
25. See also chapter 13.
26. ICCRS, *Baptism in the Holy Spirit*, 69.

contexts into the theology of baptism reaches its fullest expression in Kilian McDonnell's conclusions: "If the baptism in the Spirit belongs to those sacraments which are constitutive of the deepest nature of the church, if the baptism in the Spirit belongs to public liturgy, if it belongs to initiation as the matrix of all ministries to the church and world, then the baptism in the Spirit is normative."[27] But in the understanding of the charismatic dimension as that which is unpredictable, which comes and which goes, as the Spirit breathes, then nothing charismatic subsequent to the New Testament can be normative. The affirmation of both the institutional and the charismatic avoids both the subordination of the charismatic to the institutional (Catholic tendency) and the exaltation of baptism in the Spirit at the expense of sacramental baptism (Pentecostal tendency).

But does this mean that the attempt to relate the grace of baptism in the Spirit to the sacraments of initiation is mistaken? No, it doesn't. For as John Paul II insisted in his 1998 address, the institutional and the charismatic dimensions need each other. The charismatic is poured out into the ongoing historical body of Christ, so this grace of baptism in the Spirit in the twentieth century is poured out on the body of believers established through the full liturgy of Christian initiation in baptism, confirmation and first communion. So, as the ICCRS document acknowledges, the grace of baptism in the Spirit does infuse new life into those first brought to new life through the liturgies of initiation. It does give a new love for the sacraments, it does deepen our sense of being sons and daughters of the Father, a status we received at baptism. What I am saying here of baptism in the Spirit is true of every unexpected charismatic grace in the history of the church: all are poured out on baptized persons, on communities established on and formed by the Word of God and the sacraments; and all enhance and deepen the foundational life of sonship in trinitarian communion.

The recognition that baptism in the Spirit belongs to the charismatic dimension of the church means that it is not only the coming to deeper life or the entry into conscious experience of the graces foundationally conferred at baptism. This understanding prompts us to ask what on the one hand is a distinctive grace for our age, for this moment in the history of the church, and what on the other hand is the restoration of normality, the realization of what ought always to have been happening during the celebration of baptism. Both aspects are surely present in our experience. It may not be easy or even possible to draw a sharp dividing line between God's

27. McDonnell and Montague, *Christian Initiation*, 335–36.

charismatic gifting for our age and the invigoration of the basic baptismal grace. But the presence of both aspects requires us to say that baptism in the Spirit is a new outpouring in and for our day as well as saying that it activates the grace of sonship conferred in sacramental baptism.

The Theological Challenges

I want to identify four points on which the central grace of the Renewal calls for deeper theological reflection and research. They are all related in some way, and the first is an overarching issue and so could be said to constitute the core challenge. It concerns the sovereign character of the action of the risen Lord upon the church. This dimension embraces: (1) the claim associated with baptism in the Spirit to direct or immediate communication with the Lord; and (2) the nature of the charismatic activity of the Lord in this dimension of church life that is humanly unplanned and unforeseeable. The first is most evident in though not restricted to personal experience; the second focuses on the life of the entire church on earth. The sovereign character signifies the lordship of Jesus over the church as his body. The charismatic and prophetic impulses, manifested on the large scale in the Pentecostal and charismatic movements, recall the church to this lordship of which she remains always the servant who manages the household or tends the vineyard as in the parables of the kingdom in the teaching of Jesus.

A second challenge is posed by the claim that the basic spiritual reality being called baptism in the Spirit is fundamentally the same grace across all the different church groupings impacted by the charismatic movement. Such a phenomenon is only possible because of the charismatic character of baptism in the Spirit as an unpredictable and in some sense immediate work of the Holy Spirit. The conviction of those experiencing the charismatic renewal as an inter-confessional movement has been that this grace has produced a genuine unity in the Spirit. As a Catholic sharing this conviction, I have insisted that this experiential unity is genuine, that it has an objective character, and that it is a significant grace for moving the church towards the fullness of sacramental communion. Some in the non-denominational streams mistook this unity for the full unity desired by the Lord arguing from the immediate Holy Spirit character of this experienced unity to the irrelevance of ecumenism, dismissed as a merely human work.

A deeper investigation of this unity in the Spirit leads to the third challenge, the need to re-examine our received anthropology of the human person. It would seem that the unity between recipients conferred through the baptism in the Spirit is primarily a unity at the level of spirit that cannot be reduced to the merely emotional. The received language of soul and body does not seem adequate, not distinguishing sufficiently between the spiritual and the psychic. But as a unity in the spirit it needs to lead to a unity in understanding and a unity of will, or we could say a growing unity of soul. Without the effort to ensoul and embody this spiritual grace, its effects will be ephemeral. This challenge posed by the whole Pentecostal-charismatic phenomenon concerns the whole way that we speak about the response of the human person to God: the language of spirit, of soul, of mind, of heart, all operative in and through the human body. In fact, the Pentecostal-charismatic world generally utilizes a tripartite anthropology, though until recently it has not taken much interest in anthropological and philosophical issues.[28] Much charismatic teaching presents the ability to communicate directly with the Lord as a coming alive of the human spirit, understood to be the point in each believer through which the Holy Spirit communicates. This issue also arises in the pastoral ministry of healing with the restoration of the bodily, the psychic, and the spiritual in the practice of deliverance and exorcism.

The large ecumenical communities within the Renewal,[29] which to my knowledge all have a Catholic majority,[30] have a theological responsibility to investigate more deeply the shared life and convictions stemming from baptism in the Spirit that have made possible their common life. This kind

28. It should be remarked here that in the last decade Pentecostal scholars in the United States have begun to remedy this neglect, particularly, for example, James K. A. Smith.

29. I am using the term "ecumenical community" in a descriptive sense to refer to those communities with a membership drawn from different Christian communions because they have an ecumenical vision. This description includes Chemin Neuf that describes itself as "une communauté catholique à vocation oecuménique" (a Catholic community with an ecumenical vocation). There are of course communities with a wholly Catholic membership who profess an ecumenical vision and seek to work ecumenically.

30. I think here of the Sword of the Spirit communities; of the People of Praise (South Bend, IN); of Alleluia Community (Augusta, GA), of the Servants of Jesus (Sydney, Australia) and of Chemin Neuf. There are also several smaller communities with a mixed membership within the European Network of Communities, with main office in Vienna, Austria.

of theology requires an analysis of lived experience and cannot be done solely from a study of texts.

To affirm a genuine objective unity in the Spirit between members of separate Christian churches and communions raises many questions. One is the affirmation of loyalties that cross church boundaries and the issue of "multiple belonging" that has already been posed among those dealing with inter-church marriages. The affirmation of lived forms of communion across church boundaries challenges the reigning mentality in many traditions of an assumed total hegemony in regard to their members. Ultimately, the idea is not credible that the divided Christian world could ever pass in one moment of reconciliation from a belonging that is limited to one communion to a mutual belonging of all.

The last theological challenge I want to identify concerns eschatology. Any account of the Pentecostal-charismatic phenomenon that omits any reference to the coming of the Lord in glory is seriously defective. This is suggested by several factors, some already mentioned: first, the strong hope for the Lord's soon-coming so manifest in the beginnings of the Pentecostal movement; second, the eschatological context of the biblical references to being "baptized in Spirit"; third, the charismatic element in the rise of the Messianic Jewish movement at almost the same time as the origin of CCR. For the Jews coming to faith in Jesus (Yeshua) as their Messiah and Lord, most of whom were being baptized in the Holy Spirit it was clear that all their coming to faith belongs to the proximate preparation for the Lord's coming.

The eschatological dimension has been weaker in the charismatic renewal in the historic churches than in the free churches with a revivalistic heritage. There is a mutual antipathy here between the historic churches and the revivalist currents: the former are suspicious of all end-times enthusiasm, while the latter are suspicious of tradition and formal worship. But the Pentecostal–charismatic currents bring together both Christians from the historic churches who have been allergic to all forms of millennialism and Evangelical Christians among whom an increasing number believe in a millennial reign of Jesus on earth before the final kingdom.[31] The Messianic Jews intensify this challenge, as they cannot imagine the return of the Lord as anything other than to establish his rule on the earth. Baptism in the Spirit awakens the hope and the longing for the final completion, both

---

31. There are of course some Evangelicals within the historic churches, most notably within the Anglican communion. They can play a bridging role between the historic churches and the revivalist world.

in the Renewal within the historic churches and in the revivalist streams, Evangelical, Pentecostal, and charismatic. This grace thus has the potential to bridge this divide in the area of eschatology.[32] Here there are immense challenges on all sides, which this is not the occasion to address.[33] But as Pentecostals and Evangelical charismatics engage more with ecumenical Christians, as, for example, in the GCF, eschatology has to be a key theme in the resulting dialogue.

Finally I want to draw attention to a development within the wider charismatic movement. Some groupings issuing from the charismatic movement have abandoned the terminology of baptism in the Spirit and the term "charismatic." It is interesting that this has not been paralleled in CCR. There are two distinct categories here: one is within some historic Protestant churches, the other within new charismatic streams and networks. With the former, there is often the desire to avoid all charges of elitism and to work with others seeking spiritual revival and renewal; with the latter, one motive has been to get beyond Evangelical–charismatic opposition concerning the reception of the Holy Spirit. In both cases, especially the latter, distinctively charismatic elements are retained, such as the *charismata pneumatika* (spiritual gifts), the centrality of praise and of laying on of hands in ministry, without what is seen as the encumbrance of controversial or problematic concepts. These developments show again how important it is for theologians to reflect on the issues at stake: for example, the question as to whether the dropping of the terminology of baptism in the Spirit is merely the sidelining of a theological obstacle with no significant spiritual consequences or whether it represents a refusal to face the full challenge of the Lord thus contributing to a dilution and a loss in the work of the Holy Spirit.

32. See Hocken, *Challenges*.
33. The challenge in regard to eschatology is treated more directly in chapter 10.

PART II

Reflections on the New Charismatic
Churches and Networks

CHAPTER 6

Roman Catholics and Non-Denominational Christians

The Need for Each Other

A FIRST REASON FOR the Catholic Church to take non-denominational Christians seriously is the sheer size and scope of the non-denominational charismatic phenomenon in the world today. The *New International Dictionary of the Pentecostal and Charismatic Movements* gives a statistic of two hundred and ninety-five million.[1] At the very least, there is need for those in the historic churches, and not least in the Catholic Church, to pay attention to this development, to discover what is happening and how, and then to seek to understand it. Such understanding needs to take place at various levels and within various disciplines.

The need for non-denominationals and Roman Catholics to come together can be argued from both the size of the non-denominational movement as a charismatic phenomenon and the size and influence of the Catholic Church in worldwide Christianity. This argument is enhanced by the renewal currents encouraged and let loose in the Catholic Church by the Second Vatican Council together with the extent and the impact of the new ecclesial movements.

Where there are no relationships between the Catholic Church and the world of non-denominational Christians, there is a serious danger

---

1. NIDPCM, 284. The authors, David Barrett and Todd Johnson, use the terminology of "Neo-Charismatics" and "Third Wavers." Actually the term "third wave," unfortunate in my view, when first coined by C. Peter Wagner, did not refer to "non-denominational charismatics" but to Evangelicals being impacted by aspects of Pentecostal-charismatic practice without accepting a second-blessing theology or the "charismatic" label.

of mutual misrepresentation. For the non-denominationals, who are in-stinctively suspicious of all forms of institutional Christianity, it is easy to dismiss Catholicism as the embodiment of lifeless religion in thrall to the bondage of "religious spirits," from which its victims need to be de-livered. For the Catholics, both bishops and theologians, the new charis-matic churches have been easily placed in the category of "sects," the latest manifestation of fundamentalist Protestantism, the youngest wolf attack-ing the unsuspecting Catholic sheep. The danger of the dynamic currents of Pentecostal-charismatic Christianity and the Catholic Church simply perceiving each other as deadly enemies has certainly been decreased by the extraordinary openness shown by Pope Francis to Pentecostal and new charismatic leaders.[2] But the road from outright hostility to mutual re-spect as fellow-Christians is one that has to pass through real encounter leading to an accurate knowledge of each other. The big differences be-tween these two worlds, not so much in basic doctrine but in mentality and priorities—especially the totally different formation patterns of their leaders—makes this encounter both more difficult but also potentially far more fruitful. It is not enough for the Catholic Church to de-demonize the non-denominationals, for that would be to ignore their gifts and to fail to learn from their contemporaneity.

Gatherings in the Holy Spirit

The meetings between CCR leaders and some non-denominational char-ismatic leaders that have developed over the past fifteen years under the heading "Gatherings in the Holy Spirit" have an importance that even the participants may not have fully grasped. One priest who has glimpsed its potential is a Catholic participant not from CCR, Fr. Jim Puglisi, SA, the director of the Centro pro Unione in Rome, who has acted as a sponsor of these meetings.

In general, the Catholic participants have been those with the most contacts with the non-denominational world: Kim Kollins, an initiator of the Gatherings, herself a former "non-denom" missionary before becoming a Catholic in 1984;[3] Kevin and Dorothy Ranaghan from the People of Praise community in South Bend, Indiana (Kevin was for a long time chair of the

2. See chapter 11.

3. See Kollins, *It's Only*, 162–63. Kollins's non-denominational background is described in this largely autobiographical book.

Glencoe Committee and of NARSC that brought together charismatic leaders in the USA, both denominational and non-denominational); Charles Whitehead, chairman of ICC with non-denominational participation, and now co-chairman with a new charismatic church leader of Charismata, the annual meeting of charismatic leaders in Great Britain; deacon Johannes Fichtenbauer, one of the founding members of the *Weg zur Versöhnung* [Way to Reconciliation] that brings together in Austria denominational and non-denominational leaders, both Evangelical and charismatic; Pierre Chieux, a long-time leader of CCR in France with exposure to non-denominational streams and influences; as well as the present author. Closely related to the Gatherings have been Matteo Calisi (Catholic) and Giovanni Traettino (Pentecostal), who have worked together since the early 1990s on reconciliation between divided Christians, and who subsequently took this ministry to Argentina, where in 2006 it was fully embraced by the then Archbishop of Buenos Aires, Cardinal Jorge Mario Bergoglio SJ.[4]

On the non-denominational side, some participants have played a particularly significant role in unity initiatives. Ulf Ekman, the founder and for many years the senior pastor of Livets Ord (Word of Life) church in Uppsala, Sweden, at the center of a network of many local churches from many nations and several continents, had developed a close relationship with Msgr. Anders Arborelius, the Catholic bishop of Stockholm. For a number of years, Pastor Ekman had taken a group of pastors to Rome to introduce them to the life of the church of Rome, and he had initiated contacts with the Pontifical Council for Promoting Christian Unity.[5] In Britain, John Noble from the Pioneer network of new churches, had been chair of Charismata for many years before Charles Whitehead, and in Berlin, Germany, Pastor Peter Dippl has long nurtured ecumenical relationships with the historic churches.

A Framework for Understanding

For those active in the Gatherings in the Holy Spirit, who have built friendships over the years across this divide, it is possible more easily to move directly into constructive relationships. But for our constituencies, a wider

---

4. See chapter 11 for more details on these background relationships to the unity initiatives of Pope Francis.

5. Ulf Ekman resigned from the organizing committee when he was received into the Catholic Church in May 2014.

framework of understanding is needed to show how the Holy Spirit is at work on both sides and how the present situation fits into a bigger historical context.

The charismatic movement of the second half of the twentieth century can be seen as the latest in a series of "revival streams."[6] The term "streams" is preferable to "movements," because the term "streams" captures far more accurately the initial life-giving flow from the Lord that comes before all forms of organization.[7] The first of these, the Evangelical stream, arose around the 1730s;[8] the second, the Holiness stream in the middle decades of the nineteenth century; the third, the Pentecostal stream at the beginning of the twentieth century, and the fourth, the charismatic stream between 1950 and 1975. This schema has the merit of seeing that something truly new and creative happened around 1730: the beginning of outdoor preaching and mass evangelism,[9] the emergence of a strong missionary thrust in Protestant Christianity,[10] the first signs of a movement that was wider than particular Protestant denominations and groupings. It also recognizes the historical sources influencing the Pentecostal and charismatic streams, while understanding that they represent something distinctively new in reference to what had preceded them.

The Evangelical stream began within the existing Protestant denominations, though it contained a strong element of protest against outward lifeless formalism within those churches. Soon it began to have a few expressions outside those denominations.[11] The Holiness stream began within some Protestant denominations, particularly the Methodist and the Presbyterian—and then in England, the Anglican—but within fifty years it was giving rise to new Holiness denominations. The Pentecostal stream followed rapidly on the Holiness stream, winning over some Holiness groupings and posing a major challenge to Holiness circles. Unlike the other streams, the Pentecostals found no lasting place within the older denominations, and within ten to twenty years had become totally a movement

6. This framework is presented in more detail in Hocken, *Strategy.*

7. The revival stream character of the Pentecostal movement was constantly emphasized by Donald Gee (see chapter 3).

8. Here I follow Bebbington in his major study, *Evangelicalism.*

9. First by George Whitefield, and then by John Wesley.

10. The first major thrust for Protestant missions came from the "Pentecost" experience among the Moravian Brethren at Herrnhut, Germany, in August 1727.

11. E.g., in Britain the Countess of Huntingdon's Connexion.

of new Pentecostal denominations and independent ministries. In this respect, the charismatic stream first appears as "Pentecost outside Pentecost," to use Donald Gee's phrase, that is, the Pentecostal blessing and experience appearing—unexpectedly—within the historic Protestant churches, and then—even more unexpectedly—within the Roman Catholic Church. The spread of the charismatic stream to the Catholic Church, made possible by the Second Vatican Council, has to be of major spiritual significance, precisely because it represents the first time that a worldwide revival stream of Protestant provenance had entered and been welcomed within the communion of the Catholic Church.

However, the charismatic stream soon manifested a presence outside the existing churches and denominations in groupings that by the early 1970s were being called "non-denominational." The "non-denominational" charismatics did not identify with "renewal" in the historic churches,[12] and they did not identify with the Pentecostals. In fact, they generally thought that the Pentecostal movement had taken a major wrong turn when it became a cluster of new denominations. Perhaps for the first time[13]—or certainly in a new way—the first generation of "non-denominational" charismatics were determined not to become new denominations. Seeing the "non-denominationals" in this larger historical context makes it easier for other Christians to take this phenomenon seriously and not to dismiss it as an ephemeral fad.[14]

This history suggests that the tension and polarity between "inside" and "outside," between renewal of the existing churches and new expressions outside, reflects a "strategy" of the Holy Spirit, however difficult that may be for our received theologies on both sides. With this interaction between "outside" and "inside" we come to a deeper reason why dialogue, cooperation, and relationships are necessary between the historic churches and the revival streams. This interaction is especially necessary between the biggest of the ancient churches, the Catholic, and the most deliberately

12. A similar determination was found among many of the early Plymouth Brethren. Some non-denominational leaders, such as Arthur Wallis, deliberately contrasted Renewal, seen as insufficient, with Restoration, seen as the full purpose of the Lord.

13. There was an element of "anti-denominationalism" in the Plymouth Brethren, that certainly flowed into the "house church movement" in Britain; see Hocken, *Streams*, Appendix III, "The Ecclesiology of the Plymouth Brethren as Background to the Stream of the Charismatic Movement Associated with D. G. Lillie and A. Wallis," 201–06.

14. See chapter 7 concerning the origins of some of the major new charismatic groupings.

"outside" grouping, the "non-denominationals," resolved to avoid the fate of denominationalism.

The Distinctiveness of the New Charismatics—with a Few Questions

Before outlining some possible principles to guide a Catholic–non-denominational encounter, I want to reflect on the distinctiveness of the new charismatics. I am speaking primarily here of the phenomenon as it manifests itself in North America, Europe, and Australasia, though many of these characteristics are found on all continents.

Since the charismatic stream basically, I believe, carries the spiritual blessing of the Pentecostal stream, but in a different context, we may ask how the new charismatics are different from the Pentecostals. In their determination not to become new denominations, the new charismatic networks and assemblies are more flexible than the Pentecostals in their structures. They are also less doctrinaire, as the formation of denominations requires the formulation of doctrine in official Statements of Faith in a way that movements and networks do not. While fundamental convictions are important to them, the "non-denominational" charismatics are most concerned about "life," that faith is a living faith, that congregations are living bodies that grow and multiply. They are more contemporary in style and organization, owing more to modern patterns of social organization and business management than to inherited theology and traditional church structures. The formation of new networks and new assemblies is characteristic of the entrepreneurial spirit in a capitalist economy. This fact suggests that to treat this phenomenon as simply another instance of schism in the classical sense of divisions within an existing body would be a mistake. There is a strong factor of acculturation and of *aggiornamento*.

An aspect of their pragmatism is that they are generally less anti-Catholic than their Evangelical and Pentecostal forebears. This can make possible new forms of ecumenical relationship and collaboration. I have met non-denominational leaders who do not see themselves as either Protestant or Catholic, and who feel free to relate to both—and beyond. Their pragmatism often makes them more open than Pentecostals to symbols and prophetic gestures in their worship.[15] This greater openness is

---

15. E.g., the attraction of candles within the Cornerstone network in UK, and the openness of some Vineyard assemblies to more liturgical forms.

partly a consequence of being better educated than the first generations of Pentecostals, though their education has typically been secular—often in business-related and technological studies—rather than ecclesiastical-theological. The combination of intelligence and entrepreneurial spirit has produced a remarkable creativity, so that many initiatives have originated in these milieux. This means that they have an edge on the historic churches in leadership formation, in systems management, etc., as well as producing a disproportionate amount of new Christian music.

In terms of theological-spiritual content, many of the new charismatics are more interested in the issue of church than most classical Pentecostals have been. Related to this is the widespread belief in the restoration of the Eph 4:11 ministries,[16] which is typically seen as the restoration of the original structure of the church. This restoration is focused on the ministry of apostles and prophets, with much of the recent charismatic focus on the prophetic has been spearheaded by the new charismatics.[17] Initially, one of the major differences between the charismatics "inside" and those "outside" was the emphasis of the latter on the Eph 4:11 ministries, which led to their contrasting of "Renewal" with spiritual gifts, seen at best as a half-way house, with "Restoration" emphasizing both spiritual gifts and Eph 4:11 ministries.

Because the new charismatics represent a revival stream that resists denominationalization, it does not yet have the apparatus of denominations. This enables Catholics to see the "non-denominationals" more as new movements parallel to the new ecclesial movements in the Catholic Church, which make no claim to be church. The determination not to become new denominations is often regarded as sociologically naïve, but might it not be that this determination represents a prophetic element that is part of the Lord recalling us all to be more in movement towards the kingdom, just as the church was called "The Way"[18] in the Acts of the Apostles? Might not these features make it easier for the Catholic Church to relate to the new charismatics?

16. "And his gifts were that some should be apostles, some prophets, some evangelists, some pastors and teachers, to equip the saints for the work of ministry, for building up the body of Christ" (Eph 4:11–12).

17. New charismatic circles often recognize particular people as having the ministry of a prophet.

18. Acts 9:2; 19:9, 23. See also Acts 18:26; 22:4.

Some Putative Principles

To approach such a dialogue of "outside" and "inside" I want to propose a few principles for discussion and possible agreement. With each principle I will give a short explanation.

1. *The new revival streams arise as correctives to weaknesses, neglects, and failures of the historic churches.*

   This point is more of an historical observation than a theological principle.[19] It is not as broad as saying that all movements arising outside the churches represent elements of the Christian heritage neglected in the mainline churches—which may well also be true. It is a statement only about the four *revival streams*, which possess a particular character as outpourings from "on high" that do not arise from the genius or the insight of a founder figure. In consequence, they manifest a higher element of divine purpose in their origins than other new movements in which the human component in their origins is stronger.

2. *The God-given element in the revival streams is a force for new life, flowing from certain core convictions concerning the Christian gospel.*

   The revival streams combine a focus on a living relationship to God with core convictions concerning the gospel. They can only be understood rightly when both these elements are taken into account. The core convictions ground the objectivity of revival-renewal, and provide their biblical foundation. If the directness of relationship to the Lord is lost, the revival streams lose their dynamism and can degenerate into mere fundamentalism.

   The revival streams in their genesis and character do not mediate the whole of Christian life or the whole of divine revelation. The core convictions are normally part of the official belief of the churches in which the streams arise, but over time their life-giving power can become dimmed and largely ineffective. In the revival streams these core convictions are raised up as the energizing center that carries forward the Lord's work of revival. They do not represent or constitute church simply as streams.

---

19. Theologically, the action of God can never be adequately understood simply in terms of a response to a human situation.

In the Evangelical stream, the core convictions are that Jesus Christ is Savior from sin and Lord of all, his substitutionary atonement on the cross,[20] the unique authority of a totally-trustworthy Bible,[21] the primacy of evangelism, and the need for each believer to repent and to experience conversion. The Holiness stream adds the necessity of personal experience of sanctification, the Pentecostals the gift of the empowering Spirit in Spirit-baptism and the spiritual gifts.

3. *At the heart of the revival streams is a lifting up of the absolute lordship of Jesus Christ, accentuated in the Pentecostal and charismatic streams by the life-giving mission of the Holy Spirit that is totally directed towards the omega point of the coming of the Lord.*

The role of the revival streams is not primarily an insistence on certain doctrines, but the dissemination of an experienced dependence on the saving power and unique lordship of Jesus Christ. The core convictions are the necessary doctrinal underpinning for this existential dependence. The Pentecostal and charismatic streams emphasize that this dependence on the lordship of Jesus can only be realized in and through the Holy Spirit. The spiritual gifts that characterize these streams can only be received through a trusting faith-dependence upon the divine giver. The exercise of these charisms symbolizes for the whole Christian life the dependence on the Holy Spirit that is being received afresh at each moment. The dependence on the risen Lord and the outpouring of his Spirit orients the Christian community afresh to the coming of the Lord and his kingdom. For the cry that the Spirit gives to the bride is "Come." This subordination to the lordship of Jesus Christ and the ever-continuing gift of the Holy Spirit oriented to the coming fullness constitutes the deepest challenge of the revival streams to the church.

4. *New revival streams are given for the benefit of the whole body of Christ.*

---

20. Although Catholics do not usually use this term, it is in accordance with Catholic faith insofar as it is expressing the fundamental truth that Jesus died for our sins, and in so doing did what we were incapable of doing for ourselves. See CCC, 615 under the heading "Jesus substitutes his obedience for our disobedience."

21. I have used the word "trustworthy" to express what all Evangelicals believe about the total reliability of the Bible, and that many but not all would express in terms of inerrancy.

In God's purposes, all gifts are given for the sake of the whole. This is ultimately because in God's creation everything is connected, and in the redemption this connectedness that was disrupted by sin is being restored. This principle is expressed by Paul in relation to the giftings of the Holy Spirit: "To each is given the manifestation of the Spirit for the common good" (1 Cor 12:7). This is further explained later in the same chapter, when Paul writes, "For the body does not consist of one member but of many" (1 Cor 12:14), and then makes the comparison with the human body in which the "The eye cannot say to the hand, 'I have no need of you,' nor again the head to the feet, 'I have no need of you'" (1 Cor 12:21).

The revival streams focus on the spiritual and the inward, as a corrective to formalism and lack of life. As currents of new life given to benefit the whole body, the streams have a servant role. They are not the whole of Christianity, and never bear witness to the fullness of divine revelation. A servant vision recognizes the God-given character of much in the church heritage that needs to be preserved and revivified through renewal. If revival streams claim to be the whole, they lose this servant character and their exaggerated claims distort their original gifting. This may happen in the process of a revival stream becoming a new denomination or cluster of denominations.

5. *The revival streams are needed by the historic churches.*

To benefit the whole body of Christ, the core convictions of the revival streams have to interact with the total life of the church in all its multifaceted dimensions. This is the profound meaning of *renewal*. This interaction means encounter with a corporate way of life, with a church culture, with a heritage, with a structured institution. The church so addressed from within and from without by the revival streams has its non-negotiable convictions and core traditions. With the Catholic and the Orthodox Churches, the non-negotiable element is greater, and is not just spiritual or theological. The non-negotiable includes an element of embodiment. Here the encounter occurs within a church that understands itself as a privileged embodiment of the one church of Jesus Christ.

This encounter between revival/renewal stream and church inevitably creates tensions. The tensions come first from the challenge of the Holy Spirit to embodied and entrenched forms of church behavior.

They can be exacerbated by immature behavior by revival-renewal enthusiasts, but the call and the dynamism of revival/renewal necessarily contains a prophetic challenge to the status quo in the church. The deepest challenge is the total orientation of the Holy Spirit to the coming kingdom, that cannot be accommodated to any form of settled establishment in this world.

Profound renewal in the historic churches comes through the faithful suffering of the prophetic pioneers. Most of the great pioneer figures who prepared the way for the Second Vatican Council in the Catholic Church suffered a great deal, but the church later accepted their vision and not that of their opponents.[22] It is this perseverance through acute suffering and trial that produces a humility and a depth in the prophetic figures.

6. *However, in God's Providence some streams may develop outside the existing expressions of the church. In this case, they are still for the sake of the whole body, but for their contribution to be more widely received it may require a period of separate development.*

The first statement is a fact. Streams of revival do form and/or develop outside the existing churches, whether often or only occasionally. The key questions then are: (a) how do the existing churches regard them? And (b) how do they understand themselves?

Two gospel texts can speak into this situation: (a) a word of John the Baptist: "do not presume to say to yourselves, 'We have Abraham as our father;' for I tell you, God is able from these stones to raise up children to Abraham" (Matt 3:9); (b) a word of Jesus: "John said to him, 'Teacher, we saw a man casting out demons in your name, and we forbade him, because he was not following us.' But Jesus said, 'Do not forbid him; for no one who does a mighty work in my name will be able soon after to speak evil of me'" (Mark 9:38–39).[23] These are interesting passages, because they seem to be speaking into a situation of independence rather than one of schism.

Catholics are more accustomed to think of schism than of independence. But even with schism, there is an important biblical episode

---

22. One could mention men like Dom Lambert Beauduin, OSB, the Abbé Paul Couturier, Père Yves Congar, OP, Père Henri de Lubac, SJ.

23. I have chosen the Markan version of this saying, as it includes the mention of doing "a mighty work" in the name of Jesus, which is not present in Luke's version in Luke 9:49–50.

that mentions a schism with prophetic sanction. In 1 Kings 11–12, we read of the schism between the northern and the southern kingdoms. In this narrative: (a) the prophetic promises to David concerning the kingdom are not revoked (1 Kgs 11:34); (b) the schism is the consequence of Solomon's sin (1 Kgs 11:33); (c) the schism has prophetic sanction through the prophet Ahijah (1 Kgs 11:29–39); (d) this punishment for the Davidic kingdom will not last forever (1 Kgs 11:39).

This story should not be used to justify any kind of schism. But it does question an automatic conclusion that schism can never be justified. In this episode, the prophetic sanction for the schism states that it is because of the sin of the king, it is only for a time, and it does not represent a withdrawal of the divine promises to the lineage of David. Thus, if there is a divinely-sanctioned separation, it can only be for a time.[24] Hence, this sixth principle is not an exception to the fourth. Thus, for example, the work of the Holy Spirit among the Mennonites is ultimately for the good of the whole church, even if it takes more than 450 years for those who rejected their witness to realize it.

7. *Revival-Renewal within the existing churches and Revival-Restoration outside the existing churches play different but complementary roles in the preparation of the church for the coming kingdom.*

The irreplaceable witness of the historic churches is to the fullness of divine revelation, and the fullness of the means of grace, together with the witness to God's total faithfulness. The contribution of revival/renewal is a re-centering on the core reality and revelation, that throws light on the whole, and thus leads to the purification, the re-vivification, and the "re-dynamization" of the full Christian heritage. Renewal combines the *intensive* life and focus of the stream with the *extensive* range of the whole body.

The process of renewal is messy. There is tension, there is opposition, there are times when the witness is obscured. This is a process of the new spiritual impulses impacting the structured life of believers in the church, an interaction of the spiritual with the bodily, the intellectual and the psychic. It is this interaction in all its messiness and pain

---

24. It is significant that after the schism, when Rehoboam plans to regain his lost territories by force, the prophet Shemaiah proclaims: "Thus says the Lord, You shall not go up or fight against your kinsmen the people of Israel. Return every man to his home, for this thing is from me" (1 Kgs 12:24).

that incarnates the life-impulses in the structured body and purifies the reforming soul.

When new groupings develop outside the existing churches, they have a freedom to base their whole corporate life on the core convictions that drive them. They have a freedom to follow the Holy Spirit: in worship, in ministry, in evangelism, in formation. They can develop their own models, and determine their own priorities. With the Pentecostal movement and again in the new charismatic streams, this has meant a freedom to make the gifts and ministries of the Spirit central to their corporate worship and to their government in a way that is not immediately possible for renewal movements within historic churches. In this way, the new groupings pose a challenge to the churches to live more fully in dependence on the lordship of Jesus and in the gifting of the Holy Spirit. They confront the churches with eschatological urgency.

The contribution of the new groupings and networks outside the churches is to show forth what living by these central convictions can achieve. Their calling is, we might say, to make the churches jealous, to take an idea from Paul's teaching about the Gentiles and the Jews. But the challenge of the revival streams tends to be "one-generational." Outside the historic structures, they cannot avoid taking on new structures.[25] And their structures tend to be less flexible and their heritage more limited than that of the ancient churches that were never constituted by way of "reaction." Thus, the return challenges from the historic churches to the independent groupings are the challenges of incarnation, of fullness, and of long-term fidelity.

8. *The historic churches and the non-denominational streams need each other for the recovery of a wholeness in which the spiritual, the intellectual, and the bodily-structural elements find their right ordering from God in Jesus Christ through the Holy Spirit. This recovery is essentially related to the recovery of the Jewish roots, in which these elements were fashioned together.*

---

25. When new denominations then arise, they are forced to become more total systems in a way that revival streams are not. They have to clothe themselves, so to speak, with a comprehensive doctrine, with a form of church government, with patterns of education, particularly for pastors. Later revival streams then in their turn impact these new denominations, as the holiness and charismatic streams have interacted with the Methodist churches.

The more I grapple with these issues the more I believe the two deepest issues are the relationship between spirit, mind, and body, and the messianic hope.[26] It has to do with incarnation. But not just with incarnation understood as the Son of God becoming man, but with the incarnate God-man through his passion and death becoming a "spiritual body" (1 Cor 15:44) that is a "life-giving spirit" (1 Cor 15:45), so as to bring "many sons [and daughters] to glory" (Heb 2:10).

Since 1995, I have had increasing contact with the Messianic Jews. I believe that this is highly relevant to our encounter. One major reason is that the Messianic Jews are in several ways another form of independent church with many bonds to the Evangelical-charismatic "non-denominational" world. But from another angle, the Messianic Jews are very unlike the "non-denominational" groupings, for they claim to be a resurrection of a Jewish expression of the church that existed in the first centuries of the Christian era. The Messianic Jews are living a huge tension: as believers on the one hand with an Evangelical theology and a revivalist spirituality and on the other hand as believers connecting with the most ancient biblical heritage for whom physical descent from Abraham through a historical heritage is a constituent dimension. By their double belonging, we might say, they are caught up in this meeting of new life and ancient heritage. Ultimately, they cannot separate the spirit from the body. And the Jews still carry the messianic hope—more strongly than the gentilized church has done. It is truly remarkable that the Catholic Catechism in its section on the second coming has this extraordinary sub-title: "The glorious advent of Christ, the hope of Israel."[27]

---

26. See chapter 10.
27. *CCC*, heading above para. 673.

CHAPTER 7

A Catholic Reflection on the New Charismatic Churches

An Initial Attempt at an Ecclesial Discernment

In the 1970s, when a charismatic movement outside the existing churches was clearly developing, it was often called "non-denominational." In the second decade of the twenty-first century this term is rarely used, and virtually never by those whom it is describing. In Britain, people typically speak of the "new churches" or the "new charismatic churches." From this point, I will follow this usage, as it is both accurate and simple to use. Firstly, this expansion of the new charismatic churches is now a massive worldwide phenomenon. It has spread very rapidly, it is very varied in its manifestations, but there remains an evident commonality between all the groupings covered by this label. This category is most clear in Europe and in North America, where the new charismatic churches are clearly different from the Pentecostal movement and from denominational renewal. As to the other continents, my impression is that this category retains a validity, but there are churches and ministries that own both the Pentecostal and the charismatic labels.

A second preliminary observation is that it is more difficult to make accurate statements about this sector globally, as the relevant scholarly literature is rather thin. As yet there are no scholarly works studying this phenomenon globally or even continentally. It seems that with new revivalistic currents the first scholars to show interest are often sociologists and anthropologists. Among the first works were those by Irving Hexham and

Karla Poewe on non-denominational charismatic churches in South Africa,[1] and one by a British anthropologist, Simon Coleman, on the Word of Life Church in Uppsala, Sweden.[2] The country with the fullest data available on the new church charismatics is Great Britain, largely due to the pioneering work of Andrew Walker, the Russian Orthodox son of an Elim Pentecostal pastor, for many years Professor of Theology, Culture & Education at Kings College, London,[3] who has been followed by William Kay of the Assemblies of God.[4] Interestingly, William Kay moved in the opposite direction to Walker, starting in the Orthodox Church and later becoming Pentecostal. Stephen Hunt, another sociologist, has studied some aspects of the new charismatic churches.[5] For Africa, there is relevant information in the writings of Allan Anderson, especially on Zimbabwe and Southern Africa,[6] and in the works of Kwabena Asamoah-Gyadu, particularly on Ghana.[7]

The new charismatic grouping that has attracted the most study would appear to be the Vineyard movement led by John Wimber until his death in 1998.[8] The work of Estrelda Alexander on African American Pentecostalism has a chapter on "African American Neo-Pentecostals and Charismatic Movements" mentioning many churches and groups that belong in this category.[9] There are a handful of works by participants about their new church grouping or network that have above average reliability, and are more than mere publicity and self-promotion.

I examine the origins and developments in both Britain and the United States, both because I have done more research in these areas and because in these nations the origins go back to the 1960s. Outside the English-speaking world, the new charismatic churches almost all date from 1980 onwards.

1. Hexham and Poewe, "Charismatic," 50–69. See also the article of the same authors on South Africa in NIDPCM, 227–38.

2. Coleman, *Globalisation*.

3. Walker, *Restoring*. Walker has written numerous articles on the same subject. On which see Walker, *Notes from a Wayward Son*.

4. Kay, *Apostolic*.

5. Hunt, "Anglican Wimberites," and "Radical Kingdom."

6. Anderson, "Newer."

7. Asamoah-Gyadu, *African*.

8. The bibliography on the Vineyard movement given in the entry in NIDPCM, 1177, does not mention any of the more detailed studies: Percy, *Words*; Miller, *Reinventing*; Albrecht, *Rites*. See also Versteeg, "Prophetic Outsider."

9. Alexander, *Black Fire*.

The British Roots

In Britain, there was a stronger anti-denominational element in the origins than in the USA. This animus was first due to those who came from a Brethren background. Several of the first leaders in Britain were former Brethren. The Brethren movement had from its beginnings in the 1820s firmly adopted a "cessationist" position concerning the spiritual gifts described in the New Testament. As a result, any claim to exercise such gifts was ipso facto spurious and to be rejected. In consequence, those Brethren who spoke in tongues—the most identifiable sign of charismatic leanings—were expelled from the Brethren assemblies.

One of the first Brethren to be excluded for this reason was David Lillie from Exeter in Devon (1913–2009). Although Lillie always maintained that his teaching was totally derived from the New Testament, his understanding of the New Testament was strongly shaped by the convictions and ethos of the Open Brethren, with whom he had identified from his teenage years. Among these convictions were the authentic character and marks of the New Testament church. For Lillie, the restoration of the New Testament church was the deepest reason for the outpouring of the Holy Spirit. In the 1950s Lillie had become friends with Arthur Wallis (1922–88),[10] also from the Brethren and at that time a resident of Devon; this friendship led later in the 1950s to their convening in Devon a series of conferences devoted to this theme: Exmouth (1958), Belstone (1961), and Mamhead Park (1962).[11] One could describe these conferences as "pre-charismatic," as many of the participants later became active within the "house churches," the first designation given to the non-denominational segment of the charismatic movement in Britain. In fact, Wallis himself only entered into the charismatic dimension in 1962, just when the Devon conferences were being completed. The charismatic element was prominent on the program through the teaching and ministry of Cecil Cousen, a Pentecostal who had suffered exclusion from the Apostolic Church. There was a certain irony in the fact that Lillie and Wallis invited for their restoration-oriented conferences Cousen who had been formed in one of the only Pentecostal churches

10. I am correcting the year of birth given in NIDPCM, 1184, as Jonathan Wallis speaks of his father's sixty-fifth birthday celebration held on November 16, 1987 (*Arthur Wallis*, 303).

11. A fourth conference was held at Herne Bay in Kent in 1965. See Wallis, *Arthur Wallis*, chapter 7, 126–40, for the fullest written account of the genesis of these conferences.

that had taught and practiced the ministry of apostles and prophets, but who did not continue in this conviction after his expulsion. So while Cousen taught on the spiritual gifts, he did not refer to apostles and prophets in his Devon messages.[12] The Open Brethren vision of the New Testament was always presented by David Lillie.[13]

A second source came through Roger Forster (1933–), later founder and leader of the Ichthus network of new churches, who had been one of the youngest participants in the Devon conferences, and one of the best equipped theologically. Forster had served as assistant pastor to T. Austin-Sparks, pastor of Honor Oak Fellowship, Forest Gate in South-East London, that many years earlier had disaffiliated from the Baptist Union. Austin-Sparks had developed a teaching on the church that showed marked Brethren influences, which had some impact on the teaching of the Chinese leader, Watchman Nee, for whom Honor Oak was a major British connection.[14] Nee's teachings were widely diffused after his death and had a definite influence on charismatic non-denominationalism.[15] Forster saw himself as an heir of the Anabaptist heritage.

Another influential figure in Britain was Bryn Jones (1940–2003), a fiery Welshman, who was later to present the strongest version of Restorationism in the British house church movement. Jones had been baptized in the Spirit in 1957 at an Assemblies of God church in Aberaman, South Wales, and was a youthful itinerant evangelist before spending two and a half years with his wife as missionaries in British Guyana. How did Jones come to focus on the ministry of apostles and prophets? The Apostolic Church does not seem to have played any direct role despite its origins

12. On the ministry of Cousen, see Hocken, *Streams*, 5–10, 14–16, 18, 39–43. Cousen never embraced the ecclesiology of Lillie and was invited to the Devon conferences because of his maturity in the ministry of the Spirit. Later in his life Cousen joined the Anglican Church.

13. At Exmouth, Lillie gave the opening address on the conference theme "An Enquiry into the New Testament regarding the Church of Jesus Christ—Its Purity, Power, Pattern & Programme, in the Context of Today," and at Belstone on "The Emergence of the Church in the Service of the Kingdom." At Mamhead Park, Lillie spoke on the conference theme "The Present Ministry of the Holy Spirit" and presented a study concerning spiritual gifts from 1 Cor 12.

14. Angus Kinnear, the son-in-law of T. Austin-Sparks, became a biographer of Watchman Nee.

15. The many books bearing Nee's name were all teaching given by him at conferences, with the exception of *The Spiritual Man*, the only teaching he wrote as a book, which ran to three volumes.

in South Wales. According to Jones' own testimony, two influences stand out: "The Pentecostal men who I met in my early days, used to drum it into me that Pentecost was an experience, not a denomination. 'We are a movement,' they would say, 'not a denomination.' They were fiercely non-denominational."[16] The second factor was his reading Roland Allen's *Missionary Methods—St. Paul's or Ours?*[17] Although the foremost Pentecostal teacher of that period, Donald Gee, always remained strongly opposed to the restoration of recognized apostles and prophets, he always insisted that Pentecost was above all a movement, a movement of revival, and that denominations were a subordinate reality.[18]

In the mid-1970s, the new church movement clearly emerged in Britain, with Arthur Wallis as a father-figure and Bryn Jones as the most prophetic voice.[19] The first magazine to spread their teachings, *Restoration*, began in 1975. In its first issue Hugh Thompson wrote: "He [God] intends to restore apostles and elders, signs and wonders, joyously disciplined giving, and so much more."[20] The third issue had items on both apostles and prophets.[21] Subsequent issues had regular teachings on these themes.

The strongest new church network emerging in Britain that became the most international, and that clearly preached the restoration of the five-fold ministries, was New Frontiers International, founded and led by Terry Virgo (1940–).[22] Interestingly, New Frontiers has been the only network centered outside North America with a significant presence within the USA. Virgo emerged as a major figure in the later 1970s. First nurtured in a Baptist church and baptized in the Spirit in a Pentecostal assembly, Virgo was much impacted by the preaching of Dr. Martyn Lloyd-Jones of Westminster Chapel in London, a congregation belonging to the Fellowship of Independent Evangelical Churches (FIEC), which was firmly anti-denominational. Virgo's restorationism came from the influence and teaching of Arthur Wallis.[23] In 1985, Virgo's book *Restoration in the Church*

---

16. Cited in Hewitt, *Doing a New Thing?*, 14.

17. See ibid., 14.

18. See chapter 3.

19. On the influence of Wallis see Wallis, *Arthur Wallis*.

20. Thompson, "From 'Renewal,'" 5.

21. *Restoration* 1/4 (Sept/Oct 1975).

22. For an account of their remarkable expansion and growth throughout the world, see *New Frontiers Magazine* 4/3, July–Sept 2011.

23. There is a brief allusion to this in Virgo's autobiography, *No Well-Worn*, 101. See

was published. The self-understanding within New Frontiers International is expressed in this interview: "We don't see ourselves as a denomination, since they tend to be static and associated with rules and regulations. They have headquarters. They also don't tend to be charismatic, even if they started that way. We resist being called a denomination. Instead we see ourselves as an apostolic sphere. This is defined as the relationships which draw upon the gift of the apostle."[24]

The only British new church network that arose from a local church excluded from a mainline denomination is Multiply, at the center of which are the Jesus Fellowship and the Jesus Army.[25] It originated in Bugbrooke Baptist church in Northamptonshire, pastored by Noel Stanton. Along with Ichthus, Multiply is multi-racial with a number of black member churches. They were excluded by the Baptist Union, not for doctrinal reasons, but because their adoption of elders departed from the Baptist pattern for local church government.[26]

The North American Roots

One early impulse for the "non-denominational" current came from the Latter Rain revival which occurred at North Battleford, Saskatchewan, Canada, in 1947 to 1948. Its leaders in North Battleford were Pentecostals whose teaching and praxis were not acceptable to the Pentecostal Assemblies of Canada nor subsequently to the Assemblies of God in the USA. But the movement had a major impact on some large Pentecostal or independent Pentecostal assemblies (e.g., in Detroit and Philadelphia) and on the Elim Bible Institute about to be re-located to Lima, NY. Latter Rain leaders differed from mainline Pentecostals by promoting the five-fold ministries of Eph 4:11, and by the laying-on hands for baptism in the Spirit. Richard Riss, the chronicler of the Latter Rain revival, wrote that "Many hundreds of 'revival churches' became visible . . . most of these churches were independent and autonomous, and many became mother churches to numerous others that were established or nurtured by members of the mother

---

also Hewitt., 80.

24. Warnock, "Together," 11. See also Smith, "Account," 137–56.

25. See Cooper and Farrant, *Fire*, Hunt, "Radical Kingdom," 21–41.

26. In discussion after this paper was presented, Paul Goodliff from the Baptist Union in Great Britain, commented that Bugbrooke's exclusion would probably not have happened if it had not been for their sectarian and exclusive tendencies at that time.

church."[27] However this development was not one of the main impulses that gave rise to the clearly "non-denominational" currents of the 1970s, but nonetheless fed something into what had emerged by the 1990s, of which more in a moment.

The origins of the "non-denominational" stream in North America are especially found in the Holy Spirit Teaching Mission, founded in Fort Lauderdale, Florida, in 1966, that in 1972 was transformed into Christian Growth Ministries (CGM). CGM was led by five prominent teachers: Derek Prince (1915–2003), Don Basham (1926–89), Bob Mumford (1930–), Charles Simpson (1937–), and Ern Baxter (1914–93). What brought the CGM teachers together was a shared concern for the large numbers of Christians coming into a powerful experience of the Holy Spirit, but then lacking teaching, guidance, and formation, and so being vulnerable to deception and disillusionment. Many young people impacted by the Jesus movement were especially needy in these respects.[28]

Unlike the current issuing from the Devon conferences in England, the focus of the Fort Lauderdale group was Christian growth and discipling to facilitate growth. The focus was never on apostles and prophets, though issues of church government and authority were brought more clearly into focus by the pastoral leadership needs that preoccupied them.[29] Their ministry had brought them into contact with many Spirit-impacted believers in scattered fellowships without denominational affiliation. But, as Moore writes, "Their goal was in the beginning to renew existing churches through their teaching. As time passed, however, this would prove more and more difficult. In the end, they decided to create their own churches."[30]

In this way, the Fort Lauderdale group gave a strong impulse and a new visibility to the growth of "non-denominational" assemblies. The "non-denominational" impulse in the United States was primarily pragmatic, influenced by the surrounding entrepreneurial culture (new churches being started as any other new enterprise) and a need for freedom from institutional constraints so as to develop newer and more effective forms of communicating the gospel and forming Christian community. The only

27. Riss, "Latter Rain Movement," NIDPCM, 832.

28. See Moore, *Shepherding*, 42–45.

29. The church backgrounds of the five men were: Prince (Assemblies of God), Basham (Disciples of Christ), Mumford (Assemblies of God, then Reformed Episcopal), Simpson (Southern Baptist), and Baxter (Pentecostal).

30. Moore, *Shepherding*, 44.

one of the five leaders to advocate the restoration of apostles and prophets was Ern Baxter, who had been shaped by some Pentecostal teaching, by the healing evangelists, and by the Latter Rain movement.[31] Interestingly it was Baxter who provided a short-lived but influential point of connection between the North American and the British "non-denominational" leaders, especially connecting with Bryn Jones.[32]

By the time CGM dissolved in 1986, following the discipling controversy that had flared up in 1975,[33] the "non-denominational" currents in North America had developed strongly around a number of other leaders and ministries. Among them were Bill Hamon, Francis Frangipane, John Eckhardt, and Rick Joyner. There does not appear to have been any one major source, but several contributory factors. These include the Faith groupings, of whom the foremost was led by Kenneth Hagin, that came out of Pentecostal roots and that re-labelled themselves charismatic, perhaps for strategic and marketing reasons; the influence of those Pentecostal groups that had accepted the Latter Rain teaching;[34] the progeny of various healing ministries;[35] churches that had been under the Fort Lauderdale umbrella. A major new church network in Scandinavia and Eastern Europe, Livets Ord (Word of Life), based in Uppsala, Sweden, arose following the return of Ulf Ekman and two colleagues from their studies at Kenneth Hagin's school in Tulsa, Oklahoma.

As we have seen, the new charismatic churches in Britain mostly embraced the ministries of apostles and prophets. In the United States, the focus was first on the prophetic and only subsequently on the role of apostles. A major teacher has been Bill Hamon, who in 1990 published a book *Prophets and the Prophetic Movement: God's Prophetic Move Today.*[36] The publisher's blurb states that Hamon "has functioned in the ministry of prophet for over 36 years," had been twenty-three years a bishop, and that

31. Baxter was a Canadian, born in Saskatchewan, who ministered in British Columbia for many years before the locus of his ministry shifted to the United States.

32. See Walker, *Restoring*, 93–101. Baxter spoke at the last Capel Bible Week in 1975, and at the Dales Bible Week in 1976 and 1977.

33. For a full account of the discipling controversy, see Moore, *Shepherding*.

34. Riss gives a list of pastors and congregations so influenced by the 1970s: *Latter Rain*, 142.

35. Oral Roberts had founded the International Charismatic Bible Ministries in 1986 to provide fellowship for ministerial leaders, mostly non-denominational.

36. There is no mention here of the Kansas City prophets, a phenomenon that briefly hit the headlines around 1990.

he established the CI-Network of Prophetic Ministries in 1988. Hamon notes "The 1948 Latter Rain Movement brought the seed of revelation that there are prophets in the Church today, but the 1988 Prophetic Movement is bringing the activation and reproducing of those prophets."[37] Ten years later, in Hamon's writing, the Prophetic Movement has become the Prophetic–Apostolic Movement.[38] This later book has an account of Christian history from a restorationist standpoint.[39] "The Holy Spirit activated the Prophetic–Apostolic Movement to restore Christ's ascension-gift ministries of the apostle and prophet back into the Church."[40] According to Hamon, 2003 version, the way for the Prophetic-Apostolic Movement was prepared by the Latter Rain movement of the late 1940s, and then "John Sandford and Bill Hamon were the first to write books that prepared the way and made ready a people for the Prophetic–Apostolic Movement,"[41] which was birthed in 1988.[42] This US-centered version of the history seems unaware of what had been happening in Britain, much of it somewhat earlier in date.

The Prophetic–Apostolic movement has been non-denominational for both pragmatic and theological reasons. The pragmatic is that it is impractical to have space for recognized apostolic and prophetic ministries within the existing churches and denominations, in addition to which the Prophetic-Apostolic movement is a movement in a hurry. The theological reasons lie in the restorationist character of its vision of the church, in which restoration means in effect rebuilding the church from scratch. In this view, renewal was never more than a half-way house or rest station on the route to full-blown restorationism. Why are such restorationists so strongly resistant to the prospect of becoming new apostolic–prophetic type denominations? It is because restoration is of the church. They are building the church, and denominations can never be the church.

The most common restorationist position in the new church movement sees the restoration of the five-fold ministries of Eph 4:11 as a climactic stage in a progressive restoration that began with the Protestant Reformation. Protestantism has been marked by restorationist currents

---

37. Hamon, *Prophets*, 102.

38. Hamon, *Eternal*, chapter 26, 263–87. Wagner uses the term "The New Apostolic Reformation."

39. See next section on Restorationism.

40. Hamon, *Eternal*, 264.

41. Ibid., 271.

42. Ibid., 272.

since its beginnings, but its most typical form has been the restoration of biblical patterns of preaching, church government, and ministry in the place of what were seen as Catholic corruptions and additions. The Pentecostal movement then preached the restoration of pentecostal power, and of signs and wonders, including healing and prophecy. But there was no distinctive Pentecostal form of church government. But with the new churches and the restoration of Eph 4:11 ministries, there is a stronger form of primitivist restorationism, that abandons strict congregationalism in various ways: (i) by affirming a form of hierarchical order in the church; (ii) by accepting the trans-local character of apostolic and prophetic ministries; (iii) by creating trans-local patterns of relationships in structured networks. However, the restorationist teachers typically uphold the authority of the local pastor, with some rejecting free-lance ministries that do not defer to the authority of the local pastor in their home-base congregation.

While most restorationists present a development of the phases of restoration that sees their climax in the Prophetic-Apostolic movement, Hamon teaches that we are currently in stage five of an eight-stage restoration. Hamon's phases of church restoration are based on eight doctrines of Christ, outlined in a chart.[43] He has eight corresponding phases: the Protestant (Reformation), Holiness, Pentecostal, Charismatic, Body of Christ, Army of Lord, Queen Church, Eternal Church. For Hamon, we are at present in the fifth phase, with the last four phases being ushered in by the prophets.

The ways of avoiding denominationalism often remain very pragmatic. Dick Iverson of Ministers Fellowship International identifies three elements that "have historically caused fellowships to become denominations": credentialing, ownership of buildings, and a central missions board, all very pragmatic factors.[44] So the non-denominational answer is ordination and issuing of credentials by the local fellowship, ownership by the local fellowship and mission work organized and supervised from the same level. In this network, the three factors promoting network bonds are relationships, integrity and doctrinal compatibility.

43. Ibid., 176.

44. Wagner, *New Apostolic*, 176–77.

A Catholic Approach to these Developments

First, the issues raised concern all Christian traditions. But when I comment as a Catholic, it would seem a fortiori that if Catholics can adopt such an approach, Protestant Christians should be able to do so.[45] Any wider Christian reflection on this theme today has to be ecumenical. That is to say, it has to ask in what ways these developments can contribute to the well-being and the unity of the whole body of Christ. Its method has to be ecumenical; it has to begin not from what is problematic in the other, taking one's own position as the norm, but from what is positive, that is to say, from the work of the Holy Spirit in the other, taking the Scriptures as the foundational expression of the apostolic tradition.

The Determination to Avoid Becoming
New Denominations

It should not be hard for a Catholic of an ecumenical spirit to commend this determination. The new church networks have begun as a movement or as movements. A movement is characterized by a vision that inspires and energizes its participants and by core convictions that drive the movement forward and shape its direction. In a Christian movement, the vision is understood as coming from the Holy Spirit and as an unveiling of the purposes of the Lord, and the core convictions as faith convictions that articulate fundamental biblical and christocentric teaching. In this way, a new Christian movement never is nor can become the church. But the church needs such movements to shake it up, to challenge all forms of immobility and stagnation, and to unleash fresh dynamism from the Spirit of God. A Christian movement does not have a complete and rounded doctrine, but it emphasizes key elements from a fuller Christian heritage of doctrine and teaching. A movement does not draw up its own creed, though as it develops it will typically express in written form its own doctrinal convictions and emphases with a non-negotiable core. As a Christian movement develops, it will typically recognize distinctive ministry gifts in its members, and it will probably have forms of commissioning of new leaders, without imitating the ordination rituals of the historic churches. Movements are not territorially limited, though the English language plays a major role in their

45. Benjamin McNair Scott, an Anglican priest, has surveyed and evaluated the new charismatic churches in *Apostles Today*.

diffusion. This is all the more so in the globalized world of today with its modern means of communication and travel.

So the element in the new church movement that can be viewed wholly positively is the determination to remain movement, and to resist the process of becoming fixed and established organizations having lost their earlier movement character. This aspiration was vividly expressed in an interview by a young leader in Britain of 24–7 prayer. In answer to the question "How are you going to keep all this going?," he replied: "We're not! It's vital we don't keep it going. . . . . We don't want to become an organization, but keep as a movement."[46] We can ask: "Is this spiritual wisdom or is it sociological naiveté?"

From the standpoint of the ancient churches, the process of denominational formation has to be regarded as at best ambiguous. Much of this is best examined under the heading of restoration of the church, for which see below. But immediately one can identify some elements in this process that are theologically questionable. First, the process of "totalization" whereby the formation of a new denomination is typically the start of a process by which it becomes a complete system in itself with the tendency to adopt self-sufficient attitudes assuming that the denomination does not need interaction with, or contribution and discernment from other Christians so as to be faithful to the Christian mission. Second, there is the common pattern whereby Protestant denominations are organized on a national basis. This factor exposes the resulting denominational system to the weaknesses and limitations of merely national perspectives and in worse scenarios to nationalistic ideology. This is not to say that there are no good reasons for some organization at the national level, for example, to relate to government and public authorities. But theologically the church has three levels that go back to New Testament times. There is the *local or city* level (most New Testament uses of the word "church" refer to the local city-wide church), the *family or house* level (see Rom 16:5, 1 Cor 16:19; Col 4:15), and the *universal* level (see Matt 16:16; Eph 1:22; 3:10; 5:32; Col 1:24; 1 Tim 3:15). At all three levels, the church is an instrument of communion. Any structures are clearly to serve the communion. But with denominations organized on a national basis, whether their head offices are in the capital or elsewhere, the structures play too big a role at the expense of life and creativity. So in fact each formation of a new denomination and its

---

46. "Talking with Pete Greig," 13.

subsequent consolidation makes future reconciliation and unity with the historic churches more difficult.

Restoration of the Church

A characteristic of the new churches is that for the most part they have manifested a greater desire for church than, for example, the Pentecostal movement generally did in its origins and early development. This trend is of course strongest in those with a vision for restoration, which almost always means a restoration of the church according to the mind of Jesus. This trend to focus on church is obviously to be welcomed.

From an historic church standpoint a vision of restoration that is restoring "from scratch" dismissing the history of the Christian church for almost twenty centuries is obviously unacceptable. The real question is not tradition versus restoration, but whether there can be a truly significant element of restoration within an overall respect for tradition. The principal characteristics that the Catholic and Orthodox Churches regard as essential to be church are apostolic succession, episcopal ministry in this succession, adherence to the historic creeds, and a form of Eucharist embodying this historical continuity. Without some visible connection to this historical continuity and without a historic pattern of liturgy, I do not believe that the restorationist endeavor can succeed. It lacks embodiment (incarnation), a rooting in history, without which a real body cannot be formed.[47] As I see it, the new church movement shows a deep desire for church, with increasing attempts to form church that can produce deep patterns of Christian togetherness with increasingly ecclesial elements, but which lack a visible coherent unity. This search for church could favor real progress towards an organic and embodied unity. As the new networks overcome sectarian tendencies, further down the road a reconciliation with the ancient churches may be more feasible than with firmly established nationally-organized denominations.

Apostles and Prophets

For most of the new charismatic churches, restoration has at its heart the recovery of the fivefold ministries of Eph 4:11, which in practice means

47. See chapter 1 on the ecclesiology of Miroslav Volf.

a focus on apostles and prophets.[48] At first sight, this view of restoration appears to present a huge barrier to the possibility (and for them the desirability) of reconciliation with historic Christianity affirming an apostolic succession of bishops. But we need to distinguish between three different issues in discussing the role of apostles and prophets:

1. *The exegesis and interpretation of the biblical data.* The new church literature is mostly apologetic and/or pastoral, with little that academics would regard as scholarly. For example, you will find little recognition of the distinctive role of the Twelve, and their relationship to others described in the New Testament as apostles; there is also no mention of the connection made in the New Testament between the twelve apostles and the twelve tribes of Israel.[49]

2. The self-understanding and self-presentation of these ministries within the new charismatic churches. This typically sees the restoration of apostles and prophets to directive roles in the church as necessary for the church to be church according to the mind of God, and necessary for the fulfillment of the church's mission before the Lord comes.[50]

3. The actual organizational, behavioral and practical ways in which the new charismatic churches act and work.

I suggest that the third area is the most fruitful to be examined both by those within the new churches and by those in the older churches and denominations. We do not have to agree with the new church exegesis and incipient theology to recognize that the Holy Spirit is at work in the flexible and creative ways the new churches actually operate. In fact, this is an application to the new charismatic churches of what Walter Hollenweger was saying for many years that what Pentecostals do is much more important than their theology.

McNair Scott, an Anglican, argues for the reception by historic churches of apostles with a small "a," reserving the big A for the Twelve and Paul.[51] "From an ecclesiological perspective therefore there is nothing inherently wrong with promoting 'apostolic' ministries; conversely, there is

---

48. See earlier passage on the writings of Hamon.

49. See Matt 19:28; Rev 21:12, 14.

50. McNair Scott has a chapter on "Popular Charismatic Teachers as Apostles," examining the teaching of Derek Prince, Peter Wagner, Mike Breen, Terry Virgo, and Kenneth Hagin (*Apostles Today*, 57–88).

51. Ibid. 207.

a lot wrong with stifling this much needed gift in a time where mission is a central concern of the church in a post-Christendom society."[52]

Flexibility and Creativity

Likewise, the desire for space to be creative and to respond to the promptings of the Holy Spirit without having to pass through layers of officialdom, committees, and bureaucratic procedures can hardly be condemned. It is in their most creative contributions to the Christian world today that the older churches can and should learn the most from the new. For example:

1. The way leaders emerge, and the attention paid to encouraging young people, especially young men, to develop leadership abilities and to have opportunities for wide-ranging experience;

2. The forms of oversight and coordination played by those with "apostolic ministries," which in many ways resemble the best concepts of ecclesial episcope, not just territorial, but today exercised at all levels up to the global; the formation of networks with varying patterns of belonging;[53]

3. New patterns of mission sending and oversight, made possible in the world of jet travel and the internet;[54]

4. New patterns of local church planting and community formation; for example, the Vineyard magazine in the USA called *Cutting Edge*, has frequent contributions illustrating the experimental approach to church planting, learning lessons, making major changes, in interaction with other leaders and the people involved;[55]

5. Diversification of forms of ministry and diakonia: ministering to different categories of people, teenagers and young people, young mothers, artists, drug addicts, etc. (some ministries characterizing particular new church groupings);

6. Creativity in music and forms of worship expression, with a massive contribution to the overall Pentecostal-charismatic musical repertoire

52. Ibid., 208.

53. In a subsequent conversation to that mentioned in note 26, Paul Goodliff mentioned that some thirteen Baptist churches in Britain joined the New Frontiers network.

54. I am indebted to William Kay for this point.

55. *Cutting Edge* was earlier known as *Voice of Vineyard*.

coming from the new churches, especially for example Vineyard and Hillsong (Australia), and the creation of praise marches by Graham Kendrick (Ichthus, UK) as part of March for Jesus;

7. Houses of prayer and 24/7 prayer, spearheaded by the International House of Prayer in Kansas City, USA, led by Mike Bickle.

Let us suppose that a humbler approach could be possible from both sides. That is to say, that each side (historic churches and new church networks) could modify their more exclusive claims and seek to formulate the key gifts that each can bring to each other. It is a sifting of the authentic theology from the encroaching ideology.[56] On the Catholic side, a greater humility would entail an openness to recognizing that the Catholic Church can learn from these seemingly upstart groups (for Catholics they are like the new kids on the block), even learning something about the church, that Catholics easily regard as their prerogative. On the new church side, I would see a greater humility including a more modest estimate of their own contribution and historical significance. Instead of any thoughts that the new churches are the only New Testament churches, the restored church, or the church of the future,[57] their leaders could see themselves in a more experimental and provisional way as forerunners and trail-blazers in some areas for the whole body of Christ. Such an approach fits much better with their entrepreneurial and experimental approach and the spirit of the twenty-first century. If then they make their experience and their giftings available for the wider church, and invite genuine assessment and discernment, then I could see remarkable things happening. For such a generous servant approach to become possible, all judgmental mentalities and sectarian narrowness would need to be abandoned, e.g., "the old churches are dead," which happily are less common today as the new church streams transition to a second generation.

Is this vision completely Utopian? I don't think so, because there are already places in the world where the new church networks include local churches or communities belonging to historic churches, or who have a free church affiliation. The free church instances seem to be mostly Baptist or

56. See chapter 2.

57. "I recently came across one church stream that stated they were planting a church in that particular town because there was 'no New Testament-type church there.' . . . I didn't object to the church plant . . . . What did concern me was the attempt to monopolise the phrase 'New Testament-type church' for churches of their particular kind of organization" (Warner, *I Believe*, 157).

Assemblies of God, as their pattern of denominational structuring makes this easier. The Vineyard movement in Europe has been moving in a direction of seeking some form of agreement with the historic churches in the regions where they are planting a new church. Surprisingly there is even an instance of a Catholic charismatic community belonging to Vineyard. In this case, it was a condition from both sides that the arrangement had to have the blessing of the local bishop. The community in question in Ravensburg, Germany, received this permission from Bishop Walter Kasper, then bishop of Rottenburg-Stuttgart,[58] who himself wrote the agreement, which stipulated that all sacramental activities should happen within the Catholic framework, but accepted their being under the leadership of the wider Vineyard leadership.

In such a context, the ministries of apostle and prophet can be evaluated over time, with an ongoing assessment of the biblical exegesis and theology used to support these ministries, together with a parallel evaluation of their missionary and pastoral effectiveness. As I have already hinted, there are many elements characteristic of the new charismatic networks that fit very well with seeing them as an experimental workshop for world Christianity: their creativity, their flexibility, their subordination of structures to mission, their confidence in the power and leading of the Holy Spirit, their aversion to patterns of dogmatism and the tyranny of the conventional.

A more modest estimate of their role in the Christian world, as streams, movement, networks, that do not call themselves collectively church, would ironically make the new charismatic churches more significant in the Christian world than when their self-perception is more sectarian and self-sufficient. From this angle, the refusal to become denominations can be recognized as having a prophetic dimension. The instinct to avoid the totalizing tendencies typically arising from the formation of denominations can and should be totally affirmed, and distinguished from the question of developing the structures needed in any coherent and growing movement. The refusal to become denominations also allows for more flexible approaches to "double" or "multiple belonging," a better formulation than double or multiple membership, which is an increasing phenomenon in our mobile and fast-changing society. This is true both for individuals and families, as well as for local assemblies, as when for example a local church

---

58. Later President of the Pontifical Council for Promoting Christian Unity, and Cardinal. I am indebted to Martin Bühlmann for the information about the Ravensburg community.

affiliated to a denomination (e.g., Baptist or Assemblies of God) joins a new church network.

An abandonment of claims simply to be the restored church of the New Testament does not mean that the new charismatic churches do not have an ecclesial significance, or that they are not contributing to the restoration of the one church of Jesus Christ. The older churches need to recognize and to take seriously the genuine concern of the new charismatic churches for church. By recognizing their creativity and by seeing them as a kind of ecclesial laboratory, the older churches can enter into serious interaction with the new. They can challenge for the good of all parties the denominationalism of the Evangelical and Protestant churches, and the rigidities of the older liturgical–sacramental churches.

CHAPTER 8

Church outside Church

The Formative Work of the Holy Spirit in Pentecostal and Charismatic Churches

THE EXPLOSION OF PENTECOSTAL and charismatic churches and ministries in recent decades requires more theological attention than it has received. I have chosen this title "Church outside Church" to address the ecclesiological issues raised by this unexpected development, consciously adapting Donald Gee's phrase "Pentecost outside Pentecost" that described the Pentecostal-type outpouring of the Holy Spirit outside the Pentecostal movement. Just as the Pentecostal movement majored on Pentecost, so we can say that the Catholic Church has majored on the issue of church. Just as the pentecostal work of the Holy Spirit could not be limited to the recognized Pentecostal movement, so the formation and reality of church cannot be limited to the Catholic Church in communion with Rome or to the world of the churches committed to the ecumenical movement.

This reflection is particularly appropriate in a theological symposium convened by Word of Life Church (Livets Ord) in Uppsala, Sweden, a striking example of the creativity and impact of the new charismatic networks that have been multiplying around the world in the last thirty years. Here the appropriateness is evidenced by the greater attention given to the issue of the church in the new charismatic circles than in the Pentecostal movement. Though it is not true to say that there was very little interest in the issue of church in the beginnings of the Pentecostal movement, it would be a gross exaggeration to regard this as a major issue for Pentecostals over the past century. It has been one of the hallmarks of the writings of Simon Chan that he has stood out as a Pentecostal deeply concerned about this neglect.[1] By contrast, the concern for church, if not for a rounded theology of the church, has been a major feature in the greater part of the new charismatic world.

Challenging Pre-Ecumenical Assumptions

The official acceptance by the Catholic Church of the ecumenical movement as a work of the Holy Spirit dates from the first half of the 1960s: the establishment in the Vatican of the Secretariat for Promoting Christian Unity (1960), the invitation of official observers from other Christian churches and communions to the Second Vatican Council (1962–65), and the Council's decree on Ecumenism (1964). At the heart of the conciliar renewal was the recognition that the other Christian churches and ecclesial communities are not deprived of the Holy Spirit, and that they belong within, although "imperfectly" within, the one body of Christ. However, some of the implications of this momentous shift have not yet been adequately appropriated in Catholic theology and praxis. This section examines some of these surviving "pre-ecumenical" assumptions that stand in the way of an adequate Catholic response to the phenomenon of the new charismatic churches.

1. The first assumption to be examined is that separation from the Catholic Church in communion with Rome cuts off separated communities from the life-giving forces of the one body so that they then suffer a steady process of deterioration. The biblical image invoked would be that of the branches cut off from the vine (John 15:6) or from the olive tree (Rom 11:17, 20). Whatever the immediate consequences of separation with all the upheaval provoked by schism, it has to be asked how church communities and denominations formed over the centuries have actually fared after their separation from a "parent" church. That requires study of the patterns of decline and the patterns of revival and renewal. The evidence of the centuries since the Reformation appears to be one of ups and downs, not one of steady deterioration. The phenomenon of revival in the Evangelical world illustrates a strong "up" element. Acknowledging such positive features is part

---

1. Simon Chan from Singapore was one of the other presenters at the Uppsala symposium. On Chan, see also chapter 1.

of the turning from a priori negative judgments to an unprejudiced examination of the historical data.

2. The second assumption to be examined is an ecclesiological consequence of the first assumption. It is that in the separated communities of faith, there are *vestigiae ecclesiae*, that is to say, elements belonging to the one church that have survived the amputation and which are still life-giving despite their lack of communion with the Catholic Church.[2] When Catholics were first opening up to the ecumenical question, this concept of *vestigiae ecclesiae* was invoked as a basis for recognizing the work of God in the separated communities. It represented a way of recognizing positive elements in other Christian communions despite their separation. But it is a very static idea and belonged to a church-centered "ecumenism of return" in which the only conceivable way to unity was for the separate communities to come back to mother church. In this view, the only positive elements in non-Roman communities of faith are the Catholic elements that survived the separation. There was no consideration of the possibility of new initiatives of the Holy Spirit outside the one visible church or of the rediscovery of previously abandoned elements from the apostolic heritage. With the abandonment of the "return" model at Vatican II, the idea of *vestigiae ecclesiae* began to disappear from ecumenical vocabulary. But the assumptions behind this concept have not died away so easily.

---

2. In an article published in 1962, the great Catholic ecclesiologist and ecumenist, Père Yves Congar, wrote: "Ces éléments externes, appelés parfois vestigiae Ecclesiae, appartiennent de droit à l'Eglise et sont possédés illégitimement au-dehors d'elle. Ils n'y ont pas leur vérité parfait: le baptême n'y accompagne pas la pleine profession de la vraie foi, il n'est pas suivi des autres sacrements dans les communions Protestantes, et, même chez les Orthodoxes, où il est suivi des vrais sacrements, le baptême et l'eucharistie n'agrègent pas à la Communion ecclésiale et à son unité telles que le Christ les a voulues, à savoir présidées par le successeur de Pierre, chef du Collège apostolique." "Le mouvement oecuménique" in *Chrétiens*, 31. English translation: "These elements outside, sometimes called *vestigiae Ecclesiae*, belong by right to the church, and are illegitimately possessed outside the church. They do not have there their perfect truth: baptism is not there accompanied by the full profession of the true faith, it is not followed by the other sacraments in the Protestant communions, and, even with the Orthodox, where it is followed by true sacraments, baptism and the Eucharist do not unite them to the ecclesial communion and its unity such as Christ has willed, that is to say, presided over by the successor of Peter, head of the apostolic college."

3. Another questionable assumption concerns the application of the concept of the "sensus fidelium." In the Vatican II Constitution on the Church, the *sensus fidelium* is described in this way:

> The whole body of the faithful who have received an anointing which comes from the holy one (see 1 John 2:20, 27) cannot be mistaken in belief. It shows this characteristic through the entire people's supernatural sense of the faith, when, "from the bishops to the last of the faithful," it manifests a universal consensus in matters of faith and morals.[3]

The assumption in past Catholic writings on the *sensus fidelium* has been that the only "fideles" that count are the Catholic faithful. John Henry Newman had drawn attention to this concept in his essay "On Consulting the Faithful in Matters of Doctrine" (1859), in which he wrote: "Though the laity be but the reflection or echo of the clergy in matters of faith, yet there is something in the 'pastorum et fidelium conspiratio,' which is not in the pastors alone."[4] So while Newman understood this *sensus* only of the Catholic faithful, his teaching insisted on the essential role of the *sensus fidelium* among the unordained.[5] In this way, Newman anticipated the teaching of Vatican II on the laity in the church. But the recognition that the Holy Spirit is at work in other Christian communions and that they are within, not outside, the mystery of the church, calls for a modification of the formulation of *sensus fidelium* in an ecumenical era.[6]

The Ecumenical Challenges to These Assumptions

It is clear that the progress of the ecumenical movement challenges these earlier Roman Catholic assumptions. While the idea of ecumenism simply

3. *LG*, 12.

4. Newman, *On Consulting*, 103–4. The Latin word *conspiratio* does not easily translate into English; literally it means a bringing together of many voices in a unified whole, though today we use this Latin root more negatively as in conspiracy. So *pastorum et fidelium conspiratio* refers to the Holy Spirit's work of producing harmonious agreement between the pastors and the faithful.

5. In fact, Newman's argument was that the authentic faith of the church in the divinity of Christ was maintained in the fourth century by the lay faithful when many bishops had fallen into Arianism.

6. Since this paper was first written, the International Theological Commission in Rome has published a statement on *The "Sensus Fidei" in the Life of the Church* (2014).

as "return" has been abandoned in official Catholic documents, it has not fully disappeared from popular Catholic consciousness.

The First Assumption

The steady deterioration assumption betrays a triumphalist vision of the Catholic Church and its history. In my personal theological journey, the issue that really confronted me with the dark side of church history is the treatment of the Jewish people. It was the virtual inevitability of having to face up to the horror of the Holocaust that led the Catholic Church (and other churches) to address the questions: "How could this have happened on an officially Christian continent?" and "what responsibility does the church carry because of its preaching and attitudes?" There is evidence that examination of the historical issues concerning the Jews played an important role in the process by which John Paul II came to call for a confession of the sins of Catholics in the past. So, for instance, the pope called for such a confession in his letter *Tertio Millennio Adveniente* (1994) preparing for the great jubilee of the year 2000,[7] an appeal that was repeated in the encyclical letter *Ut Unum Sint* (1995).[8] But the pope then set up two commissions of specialists to examine (1) the Catholic treatment of the Jewish people, particularly in the second millennium, and (2) the Inquisition. The pope's presiding at a penitential liturgy in March 2000 for the sins of Catholics was immediately followed by his journey to Jerusalem and the insertion in the Western wall of his prayer confessing the Catholic sins against the Jews.

There are two areas in which the Catholic response to the sins of the past is still not addressing the full extent of the challenge. The first is the great reluctance to acknowledge that the sins were not just the responsibility of individual Catholics, even popes and bishops, but also extended to acts and decisions of gathered church leadership acting in the name of the church. The second is the area of doctrine, which is even more difficult. Here ecumenical progress requires an honest acknowledgment of the limitations, inadequacies, and distortions of prevailing Catholic theology and praxis in certain epochs, without which the divisions would probably not have occurred. The theological obstacles to the first admission were anticipated in a sentence in the Decree on Ecumenism.[9] In fact, the key teaching in

7. TMA, 33–35.
8. UUS, 34–35.
9. "Christ summons the church, as she goes her pilgrim way, to that continual

paras. 6–8 was the Council's official endorsement of the ecumenical vision of the Abbé Paul Couturier, whose spiritual genius was to have shifted the Catholic prayer for unity from a Roman-centered perspective to one that is totally Christ-centered, but ecclesially and not individualistically, i.e., from an ecclesiastical church-centeredness to an ecclesial Christ-centeredness.[10] The way forward in the second area has already been prepared by the official Catholic recognition that the responsibility for past divisions lies on both sides and by the recognition in *Ut Unum Sint* that "ecumenical dialogue is not just an exchange of ideas, but an exchange of gifts" (para. 28). If there are gifts for the Catholic Church to receive from other Christian traditions, then there are areas where the others are stronger and more gifted than the contemporary Catholic Church.

The Second Assumption

The second assumption manifests a church-centeredness or Roman-centeredness which was the inevitable psychological accompaniment of Catholic triumphalism. The assumptions that church separation begins a process of steady deterioration in the dissident bodies and that the best possible outcome for the separated body is limited to maintenance of the "vestigia" reflect the inadequate recognition of the role of the Holy Spirit in the prevailing Catholic ecclesiology. In fact, a key recognition at Vatican II was that "the Spirit of Christ has not refrained from using them [the separated churches and communities] as means of salvation," although the following phrase "which derive their efficacy from the very fullness of grace and truth entrusted to the Catholic Church"[11] can easily be understood in a vestigial way. But if the Holy Spirit is present in the separated churches and communities, the Holy Spirit is active within them, and is advancing the plan of God through them to the extent of their openness to the Spirit,

---

reformation of which she always has need, insofar as she is a human institution here on earth." (UR, 6).

10. See also chapter 12.

11. UR, 3. The first response of the Catholic Church that was in any way positive to the ecumenical movement came in an Instruction of the Holy Office in 1949, which spoke of "a growing desire amongst many persons outside the Church for the reunion of all who believe in Christ" and which commented that "This may be attributed, under the inspiration of the Holy Ghost, to external factors and the changing attitudes of men's minds but above all to the united prayers of the faithful" (cited in Bell, *Documents*, 22).

their attentiveness to the biblical revelation, and their willingness to sift the authentic from the dross in their heritage.

So, instead of the history of other Christian bodies, separated from Rome, being one of steadily increasing deterioration, we find a pattern of ups and downs, of gains and losses, that has many parallels with what was happening at the same time within the communion of the Catholic Church. We find in the twentieth century that the strong impulses of the Holy Spirit for renewal of the Catholic Church had parallels in the Protestant world: for example in the renewal of biblical and liturgical studies and the spread of liturgical renewal. In some of these areas, the renewing impulses appeared earlier in the Protestant world than in the Catholic Church. Here a study of the origins of the ecumenical movement proves very instructive. As Rome recognized in 1949, the impulse for unity comes from the Holy Spirit, but this had not been recognized in 1864 when Pius IX required Catholics to withdraw from The Association for the Promotion of the Unity of Christendom, or in 1928, with Pius XI's negative encyclical *Mortalium Animos* on the ecumenical movement.[12] In the case of the movement for unity, the Catholic Church was the last major Christian tradition to welcome this initiative of the Holy Spirit. However, having accepted it—and this is an important point—there is permanence and universality to the Catholic endorsement that is a strength also for the other expressions of the movement not in communion with Rome.

When one comes to the extraordinary outpouring of Pentecostal life and power that—along with the ecumenical movement—characterizes the twentieth century, we find that it starts "outside the gates." Rejected, despised, and/or ignored by the established Christian world, the Pentecostal phenomenon is first a movement that later, sometimes out of practical necessity, sometimes with enthusiasm, becomes a cluster of new denominations that continue to fragment and multiply. If this is the Holy Spirit at all, as I think we have to say that it is in its fundamental character and gifting, though not in its divisive tendencies, then it follows that the Lord is forming and shaping something outside the boundaries of what the existing Christian world regard as church.

The self-understanding of the Pentecostal movement was reflected in various phrases, such as Apostolic Faith and Latter Rain, both of which express a restorationist vision. The Lord is restoring elements that have been missing since the first generations of the church. As such a vision

12. See chapter 2.

with its dismissal of the intervening centuries as spiritually insignificant was clearly unacceptable—beneath serious consideration—by scholars and leaders from the older churches, this restorationist dimension was generally dropped when the Pentecostal blessing spread to the other churches and denominations in the 1950s and 1960s.[13]

However this spread of Pentecostal blessing through the charismatic movement nonetheless represented a belated recognition of this work of the Holy Spirit, necessitated by its occurring within the ranks of the historic churches. Here again, though the Catholic Church was the last in which the renewal broke out, it was the first to welcome it officially and to give it the highest encouragement. However, this encouragement was not an encouragement of the whole charismatic movement across the churches but an encouragement of CCR, generally seen as a distinct Catholic movement.

But then in another of the Holy Spirit's surprises, the Lord's work in the charismatic movement gave rise to the new charismatic assemblies and networks, of which Livets Ord in Uppsala, Sweden, is a prime example. Like the Pentecostal movement, the new charismatic churches represent a major worldwide phenomenon that is too recent to have been adequately chronicled and studied. In all these currents, the Holy Spirit is at work— it would seem with an intensifying creativity—outside the structures of church, as understood by the ancient churches, Orthodox and Catholic, and by the classical Protestant Reformation (Lutheran, Anglican, and Reformed). This element of intensifying creativity is further shown in the rise of the Messianic Jews affirming their faith in Jesus as the Messiah of Israel and Savior of the world, while insisting on their continuing Jewish identity. For in its patterns of relationship and organization, the Messianic Jewish movement is a new church phenomenon, though the word "church" is generally avoided.

The Third Assumption

The Catholic assumption in the past that the only "fideles" that count for the *sensus fidelium* are the members of the Catholic Church in communion with Rome is in fact another expression of church-centeredness or Romano-centrism. But once one admits the life-giving presence of the Holy Spirit in other Christian communions, there is something illogical in

---

13. The possibility of a Catholic acceptance of a restorationist understanding of Christian history is discussed in chapter 13.

refusing to take seriously the witness of their faithful as moved and led by the Holy Spirit.[14]

The remarkable achievement of the Catholic–Lutheran dialogue in producing the joint declaration (*Gemeinsame Erklärung*) on Justification by Faith, the only dialogue document so far to have received the official endorsement of both commissioning parties, challenges Catholic theologians to ask to what extent the Lutheran tradition and the witness of its faithful have contributed to the development of the church's teaching on justification.[15] In effect, the Catholic Church is now recognizing, however carefully this is expressed, that in some respects Martin Luther's convictions about justification by faith mediated through the Lutheran faithful were correct and are to be received, albeit belatedly.

It would also seem that the greater attention of Rome to the role of the charisms in the life of the church is a fruit of the Pentecostal and charismatic movements. While the break-through on justification by faith was the fruit of prolonged theological dialogue, the growing understanding concerning charisms is not coming from theological dialogues, but is coming from the witness of renewed Catholics including charismatics whose thinking is influenced by teaching from other Christian traditions. Is this the beginning of the reception of the witness of other Christians in these matters into the faith and theological heritage of the Catholic Church?

In a few nations, and notably in Sweden, there has been a close collaboration between new charismatic church leaders and Roman Catholic leaders, particularly in upholding traditional Christian morality. But it should be asked whether the strong convictions of church members on both sides on such matters as abortion and homosexual "marriage" are not a sign of the *sensus fidelium* among those who take seriously the Word of God once given to the saints.

---

14. In the document *"Sensus Fidei,"* the question is asked, "Can one think that the separated Christians participate and contribute in a certain way to the sensus fidelium? Here, one can reply in the affirmative without any doubt" (para. 86b). However, the conditions insisted on for an "authentic" participation include "an active participation in the liturgy, specially in the eucharist, a regular reception of the sacrament of reconciliation" (89) and adhesion to the magisterium (97), though this last point is expressed in a nuanced way. The formulation of these conditions indicates that Catholic theologians are at an early stage of grappling with the ecumenical dimension of the "sensus fidei."

15. See also chapter 13.

The Challenge of the New Charismatic Churches and Networks

The new charismatic bodies represent a major challenge to all the historic churches and to the newer denominations, including the Pentecostal. Their challenge comes first from their rapid growth and considerable impact. While this impact has been greater in the "younger" continents, it is noteworthy that even in Europe, which is the hardest soil for revival–renewal movements, the new churches have had an impact beyond anything previously achieved in the free church sector.

The comments that follow refer primarily to the new charismatic bodies and currents in Europe and North America. It is here that their "non-denominational" character is most obvious and where they draw even unconsciously from the Christian heritage. In both these respects the European and North American situation is distinctive. In Africa, the formation of independent churches has a strong indigenous motivation in addition to the factors promoting "non-denominationalism" in Europe and North America. This is probably the reason why in Africa there is no noticeable reluctance to become new denominations, and why it is not always easy to distinguish between new charismatic currents and new Pentecostal bodies.

Where do the challenges lie? I suggest that they are not first theological challenges (their focus is not first doctrinal) but prophetic, missiological, and pastoral challenges that have theological implications. As a Catholic, I have felt most challenged by the creativity of the new churches, by their freedom to think "outside the box," certainly outside the traditional ecclesiastical boxes. So the patterns of church planting and church formation, of seeking flexible easily adaptable structures, of networking, of strategizing how to impact a secular society, of apostolic oversight, of mission to other lands and cultures, of worship songs and music ministry, to the raising up of new leaders: all these show their entrepreneurial spirit and how the leaders have not absorbed the mentalities prevalent in the historic churches, but approach new possibilities like contemporary businessmen starting a new venture. In terms of visionary thinking driven by zeal for mission I am reminded of the books by the visionary Anglican missionary, Roland Allen (1868–1947).[16]

The creativity lies above all in a new way of thinking and a new way of functioning. The Messianic Jews add further dimensions, such as a different

16. E.g., Allen, *Missionary Methods*.

approach to the Scriptures and the deeply challenging idea of a bipolar ecclesiology of the church drawn from Jew and Gentile, without the assimilation of either.[17] But what does the creativity of the new churches have to do with ecclesiology? I see the most important theological issues raised by the new church form of life as ecclesiological. They are not primarily christological or even pneumatological. They approach the issue of church from a totally new angle. They do not start from the nature or essence of the church; there are no new church debates about the four marks of the church. The quintessentially new church phrase of "doing church" says it all. It is a phrase that baffles Catholics and Orthodox, if they ever hear of it. It irritated me when I first heard it. But it illustrates perfectly the new church focus on action and impact through dynamic Spirit-filled ministry and fellowship. Because there is as yet relatively little theological writing from within the new churches, it will be hard for historic church theologians to pick up the challenge from the new churches. So it is appropriate that I try to identify where some of these challenges lie.

Worship

The best starting-point may be the sphere of worship, because all Christian worship expresses however inchoately the worshipping community's theology of God, Jesus, and the Holy Spirit. It also accords with the emphasis reaffirmed by the Catholic Church at Vatican II that the church is most fully expressed and made visible in the liturgy. Worship, and specifically praise, is a distinguishing mark of charismatic Christianity. For classical Protestantism and then for Evangelicalism the core of divine worship has been the preaching of the Word, while in the new charismatic churches, the worship and praise has moved center-stage physically as well as spiritually. The focus has shifted from understanding to lived experience. The phrase "lived experience" well captures the ambiguity of the charismatic dimension. For it can mean primarily emotional uplift and in its less mature expressions "feel-good" religion, while in the best expressions it signifies deep intimacy with the Lord. As a Catholic, I would say, in its best expressions it represents the beginnings of mystical union with God. But where mature charismatic worship differs from traditional Christian mysticism is in its holistic and corporate character, the involvement in communal worship of

17. See Kinzer, *Post-Missionary*.

body, soul, and spirit, and not just the individual raising of the mind and heart to God.

The criticism constantly leveled against the Pentecostal and charismatic expressions is that they are intrinsically individualistic and not genuinely communal and corporate. I have already mentioned that the new churches show a much greater concern for church than do the Pentecostals (but also than Evangelicals). This interest is demonstrated in worship by the focus on celebration. Celebration is essentially corporate. No sane person celebrates alone! Celebration is necessarily holistic and requires a liberation in the participants to worship with body, heart, mind, and spirit. This experience reveals the church as a celebrating community, an idea that is familiar to liturgical experts though not usually in this form. My involvement with Messianic Jews led to the discovery that the people who really know how to celebrate are the Jews, who were taught how to worship by the Lord. The historic churches and the new churches need to reconnect with the Jewish roots and with each other for liturgy and real celebration to come together again. This is a key part of the renewal of the church effected by the Holy Spirit.

Celebration also relates the new church world to an element in ecclesiology being reaffirmed through biblical renewal. Catholic ecclesiology today speaks of three levels of church: (1) The domestic church (the Christian family, the church in the house); (2) The local church (diocese); and (3) The universal church. This clearly correlates to some degree with some new church teaching on celebration that distinguishes between local congregational celebration, city-wide celebration, and global celebrations, while affirming the need for all three. March for Jesus, a quintessentially new church production, illustrated the importance of city-wide celebrations. I see the Catholic Church as best placed to organize global celebrations, as at the World Youth Days launched by John Paul II, because in the ministry of the pope there is an obvious president to serve as unifying point for an incredibly diverse gathering. March for Jesus also introduced marching songs of praise, such as we find in the Psalms of Ascent sung by the Israelites as they went up to Jerusalem for the feasts. Here there was a direct link between praise and intercession in the power of the Spirit, an idea that is rarely found in liturgical celebrations.[18]

18. Singing praise while marching had characterized the worship of some of the African Independent Churches earlier in the twentieth century.

Church Leadership

We can move now from worship to church leadership. A major focus in the new churches is the importance of relationships. Here I suggest the best new church patterns are demonstrating authentic *episcope* in the way senior leaders prepare, nurture, and encourage younger emerging leaders. The Vatican II decree on Bishops states about episcopal ministry: "Their priests . . . should be the object of their particular affection. They should regard them as sons and friends."[19] The new church focus on relationships and flexible structures makes possible this kind of fatherly role in a way that is extremely difficult in church bodies that have become more bureaucratic and institutionalized. With this goes the qualities looked for in future leaders. In the best new church models, as also in many charismatic communities and some of the new ecclesial movements in the Catholic Church, the leaders keep their eyes open to spot the people with real potential for leadership and other forms of service. Catholics have often emphasized that the grace is conferred in the ordination rite, and discernment has focused, not always successfully, on eliminating the clearly unsuitable. This pattern does not tend to produce many inspiring leaders, maybe an inevitable consequence of a marked degree of institutionalization.

This question raises important theological issues. Obviously, there is the relationship between nature and grace. But I want to focus briefly on the relationships between ministry, ministries, and charisms. The charisms that characterize the charismatic movement are one of its distinctive features, and in the New Testament they are clearly gifts for the church: "To each is given the manifestation of the Spirit for the common good" (1 Cor 12:7). I believe that charismatic experience confirms this sense, that there is a distinctiveness about the *charismata pneumatika*[20] listed in 1 Cor 12:8–10, for which is needed an openness of spirit leading to a surrender of mind and spirit to the risen and ascended Lord, in a way that is not true for other charismata. All charisms are given for the upbuilding of the body of Christ, which means that they must have a distinctive place in ecclesiology, which until recently has not been the case. John Paul II endorsed the formulation that the institutional and the charismatic are both necessary

---

19. Decree *Christus Dominus*, 15. More recently, Pope Francis has been emphasizing the spiritual fatherhood of bishops as an essential quality.

20. This phrase is not found as such in 1 Corinthians. But see 1 Cor. 12:1, 31; 14:1.

and complementary elements in the constitution of the church.[21] This now requires to be incorporated into the structure of Catholic ecclesiology.

In general the new churches have majored on the ministries of Eph 4:11, namely apostles, prophets, evangelists, pastors, and teachers,[22] with most attention being paid to apostles and prophets. In the abundant new church literature on this subject, what is offered is either a straightforward biblical exposition or an apologetics rebutting Pentecostal and Evangelical critics (or both), but there is little that would be regarded in academic circles as serious theological reflection. A serious theological reflection would need to include an adequate examination of the Jewish roots of the apostolic and the prophetic (all those initially sent, including Paul, were Jews, and Israel is the soil of the prophetic) and how much the calling of the Twelve is rooted in Israel. So, for example, there were twelve apostles because there are twelve tribes of Israel,[23] and the description of Peter as "apostle to the circumcised," parallel to Paul being apostle "to the uncircumcised" (Gal 2:7–8). Another key issue is the relationship between the charismatic callings, given by the Holy Spirit "as he [the Spirit] wills" (1 Cor 12:11), and the permanent structural ministries, that was first expressed in terms of bishops and deacons, and later became the threefold pattern of bishop, presbyter and deacon. Is it significant that the roots of the permanent structural ministries go back to the earthly ministry of Jesus wholly within Israel, starting with the choice of the Twelve, and that the Eph 4:11 ministries are "post-ascension" ministries?[24] The apostleship of Paul that is totally charismatic belongs to the post-ascension category.[25]

A Way Forward?

I suggest that the most fruitful way to bridge the chasm between the historic churches and the new could be to focus on the experimental character of the new. The most characteristic feature of the new churches is their freedom to experiment, without being shackled or limited by established

---

21. See chapter 5.

22. In context, it seems that pastors and teachers are placed together, as the text only states the word "some" (τοὺς) four times and not before "teachers."

23. See Matt 19:28; Rev 21:12, 14.

24. See Eph 4:10.

25. McNair Scott begins to address the theological issues in *Apostles Today*, but does not take account of the Jewish origins.

structures and customs. But their weaknesses are also linked to this freedom. It is the price for having total freedom to experiment, which requires
an independence from traditional structures but also means, at least at the
outset, that there is little learning from the wisdom of the ages. In the new
church beginnings there was often a naiveté that assumed they would be
immune from the trials and difficulties afflicting the older denominations,
though this naiveté has generally vanished after thirty years of experience.

The historic churches have not yet developed any theology of the experimental as an element in ecclesiology.[26] But a citation from a French
Catholic theologian may ring bells in new church ears: ""The more they [the
churches] affirm the provisional character of their forms, of their structures
and of their strategies, the more they approximate to the Kingdom and the
better they bear witness to it."[27]

Pope John Paul II's vision of "ecumenical dialogue" as not merely an
exchange of ideas but as "an exchange of gifts"[28] prompts my suggestion that
the new churches understand and present themselves as an "ecclesial laboratory." That is to say, that the new churches offer to the historic churches as
their "gift" the experience and fruits of their creative experimentation, both
for evaluation and for a degree of reception. This model does not require
any sacrifice of convictions, only a modesty that hesitates to affirm these
convictions as a new orthodoxy and to make them a test of fellowship.

I believe that such a model respects the distinctiveness of both the
historic churches and the new churches. It also fits with the tendency to
be open to learning from the historic churches and to be asking: what is it
that the Lord wants us to receive from the historic heritage? This is totally a
model of Christian service. We all speak of a servant church, but this model
gives servant church a truly ecumenical dimension.

But for this model to become workable and to bear any fruit, it requires a new degree of humility from both sides. On the historic church
side, it requires an abandonment of the spirit of superiority (theological,
spiritual, historical), an abandonment of the classification of free churches

26. Karl Rahner had some observations on the experimental in "Basic Observations
on the Subject of Changeable and Unchangeable Factors in the Church," *Theological Investigations* XIII, 3–23; see 22–23. But Rahner is primarily speaking of new theological
hypotheses.

27. Duquoc, "plus elles avouent le caractère provisoire de leurs formes, de leurs
structures, de leurs stratégies, plus elles s'approchent du Règne et mieux elles en té-
moignent." (*Eglises provisoires*, 97).

28. UUS, 28.

as "sects," a rejection of all slandering generalizations about new churches, and a recognition of the duty of Catholic bishops and priests to respect new church Christians and their leaders as they do other Christians accepted as ecumenical partners. On the new church side, it requires an abandonment of all claims to superiority as "the restored church" or "the church of the future," a rejection of all judgmental generalizations about the historic churches, an end to simplistic surveys of church history that see little good between the first centuries and the Protestant Reformation, and an openness to discover the wisdom of the ages.

Just as the Catholic Church needs to abandon the language of sects in relation to charismatic free churches, so the new churches need to abandon some unfortunate terminology, such as using the word "religion" as a wholly negative concept—a usage as far as I can see that has no greater antiquity than some thirty-five to forty years. It is virtually impossible to respect a Christian heritage when one uses this language.

As long as the new churches retain their flexibility and do not become established denominations, it could be much easier for the historic churches to receive from the new churches than from the recognized Protestant denominations. The fact that the gifts of the new churches are not primarily dogmatic or theological could also facilitate this process.[29]

29. A further aspect of new church relations to the older churches— the advantage of flexible network structures over classical denominational patterns—is examined in chapter 6.

PART III

The Holy Spirit, Israel, and the Church

CHAPTER 9

Continuity and Discontinuity in the Relation of the Church to Israel

WHAT A WONDROUS SIGN it is that at this gathering in Vienna there are believers from such an extraordinary range of churches, fellowships, communities, and ministries! Many different theologies, not to speak of many other differences as believers in Jesus/Yeshua, are represented. This coming together is made possible by the reappearance of a Jewish expression of faith in Jesus/Yeshua. All present recognize in some way that this initiative, Toward Jerusalem Council II, is a work of the Holy Spirit, a wonder in our eyes, an unexpected work of God that does not fit into received Christian categories. This recognition makes this coming together possible. We can say like the father in the parable of the prodigal son: "It was fitting to make merry and be glad, for this your brother was dead, and is alive; he was lost, and is found" (Luke 15:32). But in this case the brother who has come back to life is the elder brother, the first-born son.

Being faced with a newly-emerging Jewish *qehila* places us Gentile Christians in a new position.[1] Instead of differentiating ourselves from each other in our separated Christian confessions, we discover a common Gentile Christian identity. Facing the Messianic Jews we find that we are all in the same boat. Among participants in TJCII there are widely differing ecclesiologies. But one point common to all was that they made no reference to the olive tree (Rom 11:17–24) or the one new man (Eph 2:15), the New Testament images that speak of the union of Jew and Gentile in Christ. For centuries converted Jews were simply assimilated into a Christian church, whether the Catholic, the Orthodox, or one of the Protestant churches. The

---

1. Messianic Jews often use the Hebrew word *qehila* to refer to a local church as a gathered body of believers. .

distinctions that remained or arose within the church world did not include that between Jew and Gentile. Thus the appearance of the Messianic Jews, who claim a distinct identity as Jewish disciples of Jesus, presents a huge challenge to all Christian theologies of church. The challenge is not just to find a place for the Messianic Jews, a slot into which the churches can fit them. The challenge to the Gentiles is first to undo all the consequences of replacement thinking that either replaced Israel by the church or subsumed Israel into the church; the challenge is to restore the corporate Jewish witness to Yeshua to its rightful and foundational place within the body of Christ-Messiah. This can be the only authentic way to the healing of our divisions and to the manifestation of the unity of the one body.

I see all of us Gentile believers as beginners and learners in responding to the challenges raised by the Messianic Jews. It is impossible to undo all the effects of seventeen or eighteen centuries of replacement thinking in one or two decades. This will need time, there can be no fast solution. An intensive grappling with this issue is needed as we seek the Lord's way forward. The Lord is at work, and we must have confidence that he who has "began a good work" will "bring it to completion at the day of Jesus Christ" (Phil 1:6). The TJCII vision of reconciliation of Jew and Gentile in the "one new man" can only be advanced in humility and awe. I do not present myself as an expert, but as a servant seeking to discern the way forward.

Besides the Christian confession of sins against the Jewish people in general, there is a need for the churches to confess the sins against Jewish believers in Jesus. For these are sins against the unity of the body of Christ. In relation to the sins committed against the Jewish believers in Jesus, there are at least two distinct categories that need to be addressed and for which an ecclesial repentance is needed: (1) a repentance for the baptisms of Jews under coercion, sometimes even by physical force, and the subsequent harassment, arrest, and punishment of the baptized Jews for their continuation of any Jewish practice; (2) a repentance for all forms of teaching that eliminated the Jewish people from any distinctive role in the new covenant era. In the first area, the challenge especially concerns the Catholic Church, for the forced baptisms of Jews in Spain and Portugal led to the establishment of the Spanish and Portuguese Inquisitions to hunt down hidden Jewish practice among the *conversos*.[2] But in the second area of teaching and theology the challenge is equally great for all Christian churches. For we have all constructed our ecclesiologies without reference

2. See Hocken, *The Marranos*.

to the olive tree, allowing no place for the remnant of Israel. None of us have faithfully transmitted the importance of the Jewish identity of Jesus for our redemption.

Continuity and Discontinuity

The terms "continuity" and "discontinuity" in my title are crucial. The divisions in the Christian world have produced contrasting emphases concerning continuity and discontinuity. Those from the ancient churches, that believe in apostolic succession of episcopal ministry, emphasize historical continuity. Those from free church backgrounds stress the element of "discontinuity" with a focus on revival and on the direct work of the Holy Spirit in conversion and regeneration.

The Messianic Jews face the Christian churches with both elements, as indeed does the story of Israel. As a newly-emerging reality in the last forty-five to fifty years,[3] the Messianic Jewish movement faces us with discontinuity, with an irruption of the Holy Spirit in history. This discontinuity is manifest in the Messianic Jewish claim to "resurrection," invoking the imagery of Ezek 37:1–14, as the "dry bones" coming to new life in the restoration of the Jewish expression of the church after many centuries with no such expression. But as a movement insisting on its Jewishness, it cannot avoid speaking of continuity, for to be Jewish requires the assertion of an historical continuity as sons and daughters of Abraham.

In fact, the whole history of Israel is a weaving together of the continuous and the discontinuous. God intervenes in human history, God makes promises to human beings, God calls a people, and so there is a history that results from divine intervention. But the interventions are not just at the beginning, they continue among the chosen people; they shape their history and they introduce new elements: the giving of the Law on Sinai, the establishment of the Davidic kingdom, the rise of the prophets. We see these elements of continuity and discontinuity especially in the life of Jesus. They are expressed above all in the phrases of the Apostles' Creed: "conceived by the Holy Spirit" speaks of an intervention, of a discontinuity; "born of the Virgin Mary" indicates an event within human history, with the continuity being expressed in the genealogy in the first chapter of Matthew's Gospel. The incarnation, the Word becoming flesh, is an intervention.

3. In the original paper, given in 2004, the figures were thirty-five to forty years.

It is important to distinguish sharply between the kind of discontinuity that results from the direct action of God and that which results from human sin. The discontinuity arising from acts of God has characteristics that the human discontinuity of sin does not have: (1) the divine discontinuity takes its place within the bigger continuity of the plan of God hidden from all ages but now revealed in Messiah, what Paul calls the *mystērion*;[4] these acts of discontinuity fit into the one story of divine election; and (2) the acts of divine discontinuity are transformative; as the apostle Paul writes: "we all . . . are being changed into his likeness from one degree of glory to another; for this comes from the Lord who is the Spirit" (2 Cor 3:18). Here we have to note that the discontinuity in the death/resurrection of Jesus is different in some ways from that of the conception of Jesus. For in the death of the Messiah, we have the discontinuity of death, of any death, but in this case the discontinuity of a life terminated in its prime by violence. This death is then followed by the intervention of the resurrection, which is both new creation and the raising of the one who already has a significant history. All these dimensions have important consequences for the church.

The Image of the Olive Tree

At first sight, the image of the olive tree speaks more of continuity than of discontinuity. Continuity is part of this image, as an olive tree is a living organism with the continuity of all living things. This image expresses a continuity in Israel. Replacement thinking denies a continuity between the covenants with Israel and the new covenant. Replacement thinking led to a changed exegesis concerning the olive tree as early as Justin Martyr in the second century:

> In Paul, God has cut off some of the branches of Israel's old olive tree, and in their place he has grafted some wild branches—the Gentiles. In Justin, God has cut down Israel's olive tree, and in its place he has planted an entirely new tree—the church of the Gentiles. Onto this tree he has grafted a few branches from the old tree—those branches are the believing Jews.[5]

There is not just a linear continuity between the Israel before Jesus and the Israel after Jesus. The interventions of the incarnation, of the conception

---

4. Rom 16:25–26; Eph 3:4–5; Col 1:26–27.

5. Skarsaune, *Shadow*, 268.

of Jesus, and of his resurrection from the dead—thus an element of radical newness—have produced a transformation in Israel. Israel is transformed in the person of Jesus, who totally identified himself with his people. So Paul says that the Jews who have rejected this transformation, who did not believe in Yeshua, are no longer part of the olive tree, but are cut off branches "because of their unbelief" (Rom 11:20). Here the discontinuity is seen as the result of sin.[6]

For those who emphasize historical continuity, the first challenge from the olive tree is that the foundational continuity is that of Israel, not of the church. In fact, the new covenant prophesied by Jeremiah will be made "with the house of Israel and the house of Judah" (Jer 31:31). The church is founded in Israel. This is clearly why Jesus chose twelve apostles, as there were twelve tribes of Israel. But this then raises a question about later continuity: Did the olive tree die out? Did the disappearance of a visible Jewish expression of the church mean that there was no longer a living olive tree? For those who answer "Yes," then the modern reappearance of a visible Jewish expression of faith in Jesus in the Messianic Jewish movement represents "a resurrection from the dead," a kind of miraculous recreation of the olive tree that had died. Or, another interpretation, did the natural olive become a tree with its roots and lower trunk in Israel through Jesus and the apostles, but with all the branches being ingrafted from wild olives? In this view, the reappearance of a Jewish witness to Yeshua represents the re-grafting of branches of the natural olive in accordance with Rom 11:24.

Maybe we also have to ask about the status and identity of members of the church throughout the centuries who were in fact Jewish. If we say that the church was still the olive tree, rooted in Israel, even when no Jewish believer was allowed to retain any Jewish identity or maintain any Jewish practice, then we have to say that the church to this degree did not understand her own identity.[7] But there is a difference between those members of the church who still secretly and in their hearts valued their Jewishness—and at certain periods and in some places risked their lives for doing

---

6. This is not saying that all the Jews who did not believe in Jesus are subjectively "guilty" of sin in this regard, a position repudiated by CCC (597). But it is saying that there is "objective sin" in that their unbelief represented a refusal, whether conscious or not, to accept this transformation of Israel.

7. According to the *Rituale Romanum* of Paul V (II, 4), still in use under Pius XII, a converted Jew who wanted to enter the Catholic Church had to abjure the "*perfidia judaica*" as well as "Jewish superstition." Officially, this legal requirement was only abolished by the promulgation of the new *Rituale Romanum* under Paul VI in 1970.

so—and those Jewish converts who accepted total assimilation. As we pose these questions, we recognize that we cannot build a total theology from one biblical image. We have to ask what other biblical images complement the olive tree. Other pictures are those of "the one new man" in Eph 2:15 and of the "temple" in Eph 2:19–22.

Established in the Heavens

For our understanding of Christian history in relation to the olive tree, I see as a foundational point that *since the resurrection/ascension of Jesus the olive tree has its core-existence in the heavenly realms.* That is to say, that whatever happened in the church on earth, the church in heaven was gathered around the risen Jewish Messiah and his Jewish apostles—and many of us would add the Jewish mother of the Lord. Jesus did not cease to be Jewish when he rose from the dead. In the book of Revelation, the risen Jesus is described: "lo, the Lion of the tribe of Judah, the Root of David, has conquered" (Rev 5:5). The continuing Jewishness of the twelve apostles is indicated in the prophetic word of Jesus to the twelve that "when the Son of man shall sit on his glorious throne, you who have followed me will also sit on twelve thrones, judging the twelve tribes of Israel" (Matt 19:28). In Ephesians 2, Paul makes the contrast between the condition of the Gentiles before and after conversion: those who had been "separated from Christ, alienated from the commonwealth of Israel, and strangers to the covenants of promise, having no hope and without God in the world" (2:12) are now "fellow citizens with the saints and members of the household of God, built upon the foundation of the apostles and prophets, Christ Jesus himself being the cornerstone" (2:19–20). This is not talking about the past, but about the present. Messiah Jesus is the cornerstone in his glory, where he is the "great priest over the house of God" (Heb 10:21), "in whom the whole structure [of the church] is joined together and grows into a holy temple in the Lord" (Eph 2:21).

While Jesus has not yet been enthroned as Messiah on earth on the throne of David, he has been enthroned as Messiah in his resurrection and ascension: "Let all the house of Israel therefore know assuredly that God has made him both Lord and Messiah, this Jesus whom you crucified" (Acts 2:36). Here Jesus enters the glory of his Father as the obedient servant, who fulfills the calling of Israel in his person. In his resurrection, the olive tree that is Israel is definitively established—unlike the olive tree of Jeremiah 11:

"The Lord once called you, 'A green olive tree, fair with goodly fruit'; but with the roar of a great tempest he will set fire to it, and its branches will be consumed" (Jer 11:16). I wonder then whether it is right to describe either Israel or Jesus as only being the trunk or the root. I suggest that as Israel is the olive tree, so Jesus is the olive tree, transformed in his resurrection-ascension. Does this parallel in some way the teaching of Jesus when he says "I am the vine, you are the branches" (John 15:5)?

In Hebrews 12 we read: "you have come to Mount Zion and to the city of the living God, the heavenly Jerusalem" (Heb 12:22). Is this referring to the heavenly church made up of Jews and Gentiles? Does "the assembly of the first-born who are enrolled in heaven" (Heb 12:23), refer to the Jewish believers, since the Lord calls Israel "my first-born son" (Exod 4:22)? In the same way might the phrase "the spirits of just men made perfect" (Heb 12:23) refer to the Gentile believers, in line with the Jewish concept of the righteous among the Gentiles?

If the olive tree now has its foundation in the heavens, then the birth and ingrafting of new members happens through incorporation into the risen Messiah. I won't treat the relationship of baptism to the death and resurrection of Jesus, but just say that the initiated Christian is established in the heavenly realms. "For you have died, and your life is hid with Christ in God" (Col 3:3). God has "raised us up with him, and made us sit with him in the heavenly places in Christ Jesus" (Eph 2:6). So I suggest that since the ascension of the Lord the continuity of the olive tree is first found in the heavens, and that the only Christ into whom we can be baptized is and remains Jewish. It would be wrong then to say that the natural olive has not existed for many centuries. What has not existed continuously is the earthly expression of the church from the circumcision as the manifestation on earth of the olive tree into which the Gentiles are grafted.

"Thy will be done on earth, as it is in heaven." The church on earth is to reflect the church in heaven. The living connection between the church on earth and the church of heaven has been maintained more strongly by the churches of the East than by the Western church, though as far as I know the understanding of the heavenly as the glorification of Israel did not persist.

What about the Church on Earth?

The origins of replacement theology and the marginalization of the Jewish *qehila* seem to go back to the two Jewish rebellions that issued in the catastrophic events in Jerusalem in the years 70 and 135 CE. When there was no longer a Jewish *qehila* in Jerusalem, the consciousness of the Jewish root declined. This raises the question of the theological significance of the end of the Jewish church of Jerusalem in 135 CE. The Gentile believers came to interpret the events of the years 70 and 135 in a replacement sense—for them the destruction of the temple and of the holy city demonstrated God's rejection of the Jews. On the other hand, the Jewish believers would have understood this tragedy in the same way as the prophet Jeremiah understood the tragedy of 587 BCE. The devastation was a punishment for their sins, but in no way was God reneging on the election of Israel.

While we recognize the wrongness of replacement teaching, we have to confess the element of punishment for the sins of Israel in these events. Jesus had himself foretold the destruction of the temple (Matt 24:2) and the desolation of Jerusalem (Luke 19:44; 21:20),[8] and he had done so in terms that indicated a second exile for his people: "they will . . . be led captive among all nations; and Jerusalem will be trodden down by the Gentiles, until the times of the Gentiles are fulfilled" (Luke 21:24). Did this new exile from Jerusalem mean that it was virtually inevitable that the Jewish *qehila* would disappear for this time? According to Oskar Skarsaune, a distinctively Jewish church probably only ever existed in Erez Israel and in the immediately surrounding lands, including Syria, and that in the wider diaspora, the original pattern was of Jewish and Gentile believers being united in the same local church.[9] But whatever the historical probabilities the model of the "one new man" expressed in Ephesians 2 and 3 did not survive the catastrophes in Jerusalem. Its survival would have involved an honoring by the fast-growing church in the Gentile world of a small Jewish remnant separated from its own land and scattered throughout the nations. Perhaps that would have been the only way for the church to have avoided all triumphalism and to have remained truly humble.

Is it right in the light of history to speak of "the Jewish church" and "the Gentile church"? The term "church" is used in the New Testament both of the final universal cosmic church of Jesus Christ, as, for example, in Ephesians, and of local embodiments of the one church in cities such as Thessalonica and Corinth. I say "cosmic" in relation to the universal

---

8. It is interesting that the prophetic words of Jesus that "there will not be left here one stone upon another" are applied by Matthew to the temple and by Luke to the city of Jerusalem.

9. Skarsaune, *Shadow*, 203, 205.

church, because when the New Testament speaks of the one church, it is not just referring to the church on earth.[10] In terms of universal usage, there is a long tradition that speaks of the *ecclesia ex Judaeis* (the church from the Jews) and the *ecclesia ex gentibus* (the church out of the nations). While this terminology is not directly biblical, it derives from the letter to the Galatians where in the second chapter Paul speaks first of the gospel (verse 7) and then of apostleship (verse 8), in relation to Peter's call to the circumcised and Paul's call to the uncircumcised, the nations.[11]

At the level of local churches, it would seem appropriate to speak of Jewish and Gentile churches, as with "the church of Jerusalem" and "the churches of the nations," though this does not exclude local churches that embody the "one new man" in their life and membership.[12] At the global level, it is possible to speak as many have done of "the Gentile church," but I suggest that this is only accurate when used in a sociological rather than a theological sense. When the church of the first millennium excluded an explicitly Jewish membership, it became sociologically a wholly Gentile church. But theologically it is impossible to make the church wholly Gentile, most fundamentally because the church is not just a this-worldly reality. Secondly, the church cannot simply be Gentile when the Old Testament is accepted as Holy Scripture. Most importantly, this was done without attributing a higher level of inspiration by the Holy Spirit to the New Testament than to the Old. The church that accepts the Scriptures as "canonical" and thus "authoritative" is not best described as simply "Gentile."[13] Thirdly,

10. An English theologian has pointed out that in *Lumen Gentium*, Vatican II uses "universal Church in two different ways: on the one hand, to refer to the final heavenly eschatological Church of all ages, the assembly of all the just 'from Abel . . . to the last of the elect' (LG 2), and, on the other, to refer to the present worldwide Church of today (e.g. LG 25)." (McPartlan, "The Local Church," 22). McPartlan sees both Ratzinger and Kasper as basing their arguments on the second meaning of "universal church" and overlooking the first and deeper eschatological sense, insisted on by the Orthodox Zizioulas.

11. In verse 7, Paul "had been entrusted with the gospel to the uncircumcised (*tō evaggēlion tēs àkrobustías*), just as Peter to the circumcision (*tēs peritomēs*)," whereas verse 8 speaks of Peter's apostleship to the circumcision (*eis àpostolēn tēs peritomēs*) and Paul's "to the nations" (*eis tà èthnē*).

12. Thus Rossi de Gasperis uses the term "chiese" (churches) of the Gentiles, as in note 13 below.

13. "una tale centralità [della comunità giudeocristiana] fu altamente operativa e strutturalmente dominante per tutto il primo secolo, e specialmente durante la terza generazione cristiana, tra l'anno 70 e l'anno 135 d.C., giungendo a influenzare in modo determinante la redazione dell'intero Nuovo Testamento che rimane la regola canonica insostituibile della fede, della spiritualità e della teologia di tutte le successive chiese

because—replacement thinking notwithstanding—much that characterized Israel marked the life and particularly the worship of the Christian church. The structure of the liturgy of the Word is foundationally Jewish, as is the pattern of the "liturgy of the hours,"[14] with a definite Jewish influence on the development of the eucharistic prayers. The liturgical renewal of the twentieth century has been recovering the Jewish roots of the worship patterns of the church of the Fathers—as, for example, in the concepts of blessing (*berekah*) and of memorial (*anamnēsis*). When the leaders of TJCII went together to Ethiopia, they discovered that the Coptic Church of Ethiopia retained more Jewish elements than any other ancient church, even if they were not well understood: observance of Sabbath, dietary laws, model of the ark of the covenant in every church. The Ethiopian church seems at least to some degree to represent a church converted from Judaism rather than from paganism. As such, it is not accurately described simply as a "Gentile church."

This challenge concerning the early history and development clearly confronts the ancient churches the most strongly. As a Catholic, I want to acknowledge the ways in which the marginalization and then the outlawing of a Jewish expression of the church caused deviations from the Lord's purposes. But I also see that while deviation is always possible it is not so easy to destroy and totally efface the Lord's handiwork as some who emphasize "discontinuity" seem to imagine. The church's Jewish character can never be wholly eliminated, even though it was not rightly understood, and the exclusion of an explicit Jewish component represented a serious wound.

---

dei Gentili, come pure di tutte le future possibili chiese cristiane." (Rossi de Gasperis, *Cominciando*, 125). English translation: "such a centrality [of the Judeochristian community] was highly operative throughout the first century, and especially during the third Christian generation, between the year 70 and the year 135, joining to influence in a decisive way the redaction of the entire New Testament that remains the non-substitutable canonical rule of the faith, of the spirituality, and of the theology of all the successive churches of the Gentiles, as also for all future possible Christian churches."

14. "In its characteristic structure the Liturgy of the Word originates in Jewish prayer. The Liturgy of the Hours and other liturgical texts and formularies, as well as those of our most venerable prayers, including the Lord's Prayer, have parallels in Jewish prayer. The Eucharistic Prayers also draw their inspiration from the Jewish tradition." (*CCC*, 1096).

A Challenge to the Ancient Churches

A consequence of the disappearance of a Jewish expression of the church is that the Catholic Church has formulated its ecclesiology in universal terms without reference to the Jewish people since the incarnation. An Italian Jesuit scholar, Francesco Rossi de Gasperis, has described better than anyone else I know how the distancing from the particularity of Israel exposes the church to ideological tendencies. When the Jewish component in the church is forgotten, our protection against ideology—the idolatry of the mind—is removed. Christianity without Israel is in danger of becoming an ideology.[15] Rossi de Gasperis writes: "The Jewish presence in Jerusalem frees me from every ideology of a Constantinian type, from a Christianity that is *Judenrein*;[16] from that of an unhistorical Christianity, reduced to a humanism of nature, of law, of socio-political liberation or of ecology."[17] From this angle we can say that the renewal of our theology of the church requires a liberation from all forms of ideology. Our "-isms" express ideology more than we realize, whether Catholicism or Evangelicalism.[18]

In the twentieth century renewal of Catholic ecclesiology we can see an increasing attention to Scripture, a shift from the emphasis on the institutional to an emphasis on the organic, an increased awareness of the church as a pilgrim people in history, and a coalescence around the theme of communion. But as long as we have not discovered the essence of the church in the union of Jew and Gentile and the necessary orientation of each to the other, we cannot be totally free from the ideological vision of a universal church that is monopolar and self-sufficient. Perhaps Catholicism reached its most ideological expression in the idea of the church as

15. "Con la scusa di affermare una 'giustizia' che valga per ogni uomo, esso cerca in tutte le maniere di 'ridurre' la storia alla natura, la fede biblica a una filosofia e a una religione dell'Uomo, o l'evangelo a una causa del Povero, Gesù di Nazaret a una parabola dell'Uomo, lo Spirito Santo all'energia del cosmo, la redenzione dal peccato a una liberazione psichica o socio-politica, la chiesa a una potenza di questo mondo." (Rossi de Gasperis, *Cominciando*, 485). English translation: "On the pretext of upholding a 'justice' that is valid for every person, this [way of thinking] seeks in every respect to reduce history to nature, biblical faith to a philosophy and a religion of Man, or the gospel to the cause of the poor, Jesus of Nazareth to a parable of Man, the Holy Spirit to the energy of the cosmos, redemption from sin to a psychic or socio-political liberation, the church to a power of this world."

16. Free of all Jews in the Nazi terminology.

17. Ibid., 514.

18. See chapter 2.

a perfect society (*societas perfecta*). A church still in thrall to ideology is unable to face the messiness of her history. It is then impossible to discuss the dichotomy between the beautiful theology and the much less admirable reality on the ground. The Israel-Jewish issue then confronts the Catholic Church with a profound call to purification.

The Challenge to the Evangelicals and to the Free Churches

The challenges from the "one new man" model of the church not only concern the historic churches. The vision of TJCII is equally challenging to the Evangelicals and to the free churches. Here the challenge concerns the rightful place of continuity, and the link between the continuous and the organic. An emphasis on the direct interventions of the Lord without a corresponding focus on continuity in history results in a lack of organic unity. While we can see in much of the free church world a growing longing for a unity that is truly organic, without Israel it lacks the glue. Both the historic churches and the free churches need Israel. The ancient churches need Israel so as to be freed from the ideological distortions that have provoked the Protestant and Evangelical reactions, especially in the West. But the ancient churches have retained an understanding of the body that is expressed in Paul's principle "it is not the spiritual which is first but the physical, and then the spiritual" (1 Cor 15:46). Organic unity is grounded in the physical, which is then transformed by the spiritual. The transformation of the olive tree in Yeshua is the perfect illustration of this principle. There is a connection between the issue of the land and the question of the body: the link between land and body is through the people of the land. That is why the recovery of an organic unity, also for the free churches, can only be received through Israel.

But for an organic unity to come through Israel, the Jewish believers in Yeshua must be visibly one among themselves and one with their own people. Here we encounter the challenge to the Messianic Jews. For wonderful as is the reappearance of this Jewish expression, it would not seem that the Messianic movement has yet arrived at a unity that can be recognized as organic. However, it seems to me as an "outsider" that while the Messianic movement exhibits many tensions and experiences divisions, it has a coherence that is different from the commonality in the Evangelical world: a coherence that has a physical basis in its Jewishness. All Messianic

Jews know that their brethren whose theology they don't accept and of whose practice they disapprove are all fellow Jews.

The organic unity of the body of Messiah was formed in Israel. I believe that it can only be restored in Israel. Ezekiel 37 can help us. In this chapter, we have two elements: first, the resurrection of the "dry bones," and secondly the uniting of Israel and Judah. Both parts speak of the return to the land. Both are the work of the Lord. The first part speaks of resurrection, the second of unity. I am struck particularly by the phrase: "I will make them one nation in the land, upon the mountains of Israel" (Ezek 37:22).

Just as the opening up of the church to the Gentiles in the Acts of the Apostles was totally a work of the Holy Spirit, so is and will the resurrection of the Jewish expression of the church equally be a work of the Holy Spirit. For the Messianic movement to be what the Lord calls it to be requires a constant guidance by the Spirit. If the organic unity, the "body" character, is to be restored out of Israel, it means that it will not be the work of sociologically Gentile churches. To be a friend of the Messianic Jews as a Gentile Christian requires great forbearance! As Gentile friends, indeed sisters and brothers, we can *encourage* our fellow Jewish believers, we can *challenge* them; we can *warn* them of dangers; and we can and must *intercede* for them. But it cannot be our work. How will the Lord do this? I do not know. But I do know that it will be the work of the Holy Spirit revealing the Lord's purpose to Israel, in Israel, and out of Israel. I suspect that an important role may be played by the hidden believers in Jesus within the Jewish community, because they form a stronger link with the historic Jewish community. The Jewish believers within the historic churches could also play a valuable role as they are recognized and given a full freedom to be who they are in Messiah.

The vision of TJCII as a process of profound interaction leading to acceptance and reconciliation can help the Messianic movement to arrive at an organic unity that will be at the same time an expression of its authentic Jewishness. First, because neither the Jewish expression of the church nor the Gentile expressions can be what they are called to be without each other. Secondly, because in this extraordinary range of Christian convictions and theologies represented in our gathering are to be found the different elements that are required for the goal to be reached. Does this not contradict what I have just said that it cannot be the work of the Gentiles? No, because in our interaction, the Jewish believers are to receive what the

Holy Spirit wants them to receive, not what we Gentiles want to impose; even with what the Holy Spirit leads the Messianic believers to learn from the Gentiles, they are to receive from the Lord in a purified form. But even here the biggest part will involve the Jewish believers, above all in Israel and Jerusalem, receiving directly from the Lord and out of their own Scriptures and heritage, and so discovering afresh with new purity and power the authentic riches that Gentile Christianity has preserved in its divided state.

CHAPTER 10

Eschatology: The Complementarity of the Jewish and Christian Contributions

THE BASIC CONVICTIONS ANIMATING the Toward Jerusalem Council II (TJCII) initiative—the complementarity of Israel and the nations, the church as the union of Jew and Gentile through the cross of the Messiah, the ingrafting of the Gentile believers into the natural olive tree of believing Israel, the need of the Jewish and Gentile disciples of Jesus for each other—now need to be applied in the area of eschatology. As a vision for Jewish and Gentile reconciliation in Messiah, TJCII requires the reconciliation of the Jewish and the Christian contributions to eschatology, to our faith in the end-times, and for the restoration of all things in Messiah.

The ongoing distinction between Israel and the nations has major implications for eschatology. In Romans, Paul uses the term "fullness" (*plerōma*), first of Israel (11:12), and then of the nations (11:25). "Now if their trespass [that is, of Israel] means riches for the world, and if their failure means riches for the Gentiles, how much more will their full inclusion [*plerōma*] mean!" (Rom 11:12). Later in the same chapter he continues, "I want you to understand this mystery" (i.e., this is part of God's eternal plan): "a hardening has come upon part of Israel, until the full number [*plerōma*] of the Gentiles has come in. And so all Israel will be saved" (Rom 11:25–26). The fullness of Israel and the fullness of the nations are interrelated; they cannot be realized independently of each other. This connectedness was expressed in a different way by Yeshua himself: "they [the Jews] will fall by the edge of the sword, and be led captive among all nations; and Jerusalem will be trodden down by the Gentiles, until the times of the Gentiles are fulfilled" (Luke 21:24). This phrase "The times of the Gentiles" is related to the time of gospel proclamation to the nations mentioned in Matthew's Gospel: "And this gospel of the kingdom will be preached throughout the whole world, as a testimony to all nations; and then the end will come" (Matt 24:14). "For if their rejection [*apobolē* = setting aside, that is, of Israel] means the reconciliation of the world, what will their acceptance mean but life from the dead?" (Rom 11:15).

From the Church of the One New Man to One Universal Church

The church of Jew and Gentile together in one body, that following Eph 2:15 may be called the church of the one new man, did not last. The warnings of Paul against Gentile boasting over the Jews were not heeded (see Rom 11:18, 20, 25). By the fourth century, the church neither permitted converted Jews to retain a Jewish identity nor to continue any Jewish practices. The church understood itself to be universal embracing all nations; the main model for unity increasingly became the unity of the Roman-Byzantine Empire. Several fathers of the church recognized that the Jews would enter at the end, but this was understood as their finally entering the kingdom, unrelated to Israel, not as restoration of the one new man nor as the fulfillment of Old Testament prophecies.[1]

This process had major repercussions in a number of areas, including church unity and eschatology. It had negative effects on eschatology because the Jewish people are the bearers of the messianic promises: "to them belong the sonship, the glory, the covenants, the giving of the law, the worship, and the *promises*" (Rom 9:4). Jewish life is rooted in the covenant with Abraham and in the Torah, being oriented to the messianic promises. The references to past and to future are expressed and celebrated in the feasts of Israel. The promises given to Abraham, to David, and through the prophets, concern the coming Messiah-King-Deliverer and the coming messianic age/kingdom of righteousness and peace that is established in and from Zion. When there is no longer an explicit Jewish presence in the church, their strong messianic orientation towards the final fulfillment is removed.

Was this orientation to the final fulfillment completely lost in the church? No, and for two reasons. First, the church rejected the attempt of

---

1. "At best, the Jews might be able to give up their identity and be gathered into the Church. But it would be a Church that had been constituted apart from them, and they would be the humblest element within it." (Simon, *Verus*, 171).

Marcion to remove the Old Testament from the Christian Bible. The Scriptures of Israel remained foundational for the church. Second, the liturgies of the church retained the orientation to the completion that had come from their Jewish origins. But nonetheless in the living hope of the Christian people and in the teaching on eschatology something had been lost.

Effects on Eschatology of Distancing from Israel

How then did the distancing of the church from its Jewish roots weaken the eschatological hope? Christians began to speak of the church as the new Israel, saying that the church has become heir to all God's promises, with the assumption or explicit statement that the promises have been transferred to the church because of Israel's unbelief. When this happened, the promises were re-interpreted in a spiritualizing sense—so that the promised land becomes heaven, the earthly Jerusalem is replaced by the heavenly, and the rule of the Messiah becomes the glorified Christ's rule from heaven. In this process, the new realities with the coming of the Christ are seen as superior to the material things characterizing the covenants with Israel: the Jews are seen as carnal, the Christians as spiritual. The Jewish reading of the Old Testament is dismissed as carnal. Christians search the Old Testament for everything that can be interpreted as a type of Christ; this Christian typological reading is lauded as spiritual.[2]

This form of spiritualizing produces a rupture with the messianic hope of Israel. Why? It is not because all typological interpretation of the Old Testament is mistaken; we find typological interpretation in the New Testament, for example, "the Rock was Christ" (1 Cor 10:4), and in the description of Jesus as the Lamb of God (John 1:29, 36). Why then? First, because the only value of the type became its christological signification— the covenants with Israel and the Jewish rites have no more value in themselves. Second, the messianic promises were seen as totally fulfilled in the first coming of the Christ. This is the fundamental reason why the historic churches have great difficulty in seeing any fulfillment of messianic promises in contemporary events concerning Israel and the Jewish people. This

2. Marcel Simon indicates that this characterization goes back at least to Justin Martyr in the middle of the second century. Simon describes this Christian position: "It is a 'pneumatic' interpretation which is the only legitimate one, which throughout controls the Christian proof. It rests on the postulate, without which the revelation makes no real sense at all, that Christ and Christianity are manifest in every line of the sacred text." (Simon, *Verus*, 147).

conviction—total fulfillment in the first coming—cuts off the messianic expectation of Israel: no more messianic fulfillment, just the outworking of the consequences of the first coming understood in a spiritualizing sense. If Paul had believed that, he could not have told the Jews of Rome: "it is because of the hope of Israel that I am bound with this chain" (Acts 28:20).

I should add that some promises that did not fit the spiritualizing reinterpretation were simply left out of Christian theology and preaching: for example, the words of Jesus to the Twelve, "Truly, I say to you, in the new world, when the Son of man shall sit on his glorious throne, you who have followed me will also sit on twelve thrones, judging the twelve tribes of Israel" (Matt 19:28; see also Luke 22:30). This also applies to the words of Jesus at the Last Supper, "I tell you that I shall not drink again of this fruit of the vine until that day when I drink it new with you in my Father's kingdom" (Matt 26:29). Understanding this last text literally did not immediately cease in the early church, as we find St. Irenaeus of Lyon explaining around the year 200:

> In promising to drink there of the fruit of the vine with his disciples, he [Jesus] made two things known: the inheritance of the earth, in which will be drunk the new fruit of the vine, and the bodily resurrection of his disciples. For the flesh that will be raised in a new condition is also that which will share in the new cup. It is not in fact when he will be with his disciples in a superior and supra-heavenly place, that the Lord can be thought of as drinking the fruit of the vine.[3]

For the Christians who saw the messianic fulfillment totally in the first coming of the Lord understood this fulfillment as taking place above all in the resurrection and ascension of Jesus. There is of course something fundamentally right in this. The resurrection and ascension of Jesus was for Jesus himself being "made perfect" (Heb 5:9). This opened up the heavenly dimension, which becomes a characteristic element in New Testament faith. So, for example, Paul writes: "But our commonwealth [*politeia*] is in heaven" (Phil 3:20) and "Set your minds on things that are above, not on things that are on earth. For you have died, and your life is hid with Christ in God" (Col 3:2–3). But seeing the fulfillment of all the promises in the first coming overlooks the total orientation of the first coming to the second. This becomes more serious when the role of the Holy Spirit preparing

3. Irénée de Lyon, *Adversus Haereses*, V, 33, 1 (author's translation from French) SChr 153, 407/09.

for the second coming from Pentecost onwards is forgotten. As a result the second coming of Jesus in glory is no longer seen as the final fulfillment of the messianic promises. It is now assumed that Jesus comes in order to take us out of this creation up to heaven. So the church developed an eschatology that is markedly different from the hope of Israel. In general, the church has looked to a heavenly fulfillment, and Israel to an earthly deliverance and fulfillment. The church sees the fulfillment as outside and above human history, whereas for the Jewish people the fulfillment is within this creation and is the climax to human history. This is one of the most serious results of the separation of church and synagogue.

With the separation of the church and the synagogue through the centuries we have inherited a situation in which the church affirmed the newness of resurrection and glorification through the cross, while the Jewish people affirmed the continuing validity of the promises concerning the land of Israel and the city of Jerusalem. From the fourth century, Christian eschatology had no place for Israel as a distinct people. It developed differently in the Eastern churches from the West. Some of what I write applies more particularly to Western Christianity, both Catholic and Protestant, and I leave it to Orthodox readers to discern how much this also applies to the Orthodox Church and its reading of the Scriptures. In general, this distancing of the church from the Jewish people intensified over the centuries leading to very negative presentations of the Jews by preachers and people.

More positive approaches began slowly following the Protestant Reformation. With the Protestant emphasis on the Bible, more Christians studied Hebrew, and some scholars began to understand that the promises to Israel were permanent, and that many Old Testament prophecies remained unfulfilled. The number of Reformed and Evangelical scholars who believed in a future return of the Jews to the land of Israel and in their coming to faith in Jesus had increased by the nineteenth century. But here a complication entered. One Protestant who saw the contrast between the Jewish earthly hope and the Christian heavenly hope was John Nelson Darby, a founding figure among the Plymouth Brethren. Darby, who became a major architect of pre-millennial dispensationalism, sought to solve the dilemma by separating Israel and the church even more, so he taught two distinct destinies, an earthly destiny for Israel and a heavenly destiny for the church. In Darby's scheme the church had to be removed from the earth before Israel's destiny on earth could begin to unfold. The teaching of an invisible rapture of "the church" before the visible coming of the Lord in glory removes a key element in the role of the church of Jew and Gentile to prepare the way for the coming of the Lord. In this schema the whole church is already in heaven for a period before the coming of Jesus in glory.[4] The Darbyite schema also has other disastrous consequences; among them is the separation of Jesus as Israel's Messiah, who fulfils the kingdom promises of the Old Testament, from his role as Savior and baptizer in the Holy Spirit for Christians who have a heavenly destiny.[5]

We have to hold Israel and the church together, recognizing that their hopes belong together, even if we cannot yet understand how, and so affirm that the church is the union of Jew and Gentile in one new man. It will only be possible for the Jewish and the Christian worldviews to be brought together by the light and operation of the Holy Spirit. What then is it that has to be brought together?

The Central Christian Witness: Death and Resurrection

Central to the newness of the New Testament, the new covenant is the resurrection of Jesus from the dead. Jewish belief in the resurrection of the dead on the last day, or at least the resurrection of the righteous, had been spreading during the last two centuries of the Old Testament era, particularly among the Pharisees (see Luke 20:27–40; Acts 23:8). This expectation was for the general resurrection on the last day. The claim that one man had been raised by God from the dead, not just brought back to a mortal life, but glorified for ever, this was totally unprecedented.

The resurrection of Jesus is at the heart of the good news of the gospel. The power of death is defeated. Sin can be forgiven. The heavens are opened. With the risen and ascended Jesus, there is a new realm of human existence with God in the heavenlies. The Holy Spirit is poured out on the disciples through his glorified humanity on the day of Pentecost. The account of the martyrdom of Stephen, says that "he, full of the Holy Spirit, gazed into heaven and saw the glory of God, and Jesus standing at the right hand of God; and he said, 'Behold, I see the heavens opened, and the Son of man standing at the right hand of God'" (Acts 7:55–56). It is from heaven that the risen Jesus will come in glory "in the same way as you [the apostles] saw him go into heaven" (Acts 1:11).

4. On Darby and the doctrine of the rapture, see also chapter 4.

5. See Bass, *Backgrounds*, 128–40.

The Christian tradition witnesses to a completion-fulfillment already realized in Jesus Christ. "For in him the whole fullness of deity dwells bodily, and you have come to fullness of life in him, who is the head of all rule and authority" (Col. 2:9–10). This fulfillment already realized in Jesus is in his resurrection-ascension to glory. Jesus has reached the goal, this total transformation or glorification, through his bodily resurrection and his ascension as man to the glory of the Father. But this completion in the person of Jesus has still to be achieved in the relationships of Jesus to the church, the world, and the whole creation, and thus on earth. So the Old Testament promises that are not yet fulfilled apply to the fulfillment in the creation, on earth, and in the church.

Here the resurrection of Jesus reveals our own destiny. According to the New Testament the resurrection of the dead will take place with the coming of the Lord Jesus in glory. The most explicit formulation is found in Paul's teaching on the resurrection of the body, which we find in 1 Cor 15. "But in fact Christ has been raised from the dead, the first fruits of those who have fallen asleep. . . . For as in Adam all die, so also in Christ shall all be made alive. But each in his own order: Christ, the first fruits, then at his coming those who belong to Christ" (1 Cor 15:20, 22–23).[6]

The life of the Christian and of the Christian community between Pentecost and parousia, which is "the age of the church,"[7] is a continual immersion in the death and resurrection of Jesus. Paul writes: "Do you not know that all of us who have been baptized into Christ Jesus were baptized into his death?" (Rom 6:3). The death and resurrection of Jesus is for the sake of our death and resurrection, our death to sin and our rising to new life, both in our bodies. "For if we have been united with him in a death like his, we shall certainly be united with him in a resurrection like his" (Rom 6:5). The Christian is fed on the death and resurrection of the Lord: "For as often as you eat this bread and drink the cup, you proclaim the Lord's death until he comes" (1 Cor 11:26). We feed on his body given for us and drink of his blood poured out for us. In this way we are being given over to death in preparation for our resurrection on the last day: "he who eats my flesh and drinks my blood has eternal life, and I will raise him up at the last day" (John 6:54).

Life in Christ, life in the Spirit, is always entering into the suffering of Jesus so that we may be glorified in and with him. If we are "children

6. See also 1 Thess 4:15–16.

7. CCC, 1076.

[of God], then heirs, heirs of God and fellow heirs with Christ, provided we suffer with him in order that we may also be glorified with him" (Rom 8:17). These sufferings of the present time "are not worth comparing with the glory that is to be revealed to us" (Rom 8:18). "If we have died with him, we shall also live with him; if we endure, we shall also reign with him" (2 Tim 2:11–12).[8] The dying to self and sin is continuous in the Christian life. The opposition and the outbreaks of persecution will culminate in a final unleashing of the powers of darkness before the Lord's coming. So the Catholic Catechism teaches that "The Church will enter the glory of the kingdom only through this final Passover, when she will follow her Lord in his death and resurrection."[9]

First Challenge

The first challenge to the Messianic Jews concerns the resurrection of Jesus. With their reclaiming of the messianic hope of Israel—for example, the return of King Yeshua to Jerusalem and his rule over the nations in righteousness—it can happen that full justice is not done to the genuine newness introduced by the resurrection and ascension of the Messiah that is at the heart of the new covenant. This newness is the bodily resurrection to a glorified bodily existence that is a greater transformation than could ever have been imagined, even by those Jews who believed in the resurrection from the dead.

The Christian challenge to the Messianic Jews from the resurrection of Jesus also concerns the relationship of the Shabbat (Saturday) to Sunday. Messianic Jews are more conscious than Christians of the many ways in which replacement theology removes Israel from the new covenant heritage, and any ongoing significance of the Jewish people is denied. For this reason they can be easily attracted to the false idea that the Christian observance of the first day of the week was designed as a replacement for Shabbat. No, the first day of the week was originally observed because it was the day of the resurrection of the Lord. This has eschatological significance, because the first day is also the eighth day, which symbolizes the final fulfillment after the Shabbat rest. It was no coincidence that the body of Jesus lay in the tomb on the day of rest. Not to honor the first day of the week can take attention away from the resurrection of Jesus as the core

8. See also Phil 3:10; 1 Pet 4:12–19.

9. CCC, 677.

of new covenant faith. Not celebrating the resurrection constantly exposes believers to the danger, from which not all Christians are exempt, of reducing the significance of the resurrection to a proof of the divinity of Jesus.

Second Challenge

The second challenge from the Christian tradition to the Messianic Jews concerns what will happen as the end approaches and arrives. Messianic Jewish teaching on the coming of the Messiah follows many Evangelical presentations in teaching about the "great tribulation" preceding the climax, without any emphasis on the believer's suffering with Christ so as to enter into his glory.[10] The fear of a works-righteousness weighs heavily. As a result, the messianic vision for the glorious return of Jesus to Jerusalem easily lacks the element of mighty transformation. The return of Jesus to Jerusalem as victorious Son of David to the acclamation of the Jews who will say, "Blessed is he who comes in the name of the Lord" (Matt 23:39) is seen as his coming to rule in righteousness, but often without any reference to the transformation of the resurrection.

To understand the challenges more clearly, it may help us to look at the three phases of the Holy Spirit's action upon Jesus as man. The first is clearly that Jesus is conceived by the Holy Spirit in the womb of the Virgin Mary. The second is his baptism in the Jordan. Here the Holy Spirit descends upon Jesus, in consequence of which he begins his public ministry in the power of the Spirit. As Luke says, "Jesus returned in the power of the Spirit into Galilee" (Luke 4:14). But there is a third and final filling or total penetration by the Holy Spirit that is often overlooked. It is the transformation in his resurrection and ascension. This is the greatest work of the Holy Spirit. The verse that makes this clear is Acts 2:33: "Being therefore exalted at the right hand of God, and having received from the Father the promise of the Holy Spirit, he has poured out this which you see and hear"—that is, on the day of Pentecost. Here in Peter's Pentecost message, we are told what Jesus received when he was exalted to the right hand of the Father. He is now in his humanity totally penetrated and glorified by the Holy Spirit, so that he can pour out on us this same Holy Spirit through his glorified humanity.

This same transformation is promised to the disciples. This point is emphasized by the apostle in the first chapter of Ephesians:

---

10. In fact, the emphasis has often been on the believers escaping the tribulation.

having the eyes of your hearts enlightened, that you may know what is the hope to which he has called you, what are the riches of his glorious inheritance in the saints, and what is the immeasurable greatness of his power in us who believe, according to the working of his great might which he accomplished in Christ when he raised him from the dead and made him sit at his right hand in the heavenly places, far above all rule and authority and power and dominion, and above every name that is named, not only in this age but also in that which is to come. (Eph 1:18–21)

So I suggest that the central convictions of the historic churches that the Messianic Jews need to receive are the centrality of the death and resurrection of Yeshua in the new covenant, Christian life in the age of the church as ever deeper dying and rising with Yeshua, and the mighty transformation that bodily resurrection will bring on the last day.

The Central Jewish Witness:
The Promises of the Messianic Kingdom

What is it that the churches have to receive from the synagogue? The last verse from Eph 1 presents us with a fundamental element in the biblical and Jewish worldview: the difference between this age (*aiōn*) and the age to come. Jesus mentions this in speaking of the sin against the Holy Spirit: "Whoever says a word against the Son of man will be forgiven; but whoever speaks against the Holy Spirit will not be forgiven, either in this age or in the age to come" (Matt 12:32). It is mentioned in Hebrews 6 in a warning about those who fall away, for those who have become believers in Messiah are described as "those who have once been enlightened, who have tasted the heavenly gift, and have become partakers of the Holy Spirit, and have tasted the goodness of the word of God and the powers of the age to come" (Heb 6:4–5).

The age to come is at the heart of the Jewish witness. The coming age is the messianic age, the age of the rule of the Messiah in righteousness and peace. It is the rule of the servant of the Lord: "I have put my Spirit upon him; he will bring forth justice to the nations" (Isa 42:1). The Jewish hope is for the salvation-deliverance of this world. The age to come is not a different world, but the transformation of this world. For the faithful Jew, all the promises of the Lord given to Abraham, David, and the prophets will be fulfilled—promises that concern their descendants, the land of Israel, the city of Jerusalem, and through them all the peoples of the earth. For the Messianic Jew, this fulfillment will happen in and through Yeshua (Jesus), as was promised by the angel to Mary: "the Lord God will give to him the throne of his father David, and he will reign over the house of Jacob for ever" (Luke 1:32–33); that is to say, he will reign in and from Jerusalem.

The Jewish witness exposes the wrongness of any Christian assumption that all the Old Testament promises were fulfilled in the first coming of Jesus. But precisely because the first coming of Jesus did not fulfill all the promises, the Jewish disciples had to reinterpret the messianic hope of Israel in the light of the passion, death, and resurrection-ascension of Jesus. This reinterpretation we find in the first message of the apostle Peter described after the day of Pentecost in Acts 3:18–26. Peter starts by recognizing that there has been a fulfillment: "But what God foretold by the mouth of all the prophets, that his Christ should suffer, he thus fulfilled" (Acts 3:18). Because many prophecies of the Old Testament have not yet been fulfilled, or only partially, Peter continues, "the Christ appointed for you, Jesus whom heaven must receive until the time for establishing all that God spoke by the mouth of his holy prophets from of old" (Acts 3:20–21).

Here we have the core Jewish testimony to a coming fulfillment on earth in this creation. In fact, the Greek text says *achri chronōn apokatastaseōs pantōn*, literally the times of restoration of all things, where *chrónos* indicates historical continuous time as distinct from *kairós*, an inbreaking crisis moment. In this context, it underlines an element of continuity. The age to come follows the present age. The present age is moving toward the age to come. A Messianic Jewish scholar, Joseph Shulam, relates this phrase concerning the times of restoration to the words of Jesus in Luke 21:

> Jesus himself apparently associated the task of the Son of man with the final judgment and the ultimate realization of the kingdom of heaven. . . . In this sense, Luke's reference to "until . . . all the things" . . . parallels his allusion to the "times of the Gentiles be fulfilled" (Luke 21:24).[11]

For the Jewish people, who celebrate the goodness of all creation each Shabbat, the restoration of all things ultimately means the liberation of the entire creation from the effects of evil and sin. Paul expresses this hope in Romans 8, the hope that "the creation itself will be set free from its bondage to decay and [will] obtain the glorious liberty of the children of God" (Rom

11. Shulam with Le Cornu, *Commentary,* 207.

8:21). The Jewish witness to Yeshua challenges all Christians concerning this earthly sphere of this fulfillment.

What is it then that the Christian churches need to receive from the Jewish believers in Yeshua? Without detracting from the New Testament witness to the fullness of eternal life in communion with the Father and the Son, we need to receive the Jewish vision for the messianic fulfillment in and of this creation. It is only in this context that the full significance of bodily resurrection can be understood. This will also involve rediscovering Yeshua as Messiah, and not only as Savior and Lord. As Son of David, Yeshua will rule over the kingdom that is grounded in Israel, centered in Jerusalem, and opened up to the nations. The Jewish hope for the redemption of the world will be fulfilled through Jesus in a mighty transformation of the whole created order. None of the promises to Israel will be cast aside; but they will all be fulfilled in ways beyond the imagination of the recipients of the promises.

A key question for Christians arising from the Jewish messianic expectation is what happens on or to the earth "after" the coming of Jesus in glory. It would seem to be important that the churches reconsider the concept of the millennium, of a millennial reign of Jesus on earth following the parousia. The millennium is a Jewish concept, reflecting Israel's convictions concerning time, history, and fulfillment.[12] It can be understood as historical or as meta-historical.[13] Was the church's turning away from belief in a future millennial reign the result of distancing from the Jewish heritage and acceptance of an excessive spiritualization of the promises? Though the church since the fourth century has been unsympathetic to all ideas of a millennial reign on earth following the parousia, the official position against it is prudential rather than definitive.[14] For the Messianic Jews, it is almost universally believed that Jesus is coming back to reign as king from David's throne in Jerusalem. Teaching on a millennial reign enables them to uphold

12. When the church turned away from millenarism after the time of Constantine, one argument used against belief in a millennial reign following the Lord's return was that it was a Jewish myth. See Fredricksen, *Augustine*, 406, n. 14.

13. The teaching of the Catholic Church rejects every claim "to realize within history that messianic hope which can only be realized beyond history through the eschatological judgment." (CCC, 676). The second coming of the Lord together with the resurrection of the dead must in some way be "beyond history."

14. The decree of the Holy Office in Rome, the predecessor of the Congregation for the Doctrine of the Faith gave a response in 1944 to an episcopal inquiry stating that the theory of a "mitigated millennialism" cannot be safely taught, the lowest form of negative statement used by the Catholic magisterium.

the New Testament association of the parousia with the resurrection of the dead, and at the same time to hold to the hope that all the messianic promises to Israel will be fulfilled through the Messiah, the promises concerning the people, concerning the land, and concerning Jerusalem.

What does this mean for Jerusalem? The Jewish tradition does not allow for a total displacement of the earthly Jerusalem by the heavenly. The Christian tradition does not allow for a return of Yeshua to the city of David that does not involve the mighty transformation through death to resurrection and glorification. He will come in glory. Now, the book of Revelation ends with the vision of "the holy city, the new Jerusalem, coming down out of heaven from God, prepared as a bride adorned for her husband" (Rev 21:2). It is pointless to try to imagine what the new Jerusalem will be like and how it comes down to earth. The foolishness of trying to imagine it is shown by the impossibility of imagining one tree that is found on both sides of the river that flows "through the middle of the street of the city" (Rev 22:2). But this vision tells us important things. It indicates that finally we are not taken up to God, but God comes down to us. "Behold, the dwelling [tabernacle] of God is with men. He will dwell with them, and they shall be his people, and God himself will be with them" (Rev 21:3). Later, "the throne of God and of the Lamb shall be in it [the city]" (Rev 22:3).

The Task for the Future

The task of Messianic Jews and of Christians from all traditions is to work for reconciliation in relation to "the one hope that belongs to your call" (Eph 4:3). The Christian tendency, whether Catholic or Protestant, has always been to seek a coherent synthesis in the understanding of the biblical revelation. The Jewish tendency has always been to leave options open, embracing the contradictions, out of Israel's sense of the ineffability of God.[15] Here the Messianic Jews often seem to be more Christian than Jewish in their embrace of Christian certitudes and their desire to produce a total explanation for the messianic promises and their fulfillment.

What is clear first is that it is not possible at this point in history to formulate a coherent eschatology that does full justice to both the Jewish and Christian traditions. At present none of our eschatologies do full justice to the messianic hope of both Old and New Testaments. This reconciliation for which TJCII is working requires a coming together, a profound inter-action

15. See Brueggemann, *Theology*, 107–12.

between our different faith and theological worlds. This coming together to restore the full unity of the one church from Jew and Gentile requires more than what we are accustomed to call theological dialogue. It requires a profound and continuous encounter between the lived and reflected realities of (Gentile) Christian faith in all its expressions, and the reality of Israel as lived by Jews of all kinds, including Messianic Jews. The customary patterns of theological dialogue are a Christian construction that privileges intellectual formulations to the neglect of what may be wrongly regarded as non-theological factors. These Gentile patterns are alien to the Jews.

What could a reconciled joint Jewish-Christian eschatology look like? We cannot say at this point. What we do know—and this is the distinct witness of TJCII—is that the new covenant witness of the church of Jew and Gentile requires a reconciliation of the Jewish and Christian testimonies in order to be faithful to the New Testament and for the fullness (*plerōma*) of the body of Messiah-Christ to be realized. Here I have used the term "testimonies" deliberately, as being wider and more comprehensive than the theologies.

As an initiative for Jewish–Gentile reconciliation in Jesus Christ, TJCII has followed a prophetic rather than a theological path, without denying a necessary contribution from theology. The prophetic path corrects the Gentile bias present in theological dialogue, for the prophetic has its roots in Israel and is a characteristically Israelite-Jewish phenomenon. The prophetic approach lends itself readily to the confession of sin and humble recognition of the offense given to the all holy God by the long history of separation, of mutual disdain, of self-justification, and of humiliation inflicted on the Jewish people. This confession of sin is necessary for the purification of all our theologies, so that what is from the Lord in each of them can be brought together in the one hope to which we are all called (see Eph 4:4). This applies to the ancient churches of East and West, to the churches of the Reformation and to the free churches—and it applies to the Messianic Jews.

To effect this purification, the history of the first centuries needs to be examined so as to determine what precisely were the consequences of the Christian distancing from the Jewish roots. What resulted from the mistaken thinking that God had rejected the Jewish people? What came from losing sight of the Jewish character of the New Testament? What came from not understanding the "setting aside" of the Jews during the time of the Gentiles? Was the rejection of a millennial reign on the earth a consequence of this distancing from everything Jewish? This requires a careful re-reading of all the different strands in the New Testament, not neglecting the Epistle to the Hebrews. A purification is also needed in the teaching of those pro-Israel Evangelical Christians who teach a millennial reign, because in the teaching of Darby, Scofield, and other dispensational-ists, the millennium became part of a system involving the rapture of the church, which is a very non-Jewish concept.

But the work of reconciliation cannot only be the work of scholars and specialists. The promises concern everyone. All of us have to apply the principles we have learned in reconciliation initiatives: the need for love and respect, the importance of confession of sin, the need for the purification of memories. We have to listen to one another, to study the Word together, and together to seek the leading of the Holy Spirit. Very importantly, we all have the hope within us by the gift of the Holy Spirit (see Rom 5:5; 8:23–25). We have the full hope within us, not just part of the hope, even though we may not understand it fully or correctly. For the hope belongs to the gift of the Holy Spirit.

PART IV

Pope Francis and Christian Unity

CHAPTER 11

Catholic–Evangelical Relations
Moving Center Stage

THE ELECTION OF CARDINAL Jorge Bergoglio from Argentina as bishop of
Rome, now known to the world as Pope Francis, is opening up a new era
in Catholic–Evangelical relations. Francis is the first pope to have had close
brotherly relationships with Pentecostal pastors before his election, and the
first pope to have prayed regularly with Christians accustomed to sustained
spontaneous prayer together.

Since his election, Francis has had a series of meetings with Evangelical and Pentecostal leaders, almost all unofficial and not mentioned in the
official Vatican record of papal audiences. He has also been the first pope to
visit a free church—in fact a Pentecostal church in Italy.[1] It is interesting to
piece together the connections and relationships that made these developments possible.

A Key Friendship

A major factor making possible these new relations has been the friendship,
now for thirty years, between two Italians, a lay Catholic, Matteo Calisi,
founder of the Comunità di Gesù, a charismatic community in Bari, and a
Pentecostal pastor, Giovanni Traettino, from Caserta, near Naples.[2] After
some years of friendship, Calisi and Traettino launched in 1992 a series of

1. Besides the papal visit to Caserta mentioned below, Pope Francis visited a Walden-
sian temple in Turin, Italy, on June 22, 2015, another first.

2. Calisi and Traettino first met in 1983 at a praise conference organized by Traettino. This and the details about the origins of CCI are found in Introvigne, *Aspettando*,
38–46.

reconciliation meetings between Catholics and Evangelicals, forming for this purpose the *Consultazione Carismatica Italiana* (Italian Charismatic Consultation). The occasion for the formation of CCI was a celebration of the twenty-fifth anniversary of CCR, to which some twenty Protestant pastors had been invited. Traettino proposed to Calisi that he should wash the feet of a Catholic priest as a gesture of penitence and reconciliation. The priest whose feet Traettino washed was Fr. Antonio Belpiede, whose family name literally means beautiful feet. The CCI meetings that followed each year in Italy featured two major speakers, one Catholic and one Pentecostal. Calisi and Traettino then took their witness of reconciliation to several other European countries, including Northern Ireland.

Around the turn of the millennium, Matteo Calisi began to organize a series of annual conferences in Bari with a strong ecumenical and charismatic presence, always supported by his friend Giovanni Traettino: one series called Kairos addresses critical contemporary issues in the world; one series is with Messianic Jews; and another series focuses on praise and worship.[3]

Two developments in particular helped to prepare the way for Evangelical-Pentecostal visitors to the Vatican from 2013.[4] First, the Comunità di Gesù made its first foundation of a daughter community in Buenos Aires, Argentina, following a visit of Calisi in 2003. Through this step, Calisi came to know Cardinal Bergoglio, who gave his full support to this foundation. Second, Calisi invited a young British-born South African, Tony Palmer, who had moved to Italy in 2004, to work with him ecumenically (Palmer's wife is Italian). Palmer had earlier been responsible for Kenneth Copeland Ministries in South Africa, but had subsequently linked up with a group known as the Communion of Evangelical Episcopal Churches, set up in 1995 to work for unity by holding together the sacramental-liturgical, the evangelical, and the charismatic dimensions of Christian life.[5] From that point Calisi regularly invited CEEC leaders to his Bari conferences. Through Palmer, Kenneth Copeland spoke at one of the Praise and Worship conferences. Within CEEC, Palmer was ordained priest in 2005, and

---

3. Calisi studied at the Bari Conservatory of Music and was for a time Professor of Music.

4. Some but not all of the details that follow are mentioned in Ivereigh, *Great Reformer*.

5. See Hocken, "Communion," NIDPCM, 557.

subsequently bishop in 2010. He was then given responsibility for the CEEC's ecumenical relations.

Other Linked Developments

In Italy, Calisi had become a friend of Jorge Himitian, a Pentecostal pastor from Buenos Aires. At the time of Calisi's first visit to Argentina in 2003, Calisi and Himitian founded a new group, The Renewed Communion of Evangelicals and Catholics in the Holy Spirit (CRECES), which held its first annual congress in 2004. Cardinal Bergoglio came quietly to the CRECES congresses, and just sat in the crowd, watching and praying. For their big meeting in 2006, CRECES invited Fr. Raniero Cantalamessa, the preacher to the papal household, to be the main speaker, and the meeting was held in a bigger location, the Luna Park stadium. Among the seven thousand people present were Giovanni Traettino and Tony Palmer. In the afternoon, the Cardinal was invited to come up to the platform and to say something. He first asked them all to pray for him, he knelt down, and a group of Pentecostal pastors placed their hands on his shoulders, with Fr. Raniero alongside. A well-researched biography of Francis records that a Pentecostal pastor ended by praying: "Fill him with your Spirit and power, Lord! In the name of Jesus!"[6] After this meeting, Cardinal Bergoglio met once a month with these pastors to pray together. One fruit was a retreat in 2010 for about a hundred priests led by the Pentecostal pastors, repeated in 2012 when Fr. Cantalamessa returned to Buenos Aires.[7]

Calisi also initiated another charismatic ecumenical venture in North America, known as "United in Christ." In the mid-to-late 1990s, Calisi visited the airport church in Toronto, by then renowned in some charismatic circles for what was variously called "The Toronto blessing" or "The Father's blessing." One of the fruits of Calisi's connections with Toronto has been a strong relationship with John Arnott, formerly senior pastor of the airport church, and now leader of the Partners in Harvest network of churches. Calisi has been working particularly with Bruno Ierullo, responsible for ecumenical relations at the Toronto church, so that "United in Christ" events are in practice organized jointly by Calisi and Ierullo.[8]

6. Ivereigh, *Great Reformer*, 293.
7. Ibid., 294.
8. See www.united-in-christ.com.

From Buenos Aires to Rome

What is clear now to those familiar with the Argentine background is that, as pope, Francis is continuing what he did as archbishop of Buenos Aires, not only in his lifestyle and his emphasis on the poor, but also in his relations with Evangelicals and Pentecostals. The first story that grabbed the media was a message sent by Francis in January 2014 via Tony Palmer to a Kenneth Copeland conference in the USA. But in fact, he had had a meeting in May 2013 at his residence in the Vatican with the five Pentecostal pastors he had prayed with regularly in Buenos Aires.[9]

On June 24, 2014, Francis had a meeting in his Vatican residence organized by Palmer with those present including Copeland, Arnott, James Robison from Texas, Geoff Tunnicliffe of the World Evangelical Alliance, and others. Within a week Tony Palmer was dead, with doctors unable to save his life following a motorcycle accident in England. Most unusually, he was given a Catholic funeral. At the end of November 2014 Francis had a meeting with Loren Cunningham, the founder of Youth With A Mission, and his wife. In these meetings which were much longer than usual papal audiences, they discussed what they could do together for the Lord.

At the end of July 2014, Pope Francis was the first pope to visit a Pentecostal church, when he visited the Pentecostals at their church in Caserta, led by Pastor Giovanni Traettino. There Francis asked forgiveness for the persecution suffered by the Italian Pentecostals under the Government of Mussolini that had been supported by the Catholic authorities.[10] Throughout his message, Francis kept referring to "Brother Giovanni" or just "my brother." At the end he said: "Some may be shocked: 'But the Pope went to the Evangelicals!' He went to visit his brothers."

Following the first of two synods of bishops on the family, the Vatican held a major conference inviting other Christians and non-Christians to speak about the importance of marriage and the family. Among the Protestants invited were Rick Warren, pastor of Saddleback, an Evangelical megachurch in California, and Russell Moore, a prominent Southern Baptist from the USA. Bishop Tom Wright, a prolific Anglican biblical scholar from England was also a speaker.

9. Pastors Jorge Himitian, Norberto Saracco, Carlos Mraida, Angel Negro, and Omar Cabrera. See Ivereigh., 253.

10. Many years before, Traettino had written his dissertation on the persecution of Italian Pentecostals by the state encouraged by the church.

All these developments mark a new phase in ecumenical relations for the Catholic Church. Until now, the most important relations and dialogues have been those with the Orthodox, the Anglicans, and the Lutherans, all liturgical traditions that honor the historic creeds. Relations with the free churches were less developed and seen as less important, though Methodists were higher up the ecumenical scale than the Baptists. Opposition to ecumenism and to relations with Catholics has been highest among Pentecostals and conservative Evangelicals, especially in some predominantly Catholic nations. These initiatives of Pope Francis are challenging Evangelical and Pentecostal perceptions of the Catholic Church.

A New Pattern

We should take note of key differences between previous patterns of dialogue and this series of meetings with Pope Francis. Previous patterns of dialogue between Catholics and Evangelical Christians had at least a semi-official character, and were handled on the Catholic side by a Vatican office, the Pontifical Council for Promoting Christian Unity. The participants were chosen by the parties agreeing to hold a dialogue: on the Catholic side, appointed by the Vatican normally including at least one bishop together with a team of theologians and ecumenists; in the case of dialogue with Evangelicals, some leaders and scholars chosen by the World Evangelical Alliance; in the case of the dialogue with Pentecostals, some scholars invited by the Pentecostal co-chair. These dialogues involved prepared papers, and led eventually to a report for the respective constituencies.

In these recent meetings, those taking part are typically leaders of influential networks, organizations, or congregations, not theologians or scholars but action men (sometimes sharing in the leadership with their wives). They have been meeting not with a bishop and some theologians appointed by the Vatican, but with the pope himself. In line with the character and ministries of these leaders, and the orientation of Pope Francis, the discussion has been action-oriented. If they issue in a document, it will be a document not only affirming shared convictions, but also committing to joint action.

Francis and Justin

We already have one example of a significant initiative arising from the conversations of Pope Francis with a major Christian leader. The new archbishop of Canterbury, Justin Welby, has already had two visits to talk with Francis. The two men quickly struck up a deep rapport. Both have a strong awareness of the Holy Spirit through their experience with the charismatic movement. It is interesting that this close collaboration is happening at a time when one might have expected Catholic–Anglican relations to be less warm, particularly in view of Archbishop Welby's support for women bishops.

But Francis and Justin quickly agreed to launch an initiative to combat human trafficking. They realized that such a campaign to be effective should involve leaders of other faith communities. So on December 2, 2014, in the Vatican a group of religious leaders signed a Joint Declaration against Modern Slavery. While Justin Welby was one of those signing, the whole idea was a Christian initiative arising from Welby's talks with Francis.

On Archbishop Welby's second visit to the Vatican in the summer of 2014, he took with him the Revd. Nicky Gumbel, rector of Holy Trinity parish, Brompton, London, the director of the Alpha course. Justin Welby had been a member of Gumbel's parish in London many years before, where he was deeply impacted by the Alpha course, before going off to theological college. Again, Nicky Gumbel is one of the Christian world's movers and shakers, a man combining great vision with organizational skills. In the case of this visit, there was more background than with the Evangelical and Charismatic leaders from the USA. From an early stage in the promotion of the Alpha course, Gumbel had sought to reach the Catholic Church. With the Catholic emphasis on the New Evangelization, especially since the ministry of Benedict XVI,[11] the Alpha course has been increasingly received in Catholic contexts as a major resource. Many Catholics, including bishops from different continents have taken part in Alpha promotion courses in London. Gumbel had already visited Rome to meet with several heads of Vatican offices, and had been warmly received. He has also been a friend for some years of Fr. Raniero Cantalamessa, who has been a much appreciated guest at HTB's staff summer camps in England. As a result of all these

---

11. Benedict XVI intensified the focus on a New Evangelization through setting up a Pontifical Council for the New Evangelization (2010) and choosing the New Evangelization as the agenda for the Synod of Bishops held in the fall of 2012.

developments, the Alpha course is now more widely used in the Catholic Church than in any other Christian communion.[12]

The New Direction

When we look at all these developments, we can see some common threads and a common direction. They represent a decisive move toward praying and working together as brothers.[13] If we want to understand the thinking of Francis, I suggest a careful reading of his message to the Pentecostals gathered in Caserta on July 28, 2014.

The Caserta Message

Francis begins by picking up on the welcoming words of his brother, Pastor Giovanni Traettino. He moves from Christians being "in the presence of Jesus" to "walking" in the presence of Jesus. Committed Christians are on a journey together. Walking together leads to brotherhood. Here we have Francis's model for ecumenical leadership: walking together purposefully as brothers with *parrhēsia* (boldness).

When we do not walk and we stop, we watch each other too closely, and this leads to division. This is not the work of the Holy Spirit, but of Satan, "the father of envy." Here as often with Francis we can detect Jesuit echoes of the Spiritual Exercises of St. Ignatius. So Francis asks, what does the Holy Spirit make? "The Holy Spirit creates 'diversity' in the Church. . . . [T]his diversity is so rich, so beautiful. But then the same Holy Spirit creates unity, and this way the Church is one in diversity." He refers to a Protestant author he loves very much, advocating " a diversity 'reconciled' by the Holy Spirit."[14] The Spirit "creates the diversity of charismata and then makes harmony of the charismata."

Francis then took up a word of the pastor about the incarnation. "The incarnation of the Word is at the foundation: it is Jesus Christ! God and man, Son of God and Son of man, true God and true man. . . . It is the mystery of Christ's flesh: one doesn't understand love for thy neighbour,

---

12. Statement made by Revd. Nicky Gumbel to the author in January, 2012.

13. I use the word "brother" rather than "brother and sister" because Pope Francis is speaking about "his brothers," even though some were accompanied to the Vatican by their wives-partners in ministry.

14. This is almost certainly a reference to Cullmann, *Unity*.

one doesn't understand love for thy brother, if one doesn't understand the mystery of Incarnation. I love my brother because he too is Christ, is Christlike, is the flesh of Christ. I love the poor, the widow, the slave, those in prison . . . ."

Francis then asked forgiveness of the Pentecostals for the persecution of Pentecostals in Italy under Fascism in the 1920s and 1930s.[15] "I ask your forgiveness for those Catholic brothers and sisters who understood and were tempted by the devil and did the same thing as Joseph's brothers."

Francis continued: "the truth is an encounter, an encounter between people. Truth is not found in a laboratory, it is found in life, seeking Jesus in order to find it." He then spoke of this encounter with the Pentecostals. "This encounter is beautiful. This encounter fills us with joy, with enthusiasm." He mentioned the first encounter of Andrew and John with Jesus. It was an encounter that transforms; all else follows from that encounter. Finally, he returns to this image of walking. "We are on this path of unity, between brothers and sisters."[16]

The message of Francis is not indifferentism, i.e., it doesn't matter what church we belong to. He is clear that he is addressing believing Christians with an evident love for Jesus and a real openness to the Holy Spirit. His willingness to welcome Evangelical-charismatic guests for serious discussions and to visit a Pentecostal church follows a discernment of spirits, an approach Francis learned from the Spiritual Exercises of Ignatius of Loyola. He is not examining the details of the doctrine held by these Evangelicals he is meeting; he is discerning whether they are people who stake their lives on the incarnation and the redemption, and who are sensitive to the moving of the Holy Spirit. When he finds Christians who very evidently know and love Jesus, Son of God and Son of man, and Christians who are open to the Holy Spirit, he recognizes brothers, brothers who are on the same journey. He wants to walk with them, to testify with them, to serve with them.

With real encounter in the Lord, there is transformation—it results from walking together and leads to walking together. We go out together—to the extremities, to the needy, to the suffering world.

Francis is not bothered by the fact that these brothers and sisters may be very different to committed Catholics. He rejoices in the diversity as a richness coming from the creativity of the Holy Spirit. He looks first in

15. Pastor Giovanni Traettino wrote his doctoral dissertation on the persecution of the Italian Pentecostals by the Mussolini government assisted by the Catholic Church.

16. Francis, Address.

what is different and unfamiliar for the creative grace-filled work of God. What he opposes is the arrogance that makes our church, our group, our theology, the measure for everything else. This is what he calls "spiritual worldliness." He opposes the spirit of division that makes diversity grounds for opposition and rejection. Rejoicing together in the God-given differences brings a great joy and freedom. As we welcome the diversity and celebrate its beauty, the Holy Spirit is shaping a wonderful harmony to the glory of the Father.

What Will This Mean in Practice?

We can expect many new initiatives of the Catholic Church working together with these Evangelical and Pentecostal leaders on all the issues dear to the heart of Francis: evangelization; making Jesus known; spreading the Word of God; addressing the needs of the suffering and the dispossessed, of refugees and victims of war; challenging the world economic system and the culture of greed; caring from and learning from the aged and elderly; defending the family and marriage.

The ecumenical dialogues will continue. But they will have a different context. They will no longer be the principal encounter between separated churches and communions. They will take place between communities of faith that are more and more engaged together in the church's mission in the world. The new context will involve deeper relationships across confessional divides and a greater recognition of how theology, also in past centuries, arises out of and is influenced by the situations of conflict, rivalry, and self-justification. All this will invigorate the dialogues. It will facilitate humble confession of the ways the Christian communities have sinned against God and each other, also in the area of theology and teaching. There will be a bringing together of testimony and theology, as has already been happening in the GCF.

Francis and Charismatic Renewal

The high level contacts between leading figures in the Pentecostal-charismatic world and the pope indicates how the Pentecostal-charismatic outpouring of the Holy Spirit from the twentieth century is finally having an impact on ecumenical relations. I suggest that with Pope Francis the charismatic renewal is moving center stage in the Catholic Church. Many of his spiritual emphases are those of the Renewal: personal knowledge of Jesus, openness to the workings of the Holy Spirit, the importance of strong praise. But it should be added that he brings other emphases that have not particularly characterized CCR as a whole: the primacy of the poor and dispossessed, human solidarity, humility.

That Francis is bringing charismatic renewal to the center can be seen most clearly from his two addresses in 2014 to CCR leaders: in the Olympic stadium in Rome on June 1 to fifty-two thousand people, and on October 31 to leaders in the Catholic Fraternity of Charismatic Covenant Communities and Fellowships. In both these addresses, Francis used the term "baptism in the Holy Spirit," for the first time in papal utterances.[17] On both occasions, he said: "Share baptism in the Holy Spirit with everyone in the church."[18] Another papal first was Francis's insistence at both gatherings on the ecumenical character of the Renewal. In the November meeting, he said, "Do not forget your origins, do not forget that the Charismatic Renewal is, by its very nature, ecumenical."[19] At a third meeting with CCR in July 2015, Pope Francis expanded on these same points.

These reflections suggest that what is new in ecumenical relations with the advent of Pope Francis can be seen as the contribution of the charismatic movement to Christian unity, fully embraced and preached by a pope for the first time. In the sphere of ecumenism, the call of Francis for a "pastoral and missionary conversion of the church,"[20] means a conversion in ecumenical relations.[21]

Perhaps we could speak of "a baptized in the Spirit ecumenism." This conversion-transformation is that witnessed in baptism in the Holy Spirit. A baptized in the Spirit ecumenism will emphasize the role of the Holy Spirit in the life and mission of Jesus, and his role as risen Lord pouring out the Holy Spirit without limit on his disciples. A "baptized in the Spirit ecumenism" is one in which Jesus is recognized and honored as the living Lord

---

17. Previously those responsible in the Vatican had been very cautious about Catholics using this terminology, a caution evident in the planning and administration of a consultation held in March 2011 during the preparation of the ICCRS booklet *Baptism in the Holy Spirit*. See also comments in chapter 5.

18. Francis, address to CFCCCF, Oct. 31, 2014. The earlier address on June 1, 2014, the wording was: "I expect you to share with everyone in the church the grace of baptism in the Holy Spirit."

19. Francis, address to CFCCCF.

20. EN, 25.

21. See chapter 12 on a Second Paradigm Change for Catholic Ecumenism.

who even now is guiding and forming his church. It is an ecumenism that sees other Christians first as bearers of treasures from the Holy Spirit. It is an ecumenism that seeks first the leading of the Holy Spirit, and then obeys this leading. It is this soaked-in-the-Spirit church that is God's answer to the "spiritual worldliness" criticized by Francis on numerous occasions.[22]

22. "Spiritual worldliness, which hides behind the appearance of piety and even love for the Church, consists in seeking not the Lord's glory but human glory and personal well-being." (EG, 93).

CHAPTER 12

A Second Paradigm Change
for Catholic Ecumenism?

IN THIS CHAPTER I suggest that under Pope Francis a second paradigm change is taking place in the Catholic approach to Christian unity. For this purpose I examine in turn: (1) the Catholic position prior to the acceptance of the ecumenical movement; (2) the first paradigm change pioneered by the Abbé Paul Couturier (1881–1953), later endorsed by the Second Vatican Council; (3) a second paradigm change through Pope Francis; and (4) a retrospective look at the fifty years between the Second Vatican Council and Pope Francis indicating ways in which the second paradigm shift was being prepared.

The Catholic Position Prior to the Acceptance
of the Ecumenical Movement

This section does not need much elaboration. The official position of the Catholic Church prior to the Second Vatican Council was that Christian unity could only be realized by the return of all separated Christian bodies to the Roman obedience.

In fact, at the end of the first decade of the twentieth century when the ecumenical movement was taking shape among some Protestants, a prayer initiative for Christian unity was founded by an American, Paul Wattson, who launched the Church Unity Octave. Though Wattson was an Episcopalian priest at that point, within a year he and the small community he had founded had been received into the Roman Catholic communion.[1]

---

1. That community was and is still known as the Franciscan Friars of the Atonement

Wattson's Church Unity Octave was explicitly prayer for the return of all separated Christians to Rome and quickly received an endorsement from Pope Benedict XV.

In the 1920s, there were two major international ecumenical conferences of Protestants and some Orthodox: the Life and Work conference at Stockholm (1925), and the Faith and Order conference in Lausanne, Switzerland (1927). In 1928 Pope Pius XI issued an encyclical letter, *Mortalium Animos*, rejecting the ecumenical movement in rather unfortunate terms and repeating return to Rome as the only solution:

> So, Venerable Brethren, it is clear why this Apostolic See has never allowed its subjects to take part in the assemblies of non-Catholics: for the union of Christians can only be promoted by promoting the return to the one true Church of Christ of those who are separated from it, for in the past they have unhappily left it.[2]

The First Paradigm Change

The outstanding ecumenical pioneer and "author" of the first paradigm change was the Abbé Paul Couturier, a priest school-teacher from Lyon, France. Couturier first became aware of the tragedy of Christian division through his pastoral work for refugees from the Russian revolution of 1917. He was impressed by the piety of many Russian Orthodox exiles. During the 1920s Couturier became increasingly uneasy with the missionary approach of those Catholics who saw the plight of the Russian refugees as an opportunity to make them Catholics. Following a visit to the Benedictine unity monastery at Amay in Belgium in 1932,[3] Couturier dedicated his life to promoting prayer for Christian unity. He was ill at ease with the Church Unity Octave of Fr. Wattson, as he felt in his heart that all Christians must be able to pray for unity in the same way. It was clear that hardly any Protestants or Orthodox would or could participate in the Octave based on the return to Rome model. So Couturier sought the light of the Lord, and he received his answer from the prayer of Jesus in John 17:21, "that they may all be one, even as you, Father, are in me and I am in you." All Christians could

---

with its headquarters in Graymoor, NY.

2. MA, 10. For another citation from MA indicating its hostile tone, see chapter 2, note 19.

3. The monastery later moved to Chevetogne in the Ardennes.

unite themselves to the prayer of Jesus for unity. From this point, Couturier promoted a form of prayer based on John 17:21, in which Christians prayed for "the unity that God wants, when he wants, and by the means that he wants." He called this observance "The Week of Prayer for the Unity of Christians."[4]

In fact, in seeking a way for all Christians to pray for unity, Couturier launched a paradigm change in the Catholic approach to ecumenism. It was a change from a church-centered understanding to one that was Christ-centered. It was not a change from church-centered to an individualistic Christ-centered position, but from an institutional church-centered approach to an ecclesial Christ-centered model.

Several related themes characterized Couturier's teaching on prayer for unity: deep penitence for all sins against unity; spiritual emulation of other Christians; love comes before truth; Catholic responsibility to take the lead; the need for "une théologie priante" (theology "on our knees"). Couturier's teaching was taken seriously in several monasteries, convents, and spiritual centers. One such place was the monastery of Grottaferrata, near Rome, where a Trappistine sister from Sardinia was led to consecrate her life to Christian unity. Sister Gabriella Maria Sagheddù was beatified by John Paul II in 1987.[5]

As the Abbé Couturier was beginning his ministry for unity, another French priest was providing a theological basis for a new approach to ecumenism, the young Dominican, Père Yves Congar (1904–95). In a letter to Congar, Couturier had written of "our different ways, only in part, and more complementary than different."[6]

Thirty years later, ten years after Couturier's death, his teaching on spiritual ecumenism was endorsed by the Second Vatican Council. Within the Decree on Ecumenism, it is in chapter 2, "The Practice of Ecumenism," that key paragraphs breathe the spirit and teaching of the Abbé Couturier. In this chapter the key points are:

---

4. Since this week was first observed in this form in France, I translate its title from the French, not using the usual English form "Christian unity" which is more impersonal. So, the official title of the Pontifical Council responsible for promoting ecumenism is *Pontificium Consilium ad Unitatem Christianorum fovendam* [Pontifical Council for the Promotion of the Unity of Christians]. The dates for the Week of Prayer were the same as those for the Church Unity Octave, January 18 to January 25 each year.

5. See Cusack, *Blessed Gabriella*.

6. Congar, "L'abbé Paul Couturier," 49.

1. The church is always in constant need of reform as an institution composed of human beings.[7]

2. All true ecumenism is based on conversion of heart, on all Christians and Christian communities becoming more like Jesus: "There can be no ecumenism worthy of the name without interior conversion."[8]

3. "This change of heart and holiness of life, along with public and private prayer for the unity of Christians, should be regarded as the soul of the whole ecumenical movement, and merits the name, 'spiritual ecumenism.'"[9]

In effect what Couturier understood as the foundational principles of prayer for unity, the Council fathers understood as foundational for the renewal of the whole life of the church, namely the modeling of everything on the person and life of Jesus.

Since the Council, an important contribution has been made by the Groupe des Dombes, a theological group of Catholics and Protestants launched by Couturier, who pray and study together for a week each year. Since the 1970s, the Groupe des Dombes has produced several remarkable ecumenical documents, of which one of the most important is "Pour La Conversion des Eglises."[10]

A Second Paradigm Shift with Pope Francis

Already in the spring of 2015 it is possible to affirm credibly that with Pope Francis a second paradigm shift is taking place in regard to the Catholic understanding of the ecumenical task. It may still be too soon to make definitive statements concerning this shift, not only because Francis has only served two years as pope, but also because he has not issued any teaching document directly dealing with ecumenism. But there are many illuminating comments in homilies and addresses, together with many meetings with other Christians, sometimes of an unprecedented kind. As Austen Ivereigh shows in his biography, all the actions and teachings of Francis

---

7. UR, 6.

8. UR, 7.

9. UR, 8.

10. English title: *For the Conversion of the Churches.*

flow from a profoundly thought-out and life-tested synthesis of Christian and Catholic discipleship of Jesus.[11]

We can note three major differences between the first paradigm shift and the second. First, whereas the first paradigm shift was a real conversion, an abandonment of the earlier model, a dying to the institutional church-centeredness, the second paradigm shift is of a different kind. It is not an abandonment of the ecumenism of Couturier and the Second Vatican Council to embrace an alternative model. It is a deepening, a deeper unfolding of what was already present in the first change. But to many Catholics it appears even more revolutionary, because they had not truly grasped the radicality of the first paradigm change through Couturier and the Second Vatican Council.

Secondly, there is in this change an elevation of the role of the Holy Spirit. This can be illustrated by comparing a statement from John Paul II in *Ut Unum Sint* with one from Pope Francis in *Evangelii Gaudium*. Both are original and creative statements, and the second would probably not have been possible without the first. The first from John Paul II: "Dialogue is not simply an exchange of ideas. In some way it is always an 'exchange of gifts.'"[12] This was a clear recognition that the Catholic Church can learn from other Christian communions. The second citation is from Francis: "If we really believe in the abundantly free working of the Holy Spirit, we can learn so much from one another! It is not just about being better informed about others, but rather about reaping what the Spirit has sown in them, which is also meant to be a gift for us."[13] Francis is introducing an approach in which the action of the Holy Spirit is primary, expressed in the sowing image, but in which we have a responsibility, to reap what the Spirit has sown among the others.

Thirdly, another difference concerns our ecumenical partners. The Abbé Couturier had developed relations first with the Orthodox, and then strongly with classical Protestants: Anglicans, Lutherans, and Reformed. The major opening with Francis is to the Evangelicals and the Pentecostals. Of course, Pope Francis is leading the Catholic Church in a very different situation in world Christianity from the 1930s. But we should recognize that the expansion of Catholic ecumenism from what we may call "mainline dialogue" to include a wide variety of free churches, many of whom

11. Ivereigh, *Great Reformer*.

12. UUS, 28.

13. EG, 246.

Catholics had earlier dismissed as "sects," has to be a very significant development, whose spiritual and theological implications we need to consider. This widening of ecumenical relationships is itself the fruit of the heightened focus on the Holy Spirit.

An Ecumenism of the Holy Spirit

In this second paradigm shift, the elevation of the Holy Spirit is necessarily also an elevation of Jesus. In the first paradigm shift there was a strong conversion to a Christ-centeredness. Pope Francis draws from this Christ-centeredness two practical principles: first an experiential existential emphasis in relation to the person of Jesus—the absolute necessity for every Christian of a living relationship with Jesus; second, a deep faith in and a total openness to the working of the Holy Spirit.

The Knowledge of Jesus

I will only cite some striking comments of the pope, even though many more examples could be given. Francis says that knowing about Jesus through the Catechism "is not enough": knowing him with the mind is a step in the right direction, but "in order to know Jesus, we need to enter into a dialogue with him. By talking with him, in prayer, on our knees. If you don't pray, if you don't talk to Jesus, you don't know him. It is by following him, by going with him, by walking with him, by travelling along the road of his ways. If you know Jesus with these three languages: of mind, heart and action, then you can say that you know Jesus."[14] Another word he spoke in Assisi: "being a Christian means having a living relationship with the person of Jesus; it means putting on Christ, being conformed to him."[15] In order to know Jesus, "what is needed is not a study of notions but rather a life as a disciple."[16]

Openness to the Holy Spirit

I cite a characteristic passage from *Evangelii Gaudium*:

14. Daily Meditation, Sept. 26, 2013.
15. Homily at Mass in Assisi, Oct. 4, 2013.
16. Daily Meditation, Feb. 20, 2014.

> Yet there is no greater freedom than that of allowing oneself to be guided by the Holy Spirit, renouncing the attempt to plan and control everything to the last detail, and instead letting him enlighten, guide, and direct us, leading us wherever he wills. The Holy Spirit knows well what is needed in every time and place. This is what it means to be mysteriously fruitful![17]

For Francis, openness to the Holy Spirit and being led by the Spirit are intrinsic to living under the lordship of Jesus. Handing over our control to the Lord through the Holy Spirit is the only way for our lives to be Christ-centered.

Besides this emphasis on openness to the Holy Spirit, Pope Francis is repeatedly speaking about the creativity and newness of the Holy Spirit,[18] the surprises of the Holy Spirit,[19] the diversity that the Holy Spirit forms and then brings into harmony,[20] and to have no fears of where the Spirit may lead.

All these references to the Holy Spirit express the conviction that the Spirit of God is an active agent. For Francis, the Holy Spirit is not just an invisible power behind the scenes—necessary but intangible—but One who inspires and initiates, One who creates, and One who shapes what has been created, One who prods and corrects, One who guides and protects, One whose activity can be recognized and discerned.

Mission to the Extremities

This combination of personal relationship to Jesus as Lord and of openness to the Holy Spirit produces two further characteristics of Francis: the necessity to "go out" to the margins and the extremities, the centrality of mission, and the importance of communion. He is calling for "a pastoral and missionary conversion" of the whole church.[21] "I dream of a 'missionary option,' that is, a missionary impulse capable of transforming everything, so that the Church's customs, ways of doing things, times and schedules,

17. EG, 280.

18. See address to new ecclesial movements May 18, 2013; daily meditations at Mass: July 6, 2013; Oct. 13, 2013; Jan. 20, 2014.

19. See Pentecost homily May 19, 2013; daily meditation at Mass Oct. 13, 2014.

20. See EG, 117–18,131,230. See also address to Pentecostal church in Caserta, July 28, 2014.

21. EG, 25.

language and structures can be suitably channeled for the evangelization of today's world rather than for her self-preservation."[22] This going out flows directly from the encounter with Jesus: "Its [the church's] joy in communicating Jesus Christ is expressed both by a concern to preach him to areas in greater need and in constantly going forth to the outskirts of its own territory or toward new sociocultural settings."[23]

But this going out in mission requires communion and leads to communion:

> One other consideration we must never forget is that the most precious good, the seal of the Holy Spirit, is communion. This is the supreme blessing that Jesus won for us on the Cross, the grace which the Risen Christ continually implores for us as he reveals to the Father his glorious wounds, "As you, Father, are in me, and I in you, may they also be in us, so that the world may believe that you have sent me" (John 17:21). For the world to believe that Jesus is Lord, it needs to see communion among Christians.[24]

Commentators have rightly understood that for Francis the going out to the periphery, the extremities, and the margins, means the preferential option for the poor, the dispossessed, and the suffering. But it has not been widely seen that this going out includes going out to those regarded as on the periphery or the margins of the Christian world. This is very central to an ecumenism of the Spirit. It is about a communion in the Spirit, of being brothers and sisters in the Lord, who share in his gifts. So when Pope Francis visited a Pentecostal church in Caserta at the end of July last year, he speaks of them as his brothers—brothers who are on a journey together. He had used the same language in the famous video message to an Evangelical conference in the USA earlier in 2014.[25]

A New Ecumenical Methodology?

These fresh emphases point to a transformation in ecumenical method. In order to formulate what this new method might be, I suggest that an axiom articulated by Pope Francis in *Evangelii Gaudium* may be a helpful starting

22. EG, 27.

23. EG, 30.

24. Francis, Address to Third World Congress.

25. For these two examples, see chapter 11.

point: "Realities are more important than ideas."[26] A variation is found later in the same section: "Realities are greater than ideas."[27] This principle can also be stated: "Relationships are more important than theories." So what does this mean in terms of the relative importance of relationships of communion on the one hand and Christian doctrine on the other hand? At the very least, it calls for a change in mentality.

With the first paradigm change, the Abbé Couturier was accused of disloyalty to Rome and of indifferentism (it doesn't matter what church you belong to as long as you love Jesus). Some Catholics troubled by the direction being taken by Pope Francis clearly fear that he is opening the door to relativism, and undermining the doctrines of the church. But close attention to his messages shows that this is far from the case. Francis is clear that doctrine matters. He says about this principle concerning reality and ideas: "There has to be continuous dialogue between the two, lest ideas become detached from realities."[28] Ideas become detached from realities when the Holy Spirit is left out of the picture. Francis explains this relationship further in relation to the incarnation: "This principle has to do with incarnation of the word and its being put into practice. . . . The principle of reality, of a word already made flesh and constantly striving to take on flesh anew, is essential to evangelization."[29] But it is through the Holy Spirit that the word takes on flesh, and through the Holy Spirit that it keeps taking on flesh anew.

In the light of these thoughts, I return to this second paradigm change in ecumenical method. In the past, approaching other Christian traditions and communions, Catholics typically started from doctrines and statements of faith. On this basis, Catholics were closest to those who shared a greater part of Catholic teaching and who were closer in practice, and Catholics were further from those who shared less at these levels. This meant that the Catholic Church is closest to the Orthodox Churches, whose sacraments we recognize, and furthest from the free churches, which lack any liturgical framework. According to these criteria, the Catholic Church is at the opposite end of the scale from the Pentecostals and new church charismatics. In terms of classical sacramental theology, we attached the greatest importance to the *sacramentum*, the visible signs of liturgy and sacraments.

26. EG, 231–33.

27. EG, 233.

28. EG, 231.

29. EG, 233.

What is Changing?

Francis does not look first at the externals, the outward forms—doctrines, ordained ministries, liturgies. It is not that these do not matter, but he looks first at people's hearts; he asks "Do they know Jesus?" "Do they bear witness to Jesus?" "Are they fellow travelers on the journey?" "Do they manifest the life and dynamic of the Holy Spirit?" When the answer is Yes, there is a basis for serious prayer together and for a fraternal communion in the Holy Spirit.

This could appear to be a privileging of subjective expressions of faith over objective creeds, and a downgrading of liturgy and the sacraments. But this would be a mistaken conclusion. What Francis is affirming is (1) the outward structures exist to mediate the life of Jesus in the power of the Holy Spirit; (2) this life can be present and should be honored among those who love and believe in the Scriptures, even those outside the traditional structures. This point about the Scriptures is very basic, because the Evangelical Christians welcomed by Francis know and love Jesus, because they know and love the Word of God.

Starting from Jesus, the Holy Spirit, and fraternal communion, the focus is on what has been called the *res sacramenti*, the spiritual reality that the sacraments mediate and for which they are celebrated. The recognition at Vatican II that the Holy Spirit was at work in other Christian communities of faith, even those in Catholic eyes without valid orders and sacraments, has opened the door to see that deep faith in Jesus and openness to the Holy Spirit can and does exist in Christian bodies whose ordained ministries the Catholic Church does not recognize. Indeed, it is possible that the Spirit can be more deeply received and at work in such churches and fellowships than in parts of the Catholic and Orthodox Churches that have more of the God-given structures and that doctrinally and structurally transmit more of the apostolic heritage.

How do we apply the axiom "Realities are more important than ideas" to the issue of the Eucharist for example? What is reality and what are ideas when we speak of the Eucharist and the real presence? I see the emphasis of Francis as pointing to fully lived out faith in Jesus through the power of the Spirit. I suggest that for him the reality of the Eucharist is not the real presence in the consecrated elements separated from everything else, but the total reality of communion in Christ through the Spirit lived to the fullest in the whole eucharistic celebration within which Jesus feeds his people with his body and his blood.

The emphasis on personal knowledge of Jesus greatly facilitates relationships with Evangelicals and Pentecostals, for whom such a relationship is foundational. However, the pope's teaching about the Lord and the Spirit differs somewhat from characteristic Evangelical and Pentecostal presentations. It is more communitarian and ecclesial, and it is integrated with his teaching on the preferential option for the poor. When the Evangelicals and Pentecostals pray and talk with the pope, they can receive from him as a gift from the Spirit the emphases that they lack, while the pope receives something else of the Spirit from them.

We should also note the teaching of Francis on diversity: the Holy Spirit first creates diversity, and then forms a wonderful harmony from this amazing diversity. In one talk, he compared this diversity leading to harmony with a large orchestra using a vast array of different instruments.[30] So from this perspective, Francis speaks of "reconciled diversity."[31] As seasoned ecumenists well know, "reconciled diversity" is the term used by a number of Protestant ecumenical leaders, especially Lutheran and Reformed, to their vision of unity, that was formulated in the Leuenberg agreement of 1973. They will know too that the Catholic authorities, e.g., Cardinals Kasper and Koch, have insisted that for the Catholic Church "reconciled diversity" is insufficient as a goal for ecumenism, which must remain full organic communion. Is there a contradiction between Francis and the two Cardinals? Not really. Francis is describing the process of reconciliation; he is not replacing organic communion as the ultimate goal by reconciled diversity. Nonetheless, this is a significant development, and can also portend future shifts in ecumenical methodology. At the very least, it starts by viewing diversity as positive, rather than as a potential problem. What needs to be eliminated is not diversity, but hostility and opposition. Secondly, it assumes that immediate progress is possible—through changed relationships. Thirdly, in the process of acceptance of diversity, respect grows and the Holy Spirit has room to change hearts and to pull down barriers. This approach of Francis refuses to allow the final goal of full organic communion to seem so remote and impossible that it becomes discouraging.

30. "When I think of charismatics, I think of the Church herself, but in a particular way: I think of a great orchestra, where all the instruments and voices are different from one another, yet all are needed to create the harmony of the music." (Francis, Address to CCR).

31. "Diversity is a beautiful thing when it can constantly enter into a process of reconciliation and seal a sort of cultural covenant resulting in a 'reconciled diversity.'" (EG, 230).

As we see the ecumenical approach of Francis developing, we see that he starts with different questions and assumptions from those that have largely prevailed until now. He recognizes that the Holy Spirit is already at work as the principal agent of unity. He looks first at what the Holy Spirit is already doing, and he trusts the Holy Spirit to give light as to how to flow with what the Holy Spirit has already begun—fully open to the surprises of the Spirit.

Pope Francis has spoken of his approach as "spiritual ecumenism." This has the advantage of connecting it with the Decree on Ecumenism and with *Ut Unum Sint*, that strongly commended spiritual ecumenism rooted in conversion of heart, as taught by the Abbé Couturier. But it can obscure what is new in the approach of Francis compared with Couturier and the Second Vatican Council.

A Retrospective Look at Fifty Years between Vatican II and Pope Francis

In retrospect, it is not difficult to see ways in which the Holy Spirit has been preparing the Catholic Church for this second paradigm change since the time of the Second Vatican Council.

First, the choice of the theme of Evangelization for the Synod of Bishops in 1974 and the ensuing document *Evangelii Nuntiandi* of Paul VI (1975) was launching the process of the church "going out," that is then developed in a particular way in the New Evangelization of John Paul II and Benedict XVI. With Francis it connects with the call to conversion of heart (the characteristic of spiritual ecumenism) and becomes more pro-grammatic for renewal with the pope's call for "a pastoral and missionary conversion of the church."[32] Instead of the New Evangelization being seen as another new task, albeit very important, it now becomes an element in this ecclesial conversion that is authentic renewal.

Second, in the light of the new developments with Pope Francis, we can see John Paul II's encyclical *Ut Unum Sint* as a stage of development between the conciliar decree on ecumenism and Francis. John Paul II gave great prominence to prayer together: "Along the ecumenical path to unity, pride of place certainly belongs to common prayer, the prayerful union of

---

32. EG, 25.

those who gather together around Christ himself."[33] Particularly important are the most creative elements in *Ut Unum Sint*:

1. the call to confess Catholic sins of the past against unity, and John Paul II's insight into the psychology of humble confession within a process of reconciliation;[34]

2. the importance attributed to an ecumenism of the martyrs;[35]

3. the teaching of John Paul II on the bishop of Rome as the first servant of unity.[36]

Third, the teaching of John Paul II at Pentecost 1998 on the institutional and charismatic dimensions of the church can also be seen as an important element in this process.[37] In particular, the insistence that the charismatic dimension is necessary to the constitution of the church prepares for the emphasis of Francis on the creativity and the newness of the Holy Spirit.

Fourth, the axiom of Francis, "Realities are more important than ideas,"[38] can be seen as a pithy practical formulation of the switch effected since Vatican II, particularly through the personalist philosophy of John Paul II, from a focus on human nature to the dignity of the human person.[39] For human persons are realities, and human nature is an idea, an intellectual construct.

---

33. UUS, 22.

34. UUS, 35.

35. Francis has spoken to the Renewal communities about "the ecumenism of blood we experience today." So the pope says, "For persecutors, we are not divided, we are not Lutherans, Orthodox, Evangelicals, Catholics . . . No! We are one in their eyes! For persecutors we are Christians! They are not interested in anything else." (Address to CFCCCF, Oct. 31, 2014).

36. UUS, 94.

37. See chapter 13.

38. EG, 231–33.

39. First in the Vatican II document GS, Part I, chapter I.

PART V

Concluding Reflection

CHAPTER 13

From Azusa via Rome to Zion

MY ENTRY INTO THE charismatic renewal in 1971 quickly led to association with Pentecostals. I understood immediately that the charismatic renewal entering the Catholic Church had come from the Holy Spirit and from the Pentecostals. It had to be that this Pentecostal fire was of vital significance for the church and for the world. A story begins at Azusa Street, the story of a world-wide outpouring of the Holy Spirit that is reversing the journey from Jerusalem via all Judea and Samaria to "the end of the earth" (Acts 1:8).

This journey has to pass through Rome. Why it has to pass through Rome and not terminate in Rome I only began to understand much later. When I was first impacted by Pentecostals, the idea of leaving the Catholic Church never occurred to me, first because I had become a Catholic as a young adult by my own choice. Second, during my seminary training I had been deeply marked by the Second Vatican Council and by Pope John's call for church renewal. Third, I had received a strong heart for Christian unity, and had been influenced by the vision of Catholic ecumenical pioneers, such as Dom Lambert Beauduin OSB, the Abbé Paul Couturier, and Père Yves Congar OP. So I found myself living in a Catholic world, slowly coming to terms with Vatican II, while at the same time discovering the Pentecostal world with its mixture of Holy Spirit fire and sectarian barriers. Bridges had to be built between the Pentecostal movement and the Catholic Church, however improbable this might seem and however difficult to effect.

The Catholic Church needed this new life of the Spirit. My first assumption was that Catholics needed the life, and Pentecostals needed theology. A Catholic-Pentecostal inter-action would bring more life to the Catholics and more theology to the Pentecostals. But the ecumenical significance of charismatic renewal had to be more than facilitating a dialogue between Catholics and Pentecostals. In the initial experience of charismatic renewal, there was an element of profound shared communion between those baptized in the Holy Spirit that added a new dimension to ecumenical encounter.[1] Yet there would be a long road to travel before there could be a transforming encounter between the Pentecostal and the Catholic worlds. The chapters in this book indicate some of the road already traversed, and point to the way that still lies ahead.

Major Catholic and Pentecostal Contrasts

As I came to know the Pentecostals better—both through research of Pentecostal history[2] and through participation in SPS and EPCRA[3]—it became easier to formulate the sharp contrasts between the Catholic and the Pentecostal worlds. At that time I was distinguishing between what I as a Catholic could learn from Pentecostals and what I could not receive. In effect, many elements that could be received from the Pentecostals were already being manifest in the charismatic renewal (baptism in the Holy Spirit, charisms or spiritual gifts, spontaneous praise, evangelistic zeal), though not always possessing the same dynamism. The Pentecostal element that was more strongly in Pentecostal origins than in either CCR or the Pentecostals whom I was meeting was an intense hope and longing for the coming of the Lord in glory.[4] I was aware that a real Pentecostal and Catholic encounter required first a deeper appreciation of the differences. So I single out first those differences that may at first sight appear irreconcilable, but which after almost fifty years of interaction can illustrate the message of Pope Francis that "the unity brought by the Spirit can harmonize every diversity."[5]

1. See chapter 11 and Hocken, *Pentecost.*

2. At one stage in my doctoral studies in Birmingham (1979–84), I thought of making a comparison between the origins of the Pentecostal and the charismatic movements. For a time I studied the origins of both movements in the USA, in Canada, in the UK, and in France. When this became too encyclopaedic, the dissertation topic was narrowed down to the charismatic origins in the UK (Hocken, *Streams*). But much of the unused material later found a place in numerous articles in NIDPCM.

3. In SPS from 1980 and in EPCRA from 1984.

4. I was to encounter this most strongly in the Union de Prière in France from 1989, and in the (unpublished) writings of Pastor Louis Dallière. See later in this chapter.

5. EG, 230.

Different Views of Fullness

Both for Catholics and for Pentecostals, the concept of fullness expresses something of their self-understanding as Christians. In the Catholic tradition, fullness is related to catholicity: catholic means *kat' holon*, according to the whole. The catholicity of the church concerns the whole of time (all epochs) and it extends to the whole world, even to the whole creation. The Catholic Church claims to be the teacher of a fullness of Christian doctrine, that is the fullness of divine revelation made known in Jesus Christ through the Holy Spirit, and to minister the fullness of the means of salvation.[6] By the fullness of the means of salvation have traditionally been understood the seven sacraments (baptism, confirmation, Eucharist; penance or reconciliation, and the anointing of the sick; holy orders, and matrimony). The renewal from the Second Vatican Council has brought sacrament together again with the Word, so that the Word of God is received as an essential element in the fullness of the means of salvation.

Pentecostals also have a concept of fullness. Their message is the "full gospel." In its historical context, full gospel for the Pentecostals meant not only the received Evangelical doctrine of salvation through the cross, but also the full message of Pentecost. For Pentecostals the full gospel proclaims the baptism of the Holy Spirit, which enables the preaching of the gospel with the full power of the Holy Spirit, accompanied by the same signs and wonders as had attended the ministry of the first Christians. Very importantly, full gospel meant the preaching of the imminent second coming of the Lord in the power of the same Spirit. The glorious completion is also part of the good news.

In the received Catholic understanding, the church has always had a fullness (divine revelation, means of salvation), though this fullness has been more strongly manifest in some periods than in others. For Pentecostals, fullness is something that has been restored to Christianity through the Pentecostal movement. The Catholic view of fullness is more structural, the Pentecostal view more pneumatic.

6. "For it is through Christ's Catholic church alone . . . that the fullness of the means of salvation can be obtained." (UR, 3).

Different Understandings of Church History

In their respective understandings of the working of the Holy Spirit in history, Catholics instinctively thought of continuity and succession, of life being handed down from generation to generation. Pentecostals think in terms of discontinuity manifested in new revivals sent from heaven. The Holy Spirit falls, comes down, and springs up; but the Holy Spirit is not handed down.[7]

From the first years of the Pentecostal movement, the concept of the Latter Rain expressed an important part of their self-understanding. The revival at Azusa Street was experienced as "Pentecost" today. It was more than a repetition of the pattern of past revivals, it was an outpouring of the Holy Spirit unprecedented since apostolic times. So early Pentecostals identified this new Pentecost with the latter rain, mentioned in the Scriptures, that comes before the final harvest.[8] This imagery, based on rainfall patterns in the land of Israel, both expressed their faith in the original abundance of Holy Spirit power and their conviction that this was now being bestowed again in a way unparalleled since the origins. Latter Rain means latter days, with the Pentecostal outpouring preparing for the soon-coming of the Lord. This interpretation assumes a very negative view of the spiritual condition of the church throughout the ages. The intervening history between the first century and the twentieth had known no steady seasonal rains. This view was however qualified for the period after the Reformation, which Pentecostals now interpreted as the beginning of restoration preparing the way for the Latter Rain.

From an early stage, Pentecostals understood their movement as the climax of a series of divine restorations. In this view the first stage of restoration was Luther's rediscovery of justification by faith, followed two hundred years later by John Wesley's preaching of holiness (sanctification). A third phase in the late nineteenth century saw the restoration of divine healing, with the work of restoration reaching a climax with the Pentecostal baptism in the Spirit.[9]

---

7. Later new charismatic currents introduced the idea of Holy Spirit *impartation*, which involves transference from one Spirit-filled Christian to others via signs and gestures.

8. See Deut 11:14; Joel 2:23; Jas 5:7.

9. This sequence is found in the first issue of the Azusa Street newssheet, *The Apostolic Faith* Oct. 1906, 1, col. 1.

Many of the new charismatic churches affirm a further phase of restoration, that of the Eph 4:11 ministries, especially the ministries of apostles and prophets. Some understand the contemporary work of the Holy Spirit as supremely the restoration of the New Testament church. In this view, the church is being built again from the foundations up. In its initial formulation it assumed the impossibility of the renewal of inherited church structures.[10]

The contrast between Catholic and Pentecostal readings of church history could hardly be greater. The Catholic Church emphasized apostolic succession uninterruptedly from the time of the apostles to the present generation of bishops, together with the four "marks" that characterize the church in every age: the church is one, holy, catholic, and apostolic. The mark of apostolicity guarantees the identity of the one church throughout all generations:

> The Church is apostolic. She is built on a lasting foundation: "twelve apostles of the Lamb" (Rev 21:14). She is indestructible (cf. Matt 16:18). She is upheld infallibly in the truth: Christ governs her through Peter and the other apostles, who are present in their successors, the Pope and the college of bishops.[11]

In contrast to the pessimistic reading of Pentecostals, the Catholic reading was often triumphalist. The church is the barque of Peter sailing onward through the ages, sometimes or often battered by storms, but with the church always emerging resolute and victorious. This view of church history was eloquently expressed in a well-known Anglican hymn:

> Though with a scornful wonder
> Men see her sore oppressed,
> By schisms rent asunder,
> By heresies distrest,
> Yet saints their watch are keeping,
> Their cry goes up, "How long?"
> And soon the night of weeping
> Shall be the morn of song.
>
> Mid toil and tribulation,
> And tumult of her war,
> She waits the consummation

10. Much use was made of the gospel imagery of old wineskins that cannot hold the new wine.

11. CCC, 869.

Of peace for evermore;
Till with the vision glorious
Her longing eyes are blest,
And the great Church victorious
Shall be the church at rest.[12]

My Personal Re-thinking

I had been introduced to stronger restorationist visions through study of the new charismatic churches.[13] At a time when many Pentecostals are forgetting the restorationist impulses of their origins, the new charismatic churches represent a reviviscence of a restorationist interpretation of Christian history. The new charismatic churches remind us of an important dimension of Pentecostal-charismatic faith, that theological studies of these movements need to take into account.[14] For the data suggests that some form of restorationist vision is inherent in a Spirit-impelled charismatic outpouring upon the church and the churches.

From my studies of the Pentecostal movement and the new charismatic churches, a new question arose in my mind. *Could it be possible for the Catholic Church to receive any elements of a restorationist understanding of church history?* Two issues in particular faced me with this question, the reappearance of the charisms and the rise of the Messianic Jewish movement.

Charisms

With the appearance in CCR of the spiritual gifts (charisms), such as prophecy, healing, and speaking in tongues, the question arose for Catholics as to the existence and role of these gifts in the tradition of the Catholic Church. Charismatic Catholics concerned to defend CCR against accusations of novelty quickly adduced many examples of such phenomena from the Catholic past, especially in the lives of saints and holy people.[15] Much less attention was paid to the role played by such phenomena in the past and to what was genuinely new in their modern manifestations. One obvious dif-

---

12. From the hymn, *The Church's One Foundation* by S. J. Stone (1839–1900).

13. See Hocken, *Streams,*

14. See chapters 6 to 8.

15. See for example Ensley, *Sounds,* in relation to speaking in tongues.

ference in the modern movements is the bestowal of these gifts on millions of ordinary Christians—a stark contrast to the older model of unusual phenomena largely limited to the lives of exceptionally holy and ascetic Christians. For Pentecostals (and also for the new church charismatics) the spiritual gifts are God-given equipment for building up the body of Christ, a very different perspective from the wonders found in the lives of saints.

The question then arises as to when the charisms as God's gifts for building up the body of Christ ceased to play this role as a regular part of the church's life. Answers range from the second to the eighth century.[16] Here all the churches impacted by the charismatic renewal are faced by a restoration issue. This is particularly clear with gifts of healing, whose reappearance has led to the rise of many ministries of healing, some of them recognized by church authorities.[17]

The Messianic Jewish Movement

A second and more dramatic example of restoration would face me in 1989 through my first encounter with the Union de Prière in France and the teachings of their founder, Pastor Louis Dallière (1897–1976). Dallière had encountered the Pentecostal movement in 1930 through an Elim evangelist from Britain.[18] Over the next fifteen years, he developed his understanding of the prophetic purpose of the Lord in the Pentecostal movement in his formulation of four prayer subjects for UP, founded in 1946–47: (1) revival and the conversion of souls; (2) the salvation of the Jewish people;[19] (3) the organic unity of the body of Christ; and (4) the second coming of the Lord and the resurrection of the dead. Dallière saw the first three as

16. "These three centuries saw dramatic changes in the Christian Church. In the midst of all this, the gifts of the Spirit vanished. There came a point around AD 260 at which they no longer fitted in the highly organized, well-educated, wealthy, socially-powerful Christian communities." (Kydd, *Charismatic*, 87). McDonnell by contrast writes that "the witnesses [that the charisms were sought, or expected, and received within the rites of initiation or in relation to them] extend from the end of the second century into the eighth." (*Christian Initiation*, 314). He recognizes however that his study "concentrated on the prophetic charisms." (Ibid., 314).

17. Francis MacNutt wrote a book about the almost total disappearance of the ministry of healing during the history of the church, with the original title having the striking though misleading title, *The Almost Perfect Crime*. There are healing ministries today recognized both by the Catholic Church and within the Anglican communion.

18. Douglas Scott.

19. Later amended to the illumination of Israel.

preparation for the fourth. Dallière's teachings, which I obtained in roneographed form, provided the deepest and most integrated presentation I had yet encountered on spiritual revival, the Jewish people, Christian unity, and the second coming of the Lord.[20] Dallière understood in a profound way that characterized all he did and taught that the vitality and dynamism of the church is directly connected to the strength of its eschatological hope. Because the Jewish people are the bearers of the messianic hope, this eschatological dynamism can only be fully recovered with the healing of the division between the church and Israel.

Before he died, Dallière had heard of the beginnings of the Messianic Jewish movement. I first came across the Messianic Jews during my studies of the charismatic movement in the USA, as most were charismatic believers, now determined to become Jewish disciples of their Messiah and Lord, rather than be assimilated into Gentile churches.[21] From 1995, I began to have regular involvement with Messianic Jews, both in the USA and in Israel. The Messianic Jewish movement raises the restoration issue for all the Christian churches in an even clearer way than the charisms. For the Messianic Jews claim that their movement is a restoration of "the church from the circumcision" (*ecclesia ex Judaeis*), that has not existed since the early centuries of the church. They see their movement as a resurrection of what was dead, referring both to Ezek 37:1–14 (the dry bones of the house of Israel taking on flesh and coming back to life) and to Rom 11:15: "what will their [the Jews] acceptance mean but life from the dead?"

I was blessed to be a participant in the Catholic–Messianic Jewish dialogue from its inception in the year 2000. Rather quickly, this dialogue devoted much attention to ecclesiology.[22] For the Messianic Jews, the big question was the possibility of some kind of Catholic recognition of their movement as a work of God. The core issue was the original constitution of the church as the union of Jew and Gentile in one body through the cross, as presented in Eph 2:12–22, especially verses 14–16. To accept this framework of discussion is to consider a restoration of the Jewish expression of the church. It is significant that this question was not a point of division or of tension between the dialogue participants. For the Catholics

20. Fortunately, a thorough study of the life, ministry, and teaching of Pastor Louis Dallière is nearing completion with the doctoral dissertation of pastor David Bouillon.

21. I first became aware of the Messianic Jews in 1977, when they constituted one grouping among many participating denominations at the Kansas City conference of 1977. See Kinzer, *Searching*, 33–34.

22. For the origins of this dialogue see Kinzer, *Searching*, 35–37.

did not dispute the possibility or the importance of a Jewish expression of Jesus-faith within the one church, but asked about its relationship to the petrine ministry of the bishop of Rome and connection with apostolic succession. A key moment in this process was Mark Kinzer's paper "*Lumen Gentium* through Messianic Jewish eyes" presented in 2008.[23]

The resurrection of a Jewish expression of the church is hardly imaginable without a strong thrust for the Jewish and the Gentiles expressions to be reconciled and brought into communion. The vision for a coming together of the Jewish and the Gentile believers in Christ is at the heart of the initiative Toward Jerusalem Council II, of which I was part from its origin in 1996.[24] All these developments faced me as a Catholic with the role of Jerusalem. It became clear that the journey is not from Azusa to Rome, but from Azusa to Jerusalem (Zion) via Rome.

So in an EPCRA paper in 2014 I stated: "I realized that there was a connection between the loss of the Jewish component of the church, the loss of the spiritual gifts as the equipment of all God's people, and the loss of Christian unity."[25] The reappearance of the charisms as endowments for all Christians, the re-birth of a Jewish expression of the church, and the re-establishment of the unity of the church are inter-connected elements in a major work of restoration.

Re-reading the Period since Vatican II

In reflecting on these developments, we can re-read in a new light some important progress points of the last fifty years, and find in them elements of restoration that were not seen as such at the time.[26]

The Joint Catholic-Lutheran Declaration on Justification by Faith

In October 1999 in Augsburg, Germany, representatives of the Lutheran World Federation and of the Catholic Church signed the Joint Declaration

23. This paper is included in Kinzer, *Israel's Messiah*, 156–74. See also Kinzer, *Searching Her Own Mystery*, chapter 3.

24. See chapters 9 and 10.

25. Hocken, *What Challenges*, 54.

26. The order of presentation relates to the theme of restoration and is not chronological.

on Justification by Faith. This is to date the only official reception by two churches in dialogue of the findings of their respective delegations. As has been mentioned, Pentecostals have seen Luther's teaching on justification by faith as the first in a series of restorations culminating in the Pentecostal outpouring of baptism in the Holy Spirit. With the Joint Declaration of Augsburg, the Catholic Church has accepted the rightness of the teaching on justification in its basic formulation.[27] This acceptance then suggests the question: Can the Catholic Church accept justification by faith as the first step in a restoration series as Pentecostals have later upheld—even though for Catholics the restoration is starting much later in time?

First, justification by faith is a doctrine, which makes it somewhat different from the other elements in Pentecostal schemes of restoration. There is also the question as to what extent Luther's teaching on justification by faith was a restoration. Was there not something new in Luther's formulation— unknown in that form in the first centuries of the church? These considerations suggest that there was an element of development of doctrine; but as such, the Catholic acceptance of justification by faith is an important ecumenical step as a development of doctrine that took shape outside the Roman communion. The element of restoration lies in the understanding of the saving gospel to be preached.

The Charismatic Dimension of the Church

In his Pentecost 1998 address to the new ecclesial movements, John Paul II made a remarkable statement: that at the Second Vatican Council the Catholic Church "rediscovered the charismatic dimension as one of her constitutive elements."[28] The pope was not saying that the charismatic dimension did not exist before Vatican II; that would be demonstrably false. It was a guarded admission that the Catholic Church before Vatican II had an inadequate understanding of her own nature. But is not rediscovery a more modest word for restoration?

While John Paul II did not elaborate on the charismatic dimension of the church, this declaration can be seen in retrospect as preparing the

---

27. The format of the Declaration provides an important model in starting with each point that Lutherans and Catholics hold in common, and then moves to subsidiary aspects on which differences of presentation and emphasis remain and that require further exploration.

28. Pesare, *Then Peter*, 149.

way for the emphasis of Pope Francis on the Holy Spirit, on the Holy Spirit's creativity, and on the diversity inherent in the creative work of the Holy Spirit.[29]

A New Element in the Catechism

There is one section of the Catechism of the Catholic Church that goes significantly beyond the teaching of Vatican II. It appears in the teaching on the end times and the second coming of the Lord. Here the church recognizes that the eschatological completion requires first the coming of the Jewish people to faith in Jesus their Messiah:

> The glorious Messiah's coming is suspended at every moment of history until his recognition by "all Israel," for "a hardening has come upon part of Israel" in their "unbelief" toward Jesus. . . . The "full inclusion" of the Jews in the Messiah's salvation, in the wake of "the full number of the Gentiles," will enable the People of God to achieve "the measure of the stature of the fullness of Christ," in which "God may be all in all."[30]

The conciliar and post-conciliar Catholic teaching on the Jewish people effects two break-throughs: first, in relation to the origins, in an implicit recognition that the church lost something significant at an early stage; and secondly, in relation to the end-times, that elements of restoration are needed.

Repentance for the Sins of the Past

As part of the church's preparations for the jubilee year 2000, Pope John Paul II called on Catholics to confess the sins of the past. He singled out two categories: sins against the unity of God's people, and sins of intolerance and of "violence in the service of truth."[31] While this appeal did not specifically mention the Jewish people, it is clear that the troubled Jewish-Catholic history was on the pope's mind. As part of the jubilee preparation,

29. See chapter 11.
30. CCC, 674.
31. TMA, 34–35.

John Paul II established two study commissions of scholars, one to study the Anti-Judaism in Christian history, and the other the Inquisition.[32]

As the jubilee year approached, John Paul II proposed the "purification of memory" as the goal for all work of reconciliation.[33] While there was now a clear recognition that this purification of memory was needed for the whole history of Catholic relations with the Jewish people, the appearance of the Messianic Jews raises a further dimension. It is no longer just a question of Catholic mistreatment of the Jews and the history of contempt. It faces the church with the disappearance of the church of the circumcision, the *ecclesia ex Judaeis*, and the subsequent history of outlawing any such Jewish expression of faith in Jesus.

The Catholic confession now has to be extended to the sins that were particularly directed against Jewish believers in Jesus, especially to the history of forced baptisms that have defiled the symbol of baptism in the eyes of the Sephardic Jews. Since the teaching of Vatican II on the Jewish people and its explicit repudiation of all anti-Semitism,[34] there is a higher Catholic awareness of the great suffering of the Jewish people through the ages. But much less known is (1) the suffering of those Jews who were baptized by force or under coercion against their convictions, particularly but not only in Spain and Portugal, and (2) the suffering of Jewish believers in Jesus who could only become Christians by denying their Jewish identity and ceasing all Jewish practice.

These four examples indicate that elements of restoration form part of the renewal and revitalization of the Catholic Church since the Second Vatican Council. The elements acknowledged are the charisms, including gifts and ministries of healing; a rediscovery of the basic kerygma that alone can make evangelization effective (the restoration element in justification by faith). The element at an earlier stage of reception concerns the place of the Jewish people in God's plan of restoration. Here a taking hold of the full implications of the rediscovery of Israel's election never revoked for the life of the church has been held up because the first priority has been healing the wounds between the church and the synagogue.

32. Each group held a symposium in the Vatican, whose papers have been published. On Anti-Judaism, *Radici* (congress of Oct. 30–Nov. 1, 1997) and on the Inquisition, *L'Inquisizione* (congress of Oct. 29–31, 1998).

33. "The purification of memory" was described as the goal of repentance for the sins of the past by John Paul II in the document *Incarnationis Mysterium* (1998), 11. See also International Theological Commission, *Memory and Reconciliation* (1999).

34. NA, 4.

A Possible Catholic Understanding
of Restoration

The acceptance of elements of restoration into a Catholic understanding of church history, or theologically of "the age of the church," will form part of a purification from triumphalism, and a deeper recognition of the pilgrim character of the church on her journey toward the eschatological completion.[35]

A Catholic formulation of restoration will be different from Pentecostal and new charismatic versions. First, it will refuse an overwhelmingly negative view of church history. It cannot accept the dispensational theories of the Scofield Bible applied to the church age, with their inherent pessimism, and a serial pattern of divine rejections.[36] Second, it will reject any view with an exaggerated anticipation of the coming kingdom within the church age. The church has already rejected the view of Joachim of Flora, who divided history into ages of the Father, the Son, and the Spirit, with the age of the Spirit beginning during the history of the church. For the Catholic Church, the age of the Spirit is the age of the church between Pentecost and parousia. This does not exclude an intensification of Holy Spirit blessing as the parousia approaches. But the final goal is more than restoration. It is elevation and transformation to glory. Third, it will be more organic. Rather than seeing the restorations as sudden interventions from above without much historical continuity, a Catholic view would situate each restoration within an organic historical process being guided by the Holy Spirit. Fourth, it will see more easily the inter-connectedness of different patterns of restoration. It can recognize the ecumenical and historical significance of Wesley's focus on sanctification, without making it a phase of restoration. Fifth, it would let go of triumphalistic interpretations of Catholic history, and recognize that significant elements were lost or severely weakened in the course of centuries. Christian history manifests ups and downs, and is never simply moving from glory to glory. Sixth, it could well see Pope Francis's reception of baptism in the Spirit as a key moment in the overall process.[37]

---

35. See LG, chapter VII.

36. See the comments on John Nelson Darby and dispensationalism in chapters 4 and 10.

37. See above, and chapter 11.

Entering a New Season

At the origins of the Pentecostal movement, there was widespread agreement that this outpouring from on high was for all people, the whole church, the whole world. This was always the vision of Donald Gee.[38] It was unimaginable that the purpose of the Lord in this twentieth century Pentecost was only for the creation of Pentecostal assemblies and denominations, albeit on a worldwide scale. In the same way, the first participants in CCR instinctively understood that this renewal in the Spirit was for the whole body of Christ. For this reason, major leaders in CCR have never felt comfortable with classifying CCR as one among a number of new ecclesial movements, an administrative classification that comes from the Pontifical Council for the Laity.

In both origins there was a mixture of prophetic instinct and of limited imagination. The prophetic instinct of the Pentecostals was for the universal scope of the Pentecostal revival. But the Pentecostal imagination could not embrace a transformation of historic Christian churches. The prophetic instinct of the first charismatic Catholics was that this renewal was for the whole church. Although many had a sense of the renewal's ecumenical character, their Catholic imagination could not extend to a profound Pentecostal-Catholic encounter of mutual blessing. CCR easily became comfortable with a recognized place within the Catholic Church, and Pentecostal churches have been content to embrace church growth and pray for Holy Spirit revival. The new charismatic networks may have a vision for total church restoration, but in their first and second generation this ambitious vision easily has an exclusivist character and sectarian overtones.

However, there are now signs that the prophetic instincts of the origins are within the realms of possibility beyond the imagination of most pioneers. The break-through point came in March 2013 with the election of Francis as bishop of Rome. At exactly the same time Justin Welby was installed as archbishop of Canterbury.[39] With Francis a wave of new hope has surged through the Catholic Church, not unlike that following the election of John XXIII in 1958. How does this fit into the outpourings of the Holy Spirit in the Pentecostal and charismatic movements and the process of restoration?

38. See chapter 3.

39. Several other major appointments were made around this time: Pope Tawadros II as patriarch of Alexandria of the Copts, and John X Yazigi as patriarch of Antioch.

I suggest that baptism in the Spirit is central to the Francis revolution. In his study of Francis, Austen Ivereigh notes the transformation in him that others noticed when he was prayed over by Pentecostal pastors (and Fr. Cantalamessa) in Buenos Aires in 2006.[40] In two addresses to CCR audiences in 2014, Pope Francis urged them to share the baptism in the Spirit with the whole church.[41] With this statement, the work of the Spirit in the charismatic renewal is not just given a place in Catholic life. It becomes part of the pope's vision for the "pastoral and missionary conversion" of the church.[42] Francis is constantly speaking of the newness and creativity of the Holy Spirit, of the surprises of the Spirit, and the need to be open to the Spirit's leading.[43] So when he writes of Catholics reaping what the Holy Spirit has sown among other Christians,[44] it is highly likely he is including baptism in the Spirit. Since baptism in the Spirit is at the heart of the Pentecostal movement, this development signifies a Catholic reception of the central work of the Holy Spirit among the Pentecostals. This reception has consequences for a positive Catholic acceptance of phases of restoration.

This reception is of course at a very early stage. Most Catholics are not aware of it, nor are the vast majority of Pentecostals. For this break-through to transform Catholic-Pentecostal relations globally, the arrogant Catholic dismissal of Pentecostal churches as sects and deeply-held Pentecostal suspicion of Rome have to change. It is here that the ministry of Francis is breaking down barriers.

First, Francis breaks through the mediation barrier. He has no time for any presentation of Catholic faith that is always focused on instruments of mediation, of church, of sacraments, of hierarchy, and authority. He calls this the "self-referential church," that is sick. He embodies and lives church, he celebrates sacraments, but he speaks directly of God, of Jesus, and of the Holy Spirit.[45] He turns the instruments of mediation to their real purpose, to communicate Jesus Christ in the power of the Spirit. At one stroke his order of priorities undermines the Evangelical opposition to institutional religion. The words, the gestures, the lifestyle, and the priorities of Francis all give the lie to the widespread Evangelical and Pentecostal conviction

40. Ivereigh, *Great Reformer*, 292–93.

41. See chapter 11.

42. EG, 25.

43. See chapter 11.

44. EG, 246.

45. See chapter 12.

that the institutional church will never change, and revival-renewal can only happen in individuals.

Second, Francis brings a distinctively Latin American flair to the leadership of the Catholic Church. It shows how deeply the Catholic leadership had been rooted in and shaped by European history and European assumptions. This distancing from Europe shows itself most dramatically in Francis's refusal of all survivals of papal monarchy and of a royal court. This liberation, together with the Vatican II Declaration on Religious Liberty, demonstrate an abandonment by the Catholic Church of alliances with emperors, kings, and governments. This removes another obstacle to reconciliation with the free churches, who have suffered greatly from church-state alliances in Catholic nations.

Third, the New Evangelization launched by John Paul II and Benedict XVI takes on a different hue with Francis. With his predecessors, the New Evangelization was strongly motivated by the concern to reverse the secularization of Europe and to restore its Christian heritage. With Francis the Eurocentrism has disappeared. It is the whole church that needs to hear the gospel, to be evangelized, and then to evangelize. In *Evangelii Gaudium*, there is no nostalgia for the past, and no vision for restoring a Christian Europe. Francis comes from a country that had lived through its separation from colonial domination, and is well aware of the mixed character of the original evangelization of Latin America through the conquistadores and the Spanish and Portuguese missionaries. This focus on worldwide evangelization also favors relations with Evangelicals and Pentecostals, who have no nostalgia for Christian Europe.

Fourth, Francis comes from a continent that has had to work through the tensions between reforming society and converting people. Here Francis speaks a language Evangelicals and Pentecostals can understand. His preaching is based on the gospels. He speaks simply of Jesus, about the mercy of God, and the poor. He speaks strong words against injustice, exploitation, and greed. But this is in no way a focus on the horizontal to the neglect of the vertical. There is an integration of the personal and the social in Francis that flows from his relationship with the Lord, his openness to the Holy Spirit, and his love for the poor and the suffering. This integrated Christian vision can help the growing number of Pentecostals concerned for social justice to combine this passion with Pentecostal zeal for evangelism and personal salvation.

Fifth, Francis speaks about the opposition of the devil and of evil spirits more than any other pope in a long time.[46] This awareness goes with his openness to the Holy Spirit. The pope's language here connects immediately with Pentecostal sensitivities and approaches.

Sixth, Francis has been meeting personally with major leaders from the Pentecostal and charismatic worlds.[47] These leaders represent vast constituencies. Their meetings with Francis are clearly not just theological discussions. These men are men of action, as is Francis, who has written: "If we concentrate on the convictions we share, and if we keep in mind the principle of the hierarchy of truths, we will be able to progress decidedly toward common expressions of proclamation, service, and witness."[48] So we can expect proposals for acting together in evangelization and mission that will mobilize Pentecostals, Evangelicals, Catholics, and others in a way not yet seen. It is this joint action flowing from the Holy Spirit that will do most to break down the remaining barriers.

For the reception of Francis in the Catholic world, it would seem that there may be greater receptivity in Latin America, Asia, and Africa, even though ecumenism has been less developed on these continents. CCR is a much stronger movement on these continents than in Europe and North America, and is recognized by many bishops as of major significance for the future of the church. In Latin America, CCR has grown to dimensions never seen in North America or Europe, largely unnoticed by the media and academia, that were focused on liberation theology and on Pentecostal growth on a Catholic continent.[49]

While the ecumenical expressions of CCR were largely confined to Europe and the English-speaking world, tensions between Pentecostals and Catholics had been at their highest in Latin America. This makes it all the more significant that the break-through began in Argentina, and that the

---

46. Paul VI (1963–78) spoke about the devil, as did Leo XIII (1878–1903), who composed a prayer to St. Michael archangel against evil spirits that was said at the end of each Mass until Vatican II.

47. See chapter 11.

48. EG, 246.

49. In a study published at the end of his life by a Dominican specialist in Latin America, Fr. Edward Cleary (1929–2011) wrote: "Within Latin America, Catholic Charismatics dwarfed Protestant Pentecostals, being more than twice their numbers. But Catholic Charismatics received far less attention than Protestant Pentecostals for reasons that have not been clear to me." (Rise, x).

Catholic insistence that baptism in the Holy Spirit is inherently ecumenical is coming from a Latin American pope.

Final Reflections

I suggest not only that a restorationist framework is possible to explain modern Catholic developments, but that it is necessary for understanding their significance. Only in this perspective can the church be properly oriented toward the final fulfillment. The Pentecostal distinctive of baptism in the Spirit impacts every dimension of Christian life and orients it to the coming of the Lord. Every restored element contributes to the preparation of the bride for the wedding feast of the Lamb. This conviction suggests that what was initially considered an obstacle to ecumenism, a restoration view of modern Christian history, can turn out to be a major Pentecostal contribution to the full coming together of God's people.

The remaining piece of the puzzle is Israel. Here a significant element in the restoration would appear to be still in an embryonic stage—among Jewish believers in Jesus, among Evangelicals and Pentecostals, in the Catholic Church, and among the Jewish people as a whole. There are many signs of hope here too, with Pope Francis and Archbishop Welby both conscious of the Israel dimension.[50] There would seem to be a connection between phases of restoration in the latter days, and the pattern of the end-times ingathering reversing the initial outgoing. As the gospel goes out from Jerusalem via Samaria to "the end of the earth" (Acts 1:8), the Acts of the Apostles focuses on the journey from Jerusalem to Rome, a city of Jewish exile like Babylon (see 1 Pet 5:13). Similarly, the return journey has to pass through Rome en route for Zion, with the destination exercising a purifying influence on all the Christian voyagers. Only in this way will there be a proper repentance (reversal) for all the deviations of history and the bringing of "the glory and the honor of the nations" to the new Jerusalem that descends from heaven (Rev 21:26).

---

50. Pope Francis is the first pope to have had a strong personal friendship with a rabbi before his accession to the papacy. In his first year in Rome, he welcomed a group of Latin American rabbis to his home at Santa Marta. Archbishop Welby himself has a Jewish father.

Sources

Chapter 1 was originally presented at the SPS 39th Annual Meeting in Minneapolis, Minnesota, USA, in March 2010.

Chapter 2 was originally presented to an EPCRA meeting in Uppsala, Sweden, in September 2007.

Chapter 3 was originally presented at a joint SPS-EPCRA meeting in Mattersey Hall, Mattersey, UK, in June 1995.

Chapter 4 was originally presented at the SPS 41st Annual Meeting in Virginia Beach, Virginia, USA, in March 2012.

Chapter 5 was originally presented at an international symposium on Baptism in the Holy Spirit at Sankt Niklausen, Switzerland, in March 2013. A French translation has appeared: "Sources, Histoire, Défies", *Istina* LIX/2–3 (Avril–Sept. 2014) 179–92.

Chapter 6 was originally presented at an EPCRA meeting in Riga, Latvia in November 2011.

Chapter 7 was originally presented to the Gathering in the Holy Spirit meeting in Rome in April 2003.

Chapter 8 was originally presented to a theological symposium sponsored by the Word of Life Church (Livets Ord) in Ribbinggebäck, near Uppsala, Sweden, in November, 2011.

Chapter 9 was originally presented at a TJCII consultation in Vienna, Austria, in October 2004.

A shorter version of chapter 10 was originally presented at a TJCII consultation in Kiev, Ukraine, in May 2014.

Chapters 11 and 12 were originally presented as lectures at the Catholic University of Lublin, Lublin, Poland, in January 2015.

Chapter 13 was written for this book.

Bibliography

Albrecht, Dan. *Rites in the Spirit*. Sheffield, UK: Sheffield Academic Press, 1999.

Alexander, Estrelda. *Black Fire: One Hundred Years of African American Pentecostalism*. Downers Grove, IL: IVP, 2011.

Allen, Roland. *Missionary Methods—St Paul's or Ours?* London: World Dominion, 1960.

Althouse, Peter. "Towards a Pentecostal Ecclesiology: Participation in the Missional Life of the Triune God." JPT 18 (2009) 230–45.

Anderson, Allan H. "The Newer Pentecostal and Charismatic Churches: The Shape of Future Christianity in Africa." *Pneuma* 24 (2002) 167–84.

Asamoah-Gyadu, J. Kwabena. *African Charismatics*. Leiden, Netherlands: Brill, 2005.

———. *Contemporary Pentecostal Christianity: Interpretations from an African Context*. Oxford: Regnum, 2013.

Atti del Simposio Internazionale. *L'Inquisizione*. Città del Vaticano: Biblioteca Apostolica Vaticana, 2003.

Atti del Simposio Teologico-Storico. *Radici dell'Antigiudaismo in Ambiente Cristiano*. Città del Vaticano: Libreria Editrice Vaticana, 2000.

Barratt, T. B. *In the Days of the Latter Rain*. London: Simpkin, Marshall, Hamilton, Kent, 1909.

Bass, Clarence B. *Backgrounds to Dispensationalism: Its Historical Genesis and Ecclesiastical Implications*. Grand Rapids: Baker, 1977.

Baumert, Norbert, and Bially, Gerhard, eds. *Pfingstler und Katholiken im Dialog*. Düsseldorf: Charisma, 1999.

Bebbington, David. *Evangelicalism in Britain: 1730–1980*. London: Routledge & Kegan Paul, 1989.

Bell, G. K. A., ed. *Documents on Christian Unity, Fourth Series 1948–57*. London: Oxford University Press, 1958.

Bobov, Jean. *La Grande métamorphose. Eléments de théoanthropologie tripartite, apophatique et eschatologique*. Paris: Cerf, 2014.

Brueggemann, Walter. *Theology of the Old Testament: Testimony, Dispute, Advocacy*. Minneapolis, MN: Fortress, 1997.

Carter, John. *Donald Gee—Pentecostal Statesman*. Nottingham, UK: Assemblies of God, 1975.

Cerullo, Morris. *7 Steps to Victory for Body, Soul, and Spirit*. San Diego: World Evangelism, 1974.

Chan, Simon. *Pentecostal Theology and the Christian Spiritual Tradition*. Sheffield, UK: Sheffield Academic Press, 2000.

————. *Spiritual Theology: A Systematic Study of the Christian Life*. Downers Grove, IL: IVP, 1998.

Cleary, Edward L. *The Rise of Charismatic Catholicism in Latin America*. Gainesville, FL: University Press of Florida, 2011.

Coleman, Simon. *The Globalisation of Charismatic Christianity: Spreading the Gospel of Prosperity*. Cambridge: Cambridge University Press, 2000.

Congar, Yves. "L'abbé Paul Couturier, ses intuitions, vingt-sept ans après." *Unité Chrétienne* 60 (Nov. 1980) 46–50.

————. "Charismatiques, ou quoi?" *La Croix*, 19 Janvier 1974.

————. *Chrétiens en Dialogue*. Paris: Cerf, 1964.

Congregation for the Doctrine of the Faith. Declaration *Dominus Jesus*. Online: http://www.vatican.va/roman_curia/congregations/cfaith/documents/rc_con_cfaith_doc_20000806_dominus-iesus_en.html.

Cooper, Simon, and Mike Farrant. *Fire in Our Hearts: The Story of the Jesus Fellowship/ Jesus Army*. Nether Hayford, UK: Multiply, 1997.

Cove, Gordon. *The Triangle of Man*. London: 1935.

Cox, Harvey. *Fire from Heaven: The Rise of Pentecostal Spirituality and the Reshaping of Religion in the Twenty-First Century*. Reading, MA: Addison-Wesley, 1995.

Cullmann, Oscar. *Unity through Diversity*. Philadelphia: Fortress, 1988.

Curlee, Robert, and Mary Ruth Isaac-Curlee. "Bridging the Gap: John A. Mackay, Presbyterians and the Charismatic Movement." *American Presbyterians* 72 (Fall 1994) 141–56.

Cusack, Pearse. *Blessed Gabriella of Unity: A Patron for the Ecumenical Movement*. Ros Cré, Ireland: Cistercian, 1995.

Dallière, Louis. *D'Aplomb sur la Parole de Dieu*. Valence, France: n.p., 1932.

Daniélou, Jean. *The Bible and the Liturgy*. Notre Dame, IN: University of Notre Dame Press, 1956.

Darby, J. N. *Collected Writings: Ecclesiastical No. 1*. Kingston-on-Thames, UK: Stow Hill Bible and Tract Depot, n.d.

Dayton, Donald W. *Theological Roots of Pentecostalism*. Metuchen, NJ: Scarecrow, 1987.

Dombes, Groupe des. *For the Conversion of the Churches*. Geneva: WCC, 1993.

Duquoc, Christian. *Des Eglises provisoires: essai d'ecclésiologie oecuménique*. Paris: Cerf, 1985.

Ensley, Eddie. *Sounds of Wonder*. New York, NY: Paulist, 1977.

Francis, Pope. Address to CCR, Rome, June 1, 2014. Online: http://w2.vatican.va/content/francesco/en/speeches/2014/june/documents/papa-francesco_20140601_rinnovamento-spirito-santo.html.

————. Address to CCR, Rome, July 3, 2015. Online: http://w2.vatican.va/content/francesco/en/speeches/2015/july/documents/papa-francesco_20150703_movimento-rinnovamento-spirito.html.

————. Address to CFCCCF, Rome, Oct. 31, 2014. Online: http://w2.vatican.va/content/francesco/en/speeches/2014/october/documents/papa-francesco_20141031_catholic-fraternity.html.

————. Address to New Ecclesial Movements, May 18, 2013. Online: http://w2.vatican.va/content/francesco/en/speeches/2013/may/documents/papa-francesco_20130518_veglia-pentecoste.html.

————. Address to Pentecostal church in Caserta, July 28, 2014. Online: http://
w2.vatican.va/content/francesco/en/speeches/2014/july/documents/papa-
francesco_20140728.

————. Address to Third World Congress of New Ecclesial Movements and New
Communities, Nov. 22, 2014. Online: http://w2.vatican.va/content/francesco/
en/speeches/2014/november/documents/papa-francesco_20141122_convegno-
movimenti-ecclesiali.html.

————. Daily Meditations. Online: http://w2.vatican.va/content/francesco/en/cotidie
(then enter year and day).

————. Homily in Assisi, Oct. 4, 2013. Online: http://w2.vatican.va/content/francesco/
en/homilies/2013/documents/papa-francesco_20131004_omelia-visita-assisi.html.

————. Homily on Pentecost Sunday, May 19, 2013. Online: http://w2.vatican.va/
content/francesco/en/homilies/2013/documents/papa-francesco_20130519_
omelia-pentecoste.html.

Fredricksen, Paula. *Augustine and the Jews: A Christian Defense of Jews and Judaism.* New
York: Doubleday, 2008.

Gee, Donald. "Amsterdam and Pentecost." *Pentecost* 6 (Dec. 1948).

————. "Are We Too 'Movement' Conscious?" *Pentecost* 2 (Dec. 1947).

————. "Billy Graham in London." *Pentecost* 27 (Mar. 1954).

————. "Contact Is Not Compromise." *Pentecost* 53 (Sept.–Nov. 1960).

————, "A Day with the Huguenot Pentecostal Revival." RT 12/4 (Feb. 15, 1936) 1–2.

————. "Deserving Independent Existence." *Pentecost* 75 (Mar.–May 1966).

————. "Donald Gee and the WCC." *Pentecost* 57 (Sept.–Nov. 1961) 16.

————. "I Believe in the Holy Ghost." *Pentecost* 44 (June 1958).

————. "Movement or Message?" *Pentecost* 37 (Sept. 1956).

————. "Not 'The' Assemblies of God." RT 10/1 (Jan. 1, 1943) 5.

————. "Orientation for 1960." *Pentecost* 50 (Dec. 1959).

————. "Pentecost and Evanston." *Pentecost* 30 (Dec. 1954).

————. "Pentecost Re-Valued." *Pentecost* 28 (June 1954).

————. "The Pentecostal Churches and the WCC." *Pentecost* 67 (Mar.–May 1964).

————. "Pentecostal Theology." *The Ministry* 1/1 (Jan. 1963) 23.

————. "Pentecostals at New Delhi." *Pentecost* 59 (Mar.–May 1962).

————. "Possible Pentecostal Unity." *Pentecost* 13 (Sept 1950).

————. "Sion College." RT (May 1, 1934) 9.

————. "Superfluous Sects." RT 23/5 (March 5, 1947) 2.

————. "'Tongues' and Truth." *Pentecost* 25 (Sept. 1953).

————. "The Work of the Holy Spirit in the Pentecostal Movement Especially in
Connection with Divine Healing." In *Report of International Conference on Divine
Healing.* London: London Healing Mission, n.d.

————. "The World-Wide Evangelization Crusade and the Gift of Tongues." RT 3/8 (Aug.
1927) 14–15.

————. *Upon All Flesh: A Pentecostal World Tour.* Springfield, MO: Gospel, 1947.

Gelpi, Donald L. *Charism and Sacrament.* New York, Paulist, 1976.

Gott, Lois. "Donald Gee: The Apostle of Balance." In *Essays on Apostolic Themes: Studies
in Honor of Howard M. Ervin,* edited by Paul Elbert, 173–83. Peabody, MA:
Hendrickson, 1985.

Hagin, Kenneth E. *Man on Three Dimensions: A Study of the Spirit, Soul, and Body.* 2nd ed.
Tulsa, OK: Kenneth Hagin Evangelistic Association, 1974.

Hamon, Bill. *The Eternal Church*. Shippensburg, PA: Destiny Image, 2003.

———. *Prophets and the Prophetic Movement: God's Prophetic Move Today*. Shippensburg, PA: Destiny Image, 1990.

Hewitt, Brian. *Doing a New Thing?* London: Hodder & Stoughton, 1995.

Hexham, Irving, and Karla Poewe. "Charismatic Churches in South Africa: A Critique of Criticisms and Problems of Bias." In *Charismatic Christianity as a Global Culture*, edited by Karla Poewe, 50–69. Columbia, SC: University of South Carolina Press, 1994.

Hinn, Benny. *Good Morning, Holy Spirit*. Nashville, TN: Nelson, 1990.

Hocken, Peter. "Catholic Pentecostalism: Some Key Questions." HJ (1974) 131–43, 271–84.

———. "Cecil H. Polhill—Pentecostal Layman." *Pneuma* 10 (1988) 116–40.

———. *The Challenges of the Pentecostal Charismatic and Messianic Jewish Movements*. Farnham, UK: Ashgate, 2009.

———. "The Charismatic Movement and the Church: A Response to Heribert Mühlen." *Theological Renewal* 13 (Oct. 1979) 22–29.

———. "Charismatics and Mystics." *Theological Renewal* 1 (Oct.–Nov. 1975) 11–17.

———. "Communion of Evangelical Episcopal Churches." NIDPCM, 557.

———. *The Glory and the Shame*. Guildford, UK: Eagle, 1994.

———. "The Jewish People and the Unity of the Church." *Louvain Studies* 33 (2008) 304–18.

———. *Pentecost and Parousia: Charismatic Renewal, Christian Unity, and the Coming Glory*. Eugene, OR: Wipf & Stock, 2013.

———. "The Pentecostal–Charismatic Movement as Revival and Renewal." *Pneuma* 3 (1981) 31–47.

———. "Revival and Renewal," JEPTA XVIII (1998) 49–63.

———. "The Significance and Potential of Pentecostalism." In *New Heavens? New Earth?*, 16–67. London: Darton, Longman & Todd, 1976.

———. "What Challenges Do Pentecostals Pose to Catholics? JEPTA 35 (Apr. 2015) 48–57.

Hollenweger, Walter. *The Pentecostals: The Charismatic Movement in the Churches*. London: SCM, 1972.

Hunt, Stephen J. "The Anglican Wimberites." *Pneuma* 17 (1995) 105–18.

———. "The Radical Kingdom of the Jesus Fellowship." *Pneuma* 20 (1998) 21–41.

International Catholic Charismatic Renewal Services Doctrinal Commission. *Baptism in the Holy Spirit*. Locust Grove, VA: National Service Committee, 2012.

International Consultation between the Catholic Church and the World Evangelical Alliance. "Church, Evangelization, and the Bonds of Koinonia." *Information Service*, 113 (2003) 85–101.

International Theological Commission. *Memory and Reconciliation: The Church and the Faults of the Past*. Boston: Pauline, 2000.

———. *The Sensus Fidei in the Life of the Church*. Online: http://www.vatican.va/roman_curia/congregations/cfaith/cti_documents/rc_cti_20140610_sensus-fidei_en.html.

Introvigne, Massimo. *Aspettando la Pentecoste: il quarto ecumenismo: Intervista a Matteo Calisi e Giovanni Traettino*. Padua: Ed. Messaggero di San Antonio, 1996.

Irénée of Lyon, *Adversus Haereses*, V, SC 153. Paris: Cerf, 1969.

Ivereigh, Austen. *The Great Reformer: Francis and the Making of a Radical Pope*. London: Allen & Unwin, 2014.

Jenkins, Philip. *The New Faces of Christianity: Believing the Bible in the Global South*. New York: Oxford University Press, 2006.

———. *The Next Christendom*. New York: Oxford University Press, 2007.

Kay, William K. *Apostolic Networks in Britain: New Ways of Being Church*. Studies in Evangelical History and Thought. Milton Keynes, UK: Paternoster, 2007.

———. *Inside Story : A History of the British Assemblies of God*. Mattersey, UK: Mattersey, 1990.

———. "Peter Hocken: His Life and Work." *Pneuma* 37 (2015) 82–110.

Kinzer, Mark. *Israel's Messiah and the People of God*. Eugene, OR: Cascade, 2011.

———. *Post-Missionary Messianic Judaism*. Grand Rapids: Brazos, 2005.

———. *Searching Her Own Mystery: Nostra Aetate, the Jewish People, and the Identity of the Church*. Eugene, OR: Cascade, 2015.

Kollins, Kim. *It's Only the Beginning*. Crowborough, UK: Highland, 1989.

Kydd, Ronald A. N. *Charismatic Gifts in the Early Church*. Peabody, MA: Hendrickson, 1984.

Lake, John G. *Spiritual Hunger the God-Men and Other Sermons*. Edited by G. Lindsay. Dallas: Christ for the Nations, 1976.

Lanne, Emmanuel. "Notes sur la situation d'Israël par rapport aux schismes dans l'Église chrétienne." In *1054–1954 L'Église et les Églises: neuf siècles de douloureuse séparation entre l'Orient et l'Occident*. Études et travaux sur l'Unité chrétienne offerts à Dom Lambert Beauduin, Vol. II. Chevetogne, Belgium: Éditions de Chevetogne, 1955.

Ma, Wonsuk, and Robert P. Menzies, eds. *The Spirit and Spirituality: Essays in Honour of Russell P. Spittler*. London: T. & T. Clark, 2004.

Macchia, Frank D. *Baptized in the Spirit*. Grand Rapids: Zondervan, 2006.

Massey, Richard. *Another Springtime: The Life of Donald Gee Pentecostal Pioneer*. Guildford, UK: Highland, 1992.

McDonnell, Kilian. *The Charismatic Renewal and Ecumenism*. New York, Paulist, 1978.

———, ed. *The Holy Spirit and Power*. Garden City, NY: Doubleday, 1975.

McDonnell, Kilian, and George Montague. *Christian Initiation and Baptism in the Holy Spirit*. Collegeville, MN: Liturgical, 1990.

McNair Scott, Benjamin G. *Apostles Today. Making Sense of Contemporary Charismatic Apostolates: A Historical and Theological Appraisal*. Eugene, OR: Pickwick, 2014.

McPartlan, Paul. "The Local Church and the Universal Church: Zizioulas and the Ratzinger-Kasper Debate." IJSCC 4 (2004) 21–33.

Meeking, Basil, and John Stott, eds. *The Evangelical-Roman Catholic Dialogue on Mission 1977–1984*. Grand Rapids: Eerdmans, 1986.

Miller, Donald E. *Reinventing American Protestantism*. Berkeley: University of California Press, 1997.

Miller, Paul M. *Evangelical Mission in Cooperation with Catholics: A Study of Evangelical Missiological Tensions*. Oxford: Regnum, 2013.

Moore, S. David. *The Shepherding Movement: Controversy and Charismatic Ecclesiology*. London: T. & T. Clark, 2003.

Murray, Paul, ed. *Receptive Ecumenism and the Call to Catholic Learning: Exploring a Way for Contemporary Ecumenism*. Oxford: Oxford University Press, 2008.

Myland, D. Wesley. *The Latter Rain Covenant*. Springfield, MO: Temple, 1910.

Neumann, Peter. *Pentecostal Experience: An Ecumenical Encounter*. Eugene, OR: Pickwick, 2012.

Newbigin, Lesslie. *The Household of God*. London: SCM, 1953.

Newman, John Henry. *On Consulting the Faithful in Matters of Doctrine*. Edited by John Coulson. London: Chapman, 1961.

Orellana, Luis, and Bernardo Campos, eds. *Ecumenismo del Espiritu*. Lima, Peru: Foro Pentecostal Latinoamericano, 2012.

Percy, Martyn. *Words, Wonders and Power: Understanding Contemporary Christian Fundamentalism and Revivalism*. London: SPCK, 1996.

Pesare, Oreste, ed. *"Then Peter Stood Up . . ." Collection of the Popes' Addresses to the Catholic Charismatic Renewal from Its Origin to the Year 2000*. Vatican City: ICCRS, 2000.

Pius XI. *Mortalium Animos*. Encyclical Letter, English translation. London: Catholic Truth Society, 1943.

Rahner, Karl. "Basic Observations on the Subject of Changeable and Unchangeable Factors in the Church." *Theological Investigations* 14, 3–23. London: Darton, Longman & Todd, 1976.

———. "Ideology and Christianity." *Theological Investigations* 6, 43–58. London: Darton, Longman & Todd, 1969.

———. *Mission and Grace*, Vol. 2. London: Sheed & Ward, 1964.

———. *Visions and Prophecies*. London: Burns & Oates, 1963.

Ratzinger, Joseph (Benedict XVI). *New Outpourings of the Spirit*. San Francisco: Ignatius, 2007.

Riss, Richard M. *Latter Rain*. Mississauga, ON: Honeycomb, 1987.

———. "Latter Rain Movement." NIDPCM, 830–33.

Robeck, Cecil M. *The Azusa Street Mission and Revival*. Nashville: Thomas Nelson, 2006.

———. "An Emerging Magisterium? The Case of the Assemblies of God." In *The Spirit and Spirituality: Essays in Honour of Russell P. Spittler*, edited by Ma, Wonsuk and Robert P. Menzies, 212–52. London: T. & T. Clark, 2004.

———. "Pentecostals and Christian Unity: Facing the Challenge." *Pneuma* 26/2 (2004) 307–38.

Ross, Brian R. *Donald Gee: In Search of a Church: Sectarian in Transition*. DTh diss. Knox College, Toronto, 1974.

———. "Donald Gee: Sectarian in Search of a Church." EQ 50 (1978) 94–103.

Rossi de Gasperis, Francesco. *Cominciando da Gerusalemme*. Casale Monferrato: Piemme, 1997.

Shulam, Joseph, with Hilary Le Cornu. *A Commentary on the Jewish Roots of Acts 1–15*. Jerusalem: Netivyah, 2012.

Simon, Marcel. *Verus Israel: A Study of the Relations between Christians and Jews in the Roman Empire AD 135–425*. London: Littman, 1996.

Skarsaune, Oskar. *In the Shadow of the Temple*. Downers Grove, IL: IVP, 2002.

Smith, David. "An Account for the Sustained Rise of New Frontiers International within the United Kingdom." JEPTA XXIII (2003) 137–56.

Suenens, Léon-Joseph. *Ecumenism and Charismatic Renewal: Theological and Pastoral Orientations*. Ann Arbor, MI: Servant, 1978.

———. *A New Pentecost?* New York: Seabury, 1975.

Sullivan, Frank. *Charisms and Charismatic Renewal. A Biblical and Theological Study*. Dublin: Gill & Macmillan, 1982.

"Talking with Pete Greig." *Jesus Life* 60 (2002) 12–13.

Theological and Pastoral Orientations on the Catholic Charismatic Renewal. Notre Dame, IN: Word of Life, 1974.

Thompson, Hugh. "From 'Renewal' to 'Restoration' Cliches or Scripture." *Restoration* 1/1 (Mar.–Apr. 1975) 5.

Van Beek, Huibert, ed. *Revisioning Christian Unity: The Global Christian Forum.* Oxford: Regnum, 2009.

Van der Laan, Cornelis. *Sectarian against His Will: Gerrit Roelof Polman and the Birth of Pentecostalism in the Netherlands.* London: Scarecrow, 1991.

Versteeg, Peter. "A Prophetic Outsider: Experience and the Boundaries of Meaning in a Local Vineyard Church." *Pneuma* 28/1 (2006) 72–88.

Virgo, Terry. *No Well-Worn Paths: Restoring the Church to Christ's Original Intention.* Eastbourne, UK: Kingsway, 2001.

———. *Restoration in the Church.* Eastbourne, UK: Kingsway, 1985.

Volf, Miroslav. *After Our Likeness: the Church as the Image of the Trinity.* Grand Rapids: Eerdmans, 1998.

Wagner, C. Peter, ed. *The New Apostolic Churches.* Ventura, CA: Regal, 1998.

Walker, Andrew G. *Notes from a Wayward Son. A Miscellany.* Eugene,OR: Cascade, 2015.

———. *Restoring the Kingdom: The Radical Christianity of the House Church Movement.* Guildford, UK: Eagle, 1998.

Wallis, Jonathan. *Arthur Wallis: Radical Christian.* Eastbourne, UK: Kingsway, 1991.

Warner, Rob. *I Believe in Discipleship.* London; Hodder & Stoughton, 1999.

Warnock, Adrian. "Together on a Mission 09." *New Frontiers Magazine* 3/13 (Oct.–Dec. 2009) 11.

Whittaker, Colin. *Seven Pentecostal Pioneers.* Basingstoke, UK: Marshall Morgan and Scott, 1983.

Wright, Tom. *Surprised by Hope.* London: SPCK, 2007.

Yong, Amos. *Spirit-Word-Community: Theological Hermeneutics in Trinitarian Perspective.* Reprint. Eugene, OR: Wipf & Stock, 2006.

Name Index

Subject Index